940.475

HAIG'S
MEDICAL OFFICER

To Luca and Finlay –
that they may know their great-great-grandfather.

HAIG'S
MEDICAL OFFICER

The Papers of Colonel Eugene 'Micky' Ryan

CMG DSO RAMC

Edited by EUGENE P RYAN

with a Foreword by GARY SHEFFIELD

Pen & Sword
MILITARY

First published in Great Britain in 2013 by
PEN & SWORD MILITARY
An imprint of
Pen & Sword Books Ltd
47 Church Street
Barnsley
South Yorkshire
S70 2AS

Copyright © Eugene P Ryan

ISBN 978 1 78159 316 5

The right of Eugene P Ryan to be identified as Editor
of this work has been asserted by him in accordance with
the Copyright, Designs and Patents Act 1988.

A CIP catalogue record for this book is
available from the British Library

Typeset in LaTeX by Eugene P Ryan

Printed and bound in England
By CPI Group (UK) Ltd, Croydon, CR0 4YY

Pen & Sword Books Ltd incorporates the Imprints of Pen & Sword Aviation,
Pen & Sword Family History, Pen & Sword Maritime, Pen & Sword Military,
Pen & Sword Discovery, Pen & Sword Politics, Pen & Sword Archaeology,
Pen & Sword Atlas, Wharncliffe Local History, Wharncliffe True Crime,
Wharncliffe Transport, Pen & Sword Select, Pen & Sword Military Classics,
Leo Cooper, The Praetorian Press, Claymore Press, Remember When,
Seaforth Publishing and Frontline Publishing

For a complete list of Pen & Sword titles please contact
PEN & SWORD BOOKS LIMITED
47 Church Street, Barnsley, South Yorkshire, S70 2AS, England
E-mail: enquiries@pen-and-sword.co.uk
Website: www.pen-and-sword.co.uk

D.H. - who believes that the medical profession comprises only Ryan and a few learners - telegraphed for Ryan and now will not let him go.

Brigadier General John Charteris,
At G.H.Q., Cassell & Co., London, 1931, page 72.

Eugene Ryan

Born: 29 September 1873; Templehill, Co. Cork, Ireland
University Education (Medicine):
    Queen's College, Cork & Edinburgh University
    Licentiates of the Royal College of Surgeons (LRCS), the
    Royal College of Physicians (LRCP) and the
    Royal Faculty of Physicians & Surgeons (LRFPS), 1898
Royal Army Medical Corps (RAMC):
    Lieutenant, January 1901
    South Africa (Second Anglo-Boer War), August 1901-March 1902
    Captain, January 1904
    Major, January 1913
    France & Flanders (First World War), August 1914-April 1919
    Temporary Lieutenant Colonel, September 1915
    Chevalier, Légion d'Honneur, November 1915
    Distinguished Service Order (DSO), January 1916
    Brevet Lieutenant Colonel, January 1917
    Companion of the Order of St Michael & St George (CMG), June 1918
    Médaille de la Reconnaissance Française, March 1919
    Honorary Surgeon to the Viceroy of India, April 1921
    Lieutenant Colonel, March 1923
    Honorary Physician to the King, February 1926
    Brevet Colonel, February 1926
    Retired: September 1930
Died: 11 April 1951; Cork, Ireland

In Arduis Fidelis
(Faithful in Adversity)

Royal Army Medical Corps

Contents

Foreword by Gary Sheffield

I first came across Eugene 'Micky' Ryan some years ago while researching into the life and career of Douglas Haig. I mentally noted that Ryan was an interesting character that deserved more research, but subsequently found that very little was known about him. I was therefore delighted when out of the blue I received an email from his grandson, Professor Eugene Ryan, Professor of Mathematics at the University of Bath, which said that he understood that I was writing a biography of Haig, that he had some of Micky Ryan's personal papers, and would I like to see them? I wasn't quite on the next train to Bath, but it wasn't far off.

I was able to make use of the papers in my book *The Chief: Douglas Haig and the British Army* (Aurum, 2011), but felt strongly that Micky Ryan's diaries and letters should form the basis of a publication in their own right. Well, several years later that book is in your hand, and I was delighted to be asked to contribute a foreword.

For the historian, Ryan's papers are interesting for two principal reasons: the light they shed on Douglas Haig as a man and a general, and for the insights they give into the work of a Royal Army Medical Corps officer on the Western Front in the First World War. The picture of the most controversial general in British history that emerges from Ryan's writing confirms Haig's extreme loyalty to his staff. Starting as Medical Officer on I Corps staff in 1914, he followed Haig to First Army at the end of the year. Although Ryan was allowed to go off to command a Casualty Clearing Station in August 1915, Haig brought him to GHQ in September 1916. There, one of Ryan's roles – unofficial but nonetheless important – was simply to be there for Haig. The Commander-in-Chief's loyalty to those he liked and trusted was something of a two-edged sword. His support encompassed competent subordinates like Ryan and RFC chief Hugh Trenchard, but also individuals such as his chief-of-staff Lancelot

Kiggell and head of intelligence John Charteris, men whose performances received mixed reviews from contemporaries and historians.

Ryan's papers also provide some interesting insights into Haig's personal life. Haig's personal morale depended heavily on the support of his wife, Dorothy (Doris) and young family. Given this, it is no surprise that Haig had Ryan act as doctor to Haig's family, a role that continued long after the war and included being present at the birth of Haig's only son, the late Dawyck, Second Earl Haig, in 1918. Clearly, Haig's regard for Ryan was based on both personal liking and respect for the latter's professional competence. What is also clear is that Ryan, who was no fool, had a huge regard for Haig. The views of Ryan, and other astute contemporaries such as Richard Haldane, the great (and highly intellectual) Liberal Secretary of State for War, are a counterpoint to those who, following David Lloyd George, see Haig as stupid.

Ryan's contemporary writings give a fascinating, if tantalisingly brief, view of the 1914 campaign as seen from I Corps HQ. As I remarked in *The Chief*, Charteris's famous if histrionic account of Haig losing his nerve, albeit temporarily, at Landrecies on 25 August is perhaps undermined by the fact that Ryan mentioned nothing of this and in fact remarked on Haig's calmness over the next couple of days. Haig was clearly unwell, but the nagging question remains: did Charteris exaggerate to improve the anecdote? Similarly, Ryan's letters and diaries give important insights into his role while commanding two Casualty Clearing Stations in 1915-16. There is much work on the history of the RAMC in the First World War still to be done and the Ryan papers provide very useful primary evidence on which to build.

Gene Ryan has produced a fascinating book from his grandfather's papers. Everyone with an interest in the British army of the First World War is in his debt.

Professor Gary Sheffield MA PhD FRHistS FRSA
Chair of War Studies, University of Wolverhampton
September 2013.

Preface

Eugene Ryan was born on 29 September 1873 at Templehill, a farming community a few miles to the west of Cork City in Ireland. The sixth of eight children and one of three brothers to enter the medical profession, Ryan read medicine at Queen's College, Cork (now the National University of Ireland, University College, Cork) and at Edinburgh University. In 1898, he took the Licentiates of the Royal College of Physicians (LRCP), the Royal College of Surgeons (LRCS), and the Royal Faculty of Physicians & Surgeons (LRFPS). After a period of private practice in London, Ryan was commissioned into the Royal Army Medical Corps (RAMC) on 29 January 1901. Active service in the Second Anglo-Boer War soon followed. Lieutenant Ryan embarked for South Africa in August 1901, and joined 9 Brigade at Klerksdorp in the Transvaal. Having contracted enteric (typhoid) fever in January 1902, he was invalided home in March 1902. After six months' sick leave, Lieutenant Ryan was posted to the Military Hospital, Cork, until ordered for service in Malta in February 1903. He served in Malta until February 1908. In January 1905, Ryan married Sarah (known as Sadie or Sall) O'Connor (1884–1943) of Kanturk, County Cork, Ireland.

Captain Ryan returned from Malta in February 1908. After brief periods of service with the Scottish Command (Edinburgh), the Royal Army Medical College (Millbank, London), and the Citadel, Plymouth, he was posted to Aldershot in 1909. In October 1912, he was appointed Officer Commanding the Louise Margaret Hospital, Aldershot. It was at this juncture that Ryan first met Douglas Haig, although the precise circumstances are not known.

Ryan circa 1898
©Author's collection

Sarah ("Sadie" or "Sall") O'Connor circa 1904
©Author's collection

On 9 August 1914, Major Ryan proceeded on Active Service as Medical Officer to Headquarters Staff, I Corps (under Haig), British Expeditionary Force (BEF). Following the reorganization of the BEF in December 1914, Haig took command of First Army and brought Ryan with him as Medical Officer to Headquarters Staff ('Ryan came along with me & is now on the 1st Army staff'). From August 1915 to August 1916, Ryan was Officer Commanding No 18 Casualty Clearing Station (Lapugnoy) and, briefly in August – September 1916, was Officer Commanding No 4 Casualty Clearing Station (Beauval). On 8 September 1916, he was appointed Medical Officer on the Personal Staff of the Commander-in-Chief of the Army in France (in December 1915, Haig had succeeded Sir John French in this role). Ryan remained on Haig's personal staff until 5 April 1919, when he left France to take Command of Bethnal Green Military Hospital, London.

In October 1919, Brevet Lieutenant Colonel Ryan was ordered 'to hold himself in readiness to proceed to India at an early date'. On 1 November, he embarked at Devonport and arrived in Delhi on 28 November with orders 'to enquire into the existing arrangements at Military Stations in India for the medical treatment of the wives and families of officers, NCOs and men'. On completion of this enquiry, in June 1920 Ryan was appointed Officer Commanding the British Station Hospital, Kasauli, in the State of Himachal Pradesh in northern India: he held that post until January 1925, when he embarked at Bombay for the UK.

In April 1925, Lieutenant Colonel Ryan was appointed Officer Commanding the Military Station Hospital, Edinburgh Castle and, in February 1926, was promoted to the brevet rank of Colonel. In January 1927 he embarked for China. As part of the medical arrangements for the Shanghai Defence Force, Colonel Ryan established the 7th General Hospital in Shanghai. Following his return to the UK in November 1927, he was appointed Officer Commanding the Queen Alexandra Military Hospital, Millbank, London, in January 1928: he held that position until his retirement on 29 September 1930.

Eugene and Sadie Ryan moved from London back to their native Cork in 1942. Sadie died in 1943 and Ryan in 1951.

The Haig connection

One of my earliest memories is that of the tall figure of my grandfather standing at the top of a flight of stairs pointing his walking stick in my direction. The stick (which is still in use) has a gold plate bearing the inscription:

Lt Col E Ryan D.S.O.   Xmas 1916   From Lady Haig

(in October 1914, on the Aisne, Ryan was thrown from his horse and sustained a hip injury). The friendship between the Haigs and Ryan is evident in such mementos and in the – albeit limited – correspondence that survives. In March 1918, Ryan was the doctor in attendance at the birth of Haig's eagerly-awaited son and heir, George Alexander Eugene Douglas. The inclusion of 'Eugene' amongst the names is rightly attributed to Lady Haig's association with Empress Eugénie (wife of Napoleon III): nevertheless, it is plausible that the Ryan connection may also have been an influence. The inscription on a cigarette case, given to 'Micky' Ryan in 1926, attests to the endurance of his association with the Haigs:

To/ Micky Ryan   Colonel R.A.M.C.
in grateful remembrance of many kindnesses - 1911 - 1926
Aldershot
France and Flanders
Scotland
Dorothy Haig   Haig F.M.
Xmas 1926

©Author's collection

In addition to attending to Haig and his staff in France and Flanders, Ryan kept a medical eye on Dorothy Haig and her children. For example, in a letter to his wife on 14 September 1914 (during the Battle of the Aisne), Ryan wrote: 'I enclose a prescription for Lady Haig. She can get it dispensed at the Cambridge H [*the Cambridge Hospital, Aldershot*]'. In effect, Ryan acted as the Haig family doctor. Haig's letters to his wife (archived in the Scottish National Library) contain many references to Ryan in the role: 'I saw Col. Ryan who was delighted with the children. He thought them both very hardy & fit' (1 July 1917); 'Ryan has always been so kind in looking after you as well as me' (1 October 1917); 'Ryan goes on leave tomorrow & will call in to see you & the children when he passes thro' London either going or returning' (15 October 1917); 'I am glad you saw Ryan. I hope he also saw the children as he takes such an interest in them too, and is so fond of them' (31 January 1918). Dorothy Haig's letters to Ryan also exude warmth and informality: 'I forgot yesterday to ask you to be an angel and let me know when you have seen Douglas what you candidly think of him after all this strain' (30 March 1918); 'I was amused by your remarks at tea, though you made me feel terribly shy' (2 October 1918). In Edinburgh, autumn 1926 was a period of ill health for Dorothy Haig: again Ryan was in attendance. In his letter of 25 November 1926 to Ryan, Haig comments 'I was delighted to see so much improvement in my wife's condition y'day ... you are a wonderful fellow!!'.

In the commemorative issue of the British Legion Journal (vol. 7, March 1928), following Haig's death in January 1928, Ryan writes: *I first met the late Field-Marshal at Aldershot in 1912, and from that time until his death was either with or in touch with him.*

The lasting friendship and trust between these two men begs a number of questions, religion being but one. It has often been said that Haig was hostile to Roman Catholicism. For example, in *The Good Soldier* (Atlantic Books, London, 2007, page 174), Gary Mead refers to 'Haig's strong dislike of Roman Catholicism and distrust of its adherents'. Haig's distrust of Lieutenant General Sir George Macdonogh is frequently cited as evidence. In his diary entry for 15 October 1917 (when Macdonogh was Director of Military Intelligence at the War Office), Haig comments: 'I cannot think why the War Office Intelligence Dept. gives such a wrong picture of the situation except that Genl. Macdonogh (D.M.I) is a Roman Catholic and is (unconsciously) influenced by information which doubtless reaches him from tainted (i.e. Catholic) sources'.

Whatever Haig's views of Roman Catholicism at an institutional level, there is no hint of distrust or hostility in his personal association with Ryan, a Catholic. On the contrary, Haig was godfather to Ryan's fourth son, Douglas, born in 1917.

20 Nov: 17

My dear Ryan
Herewith a cup for my godson & to wish
him all good luck,
Yrs ever
D.H.

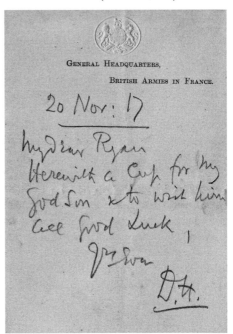

©Author's collection

There are other indicators of a relaxed attitude to Ryan's Catholicism shown by the Haigs. For example, whilst staying at the Haig home, Eastcott, in Surrey and attending to Dorothy following the birth of her son, Ryan's diary entry for 17 March (2 days after the birth) records his motoring to Mayfair, London, for Mass at Farm Street Church (Jesuits): *Motored to Farm St 11 Mass. ... Returned Eastcott for dinner. Lady H and son doing very well.*

Another issue, ingrained in the Irish psyche, remains enigmatic in Ryan's papers, namely, nationalism. Ryan's time on the Western Front, together with his subsequent years of service in India, ran in parallel with momentous events in Irish history: the Easter Rising of 1916, the Irish War of Independence leading to the Anglo-Irish Treaty of 1922 and the establishment of the Irish Free State, followed by the Irish Civil War of 1922-23 in which the charismatic Michael Collins, Chairman of the Provisional Government and a fellow Corkman, was killed in an ambush in August 1922 within 20 miles of Ryan's birthplace. Yet, with just one exception, Ryan's papers contain no references to, or comments on, Irish nationalism. One can only surmise Ryan's political colours from sparse circumstantial evidence. One piece of evidence is the exception alluded to previously: in his summary of 1917, Ryan noted the death of Willie Redmond. William Hoey Kearney Redmond, a committed nationalist (who had been imprisoned for sedition in 1882), was MP in the Irish Parliamentary Party, representing the constituency East Clare from 1892 until his death. (In the by-election, on 10 July 1917, caused by Redmond's death, the Irish Parliamentary Party lost the seat to the Sinn Féin candidate, Éamonn de Valera.) At the outbreak of war, Redmond, a dyed-in-the-wool opponent of British Government in Ireland, volunteered – at the age of 53 – to fight against Germany in the defence of the British Empire and exhorted his fellow countrymen to do likewise. This apparent paradox may be explained by his conviction that an Ireland loyal to the British Crown during the war would be better placed to achieve Home Rule in its aftermath. In *Great Irishmen in War and Politics* (Melrose, London, 1920), T P O'Connor observes 'His hope in volunteering for active service was to bring about, by his example, a feeling of mutual trust in place of the old, false distrust between nationalists and unionists both inside and outside Ireland'. It is indeed plausible that Ryan shared this outwardly paradoxical mindset. Redmond died in the Battle of Messines–Wytschaete on 9 June 1917. A second indicator of Ryan's politics is an affinity with his wife's nationalist family. The 1911 Census of Ireland records that, on 2 April of that year, Ryan's eldest child, Thomas, then aged 5, was staying at Sadie's family home in Kanturk, County Cork. While Ryan was serving on the Western Front, Sadie spent considerable time in her family home and was joined there by Ryan during several periods of leave. Ryan's father-in-law, John D O'Connor, was a nationalist in the Redmond mould. Like Redmond, O'Connor was a fervent supporter of, and activist in, the Irish Land League (a political organization – its primary aim being the abolition of absentee landlordism), as a result of which he too endured a period of imprisonment. An obituary in the newspaper *The Kerryman* (29 July 1939), records that '[h]is ardent temperament, however, could not brook restraint, and he was so strongly imbued with hatred for harsh landlordism that he threw himself heart and soul into the struggle then so fiercely waged on behalf of the tenant farmers of Ireland'. Ever active in local politics, O'Connor became Justice of the Peace and, in 1914, was Chairman of the District Council. As a career officer in the RAMC, it would have been injudicious of Ryan to nail his political colours to the mast: his association with Haig placed him in proximity to the principal players (the brothers Hubert & John Gough, in particular) in the so-called 'Curragh Mutiny'. In 1912, the Liberal coalition British government, under Herbert Asquith, introduced the Home Rule Bill for Ireland, proposing a form of self-governance through the creation of an Irish Parliament in Dublin. The Unionists responded by creating a paramilitary force, the Ulster Volunteers, which, by 1914, was estimated to be 100,000 in number. To counter the threat of violence in the event of the Home Rule Bill being passed, plans were made to move troops to Ulster. A number of senior officers, most notably Field Marshal Sir John French and Major General Sir Henry Wilson (each of Anglo-Irish descent), voiced concerns that the British Army, or sections thereof, would be reluctant to act against the Ulster Volunteers. This unrest culminated in March 1914 in an incident at the Curragh Camp, the main British army base in Ireland. Fifty seven officers, based at the Curragh and led by Brigadier General Hubert Gough, declared that they would accept dismissal rather than enforce Home Rule in Ulster. This incident caused great alarm within Asquith's government which was forced to back down, attributing the episode to an 'honest misunderstanding'. Haig was drawn into the crisis through the involvement of his principal staff officer at Aldershot, Brigadier General John Gough VC, Hubert Gough's brother. The efforts of Haig and others to pour oil on troubled waters prevailed and a mass exodus from the army was averted. The Irish Home Rule issue was quickly overtaken by the outbreak of the First World War in August 1914. In September, The Government of Ireland Act 1914 was presented for Royal Assent simultaneously with the Suspensory Act in September 1914, the latter postponing the implementation of the former for the duration of the war.

Awards & decorations

With one exception, Ryan's campaign, gallantry and other medals have survived. The exception is the Order of the Crown of Roumania, to which Ryan was admitted as Commander in 1922. The medals comprise the following:

1902: The Queen's South Africa Medal (with five clasps – Cape Colony, Orange Free State, Transvaal, South Africa 1901, South Africa 1902).
1914–1918: 1914 Star, British War Medal & Victory Medal.
1915: Chevalier, Légion d'Honneur.
1916: Distinguished Service Order (DSO).
1918: Companion of Order of Saint Michael and Saint George (CMG).
1919: Médaille de la Reconnaissance Française.
1920: Officer, Order of the Star of Roumania.

Ryan was seven times Mentioned in Dispatches.

In 1921, he was appointed Honorary Surgeon to the Viceroy of India.
In 1926, he was appointed Honorary Physician to the King.

The War of 1914-1918.

Royal Army Medical Corps

Maj. & Bt. Lt.-Col. (T/Lt.-Col.) E. Ryan, C.M.G., D.S.O.

was mentioned in a Despatch from

Field Marshal Sir Douglas Haig, K.T., G.C.B., O.M., G.C.V.O., K.C.I.E.

dated 16th March 1919

for gallant and distinguished services in the Field.

I have it in command from the King to record His Majesty's

high appreciation of the services rendered.

War Office
Whitehall, S.W.
1st July 1919.

Secretary of State for War.

Seventh Mention in Dispatches   ©Author's collection

The papers

In presenting Ryan's papers (which mainly consist of letters to his wife and an incomplete set of diaries), an attempt has been made to place events in historical context (albeit with the naïvety of a novice in military history). No attempt has been made to provide critical analyses of the underlying events and personalities (Haig, in particular, who – to this day – remains a controversial figure, polarizing the views of military historians): such analyses are the remit of professionals and have, in any case, already generated a comprehensive literature. In consequence, the words of Sir George Arthur (taken from the Foreword to his book *Lord Haig*, Heinemann, London, 1928) spring to mind: 'this little volume may be as devoid of military value as of literary merit'. The intention is solely that of charting – at a personal, informal and anecdotal level – the career of a RAMC officer spanning the Second Anglo-Boer War, Headquarters Staff British Army in France and Flanders, Casualty Clearing Stations, Armistice, service in India and with the Shanghai Defence Force. The account, in which Haig features regularly, encompasses first-hand insights into the movements, actions and milestones of the 1914-18 War juxtaposed with personal vignettes such as his treatment of Haig's illness at a crucial juncture (Landrecies) in the Retreat from Mons, football with the Prince of Wales (the future Edward VIII) on the Western Front, and attendance at the birth of Haig's son and heir in 1918. The figure of Haig also permeates the account of Ryan's postwar years: riding to hounds (Buccleugh Hunt) with Earl Haig at Bemersyde, only a matter of weeks before the Field Marshal's death in January 1928, was the occasion of their last meeting.

As already noted, Ryan's papers are mainly comprised of letters to his wife, Sadie, and his diaries. In the context of the First World War, the letters are largely confined to the years 1914 – 15 and, as a result, in presenting the papers there is an inevitable emphasis on the earlier campaigns and battles of the war: Mons, the Marne & the Aisne, First Ypres, Neuve Chapelle, Festubert, and Loos. The relative paucity of material pertaining to 1916 – 1918 has the unfortunate consequence of providing little commentary on the most controversial phases of Haig's command, namely the Somme, Third Ypres/Passchendaele and Cambrai, or on the pinnacle of Haig's command, the Hundred Days, leading to victory and the armistice in November 1918. The 1916 – 1918 material does, however, provide some insights into life at GHQ and glimpses of Haig's personal and family life – behind a well-documented austere facade of detachment, stern reserve and imperturbability.

The diaries are sparingly written, occasionally cryptic and in places illegible (Ryan's handwriting is small, and his use of pencil has resulted in fading or blurring of some entries). In both his diaries and letters, Ryan's spelling of French and Belgian place names is frequently inaccurate, occasionally to the extent of precluding their correct identification; however, in most cases, accurate identification has been possible and the corrected spelling has been inserted in the text. One oddity warrants explanation: somewhat idiosyncratically, Ryan usually ends his letters to his wife Sadie (Sall) with the phrase 'Your loving Jane'; the name 'Eugene' has the diminutive 'Gene' which, in the accent of his birthplace, is pronounced 'Jane'.

©Author's collection

To his military colleagues (and Haig in particular), Ryan was known variously as 'Micky', 'Mickey' or 'Mickie'.

Throughout the text, in mentioning military personnel, the convention of citing an individual's contemporaneous rank is adopted.

What do the papers tell of 'Micky' Ryan – the man? Most notable, perhaps, is the positivity that pervades his writing. Even in the most precarious
of times for the BEF (the retreat from Mons and First Ypres, for example), he
exudes optimism: on 31 October 1914 – a critical day for the British at Ypres
– he wrote to his wife Sadie '... a mighty German onslaught, which seems to
have fizzled out and today we are putting in a strong counter-attack & I hope
we will succeed in driving them back.' 'Jane' wrote to Sadie on an almost daily
basis; even so, on occasions, he had to endure Sadie's grumbles, to which he
responded good-humouredly: 'I think you are very naughty at grousing as I
have written to you every day'. Ryan rarely – if ever – denigrates his military colleagues, either officers or other ranks. On the contrary, he seeks to sing
their praises: 'I don't know how our splendid chaps stand perpetual shelling
– each & every one of them deserves the VC.' On the plight of the Tommies
at First Ypres, he writes 'I feel so much for those poor chaps in their sodden
trenches & clothes' and, with relief promised, he continues 'I am simply counting the days to see those chaps out of their trenches'. In contrast with conditions at the front line, Ryan's attachment to headquarters staff meant that his
war was one of relative comfort and safety; nevertheless his own fortitude is
evident. Ryan's tending a wounded colleague under heavy shelling at an Advanced Reporting Station at Ypres (at so-called 'Hellfire Corner' on the Menin
Road) in November 1914 is described as 'splendid' by Brigadier General John
Charteris (Haig's Intelligence Officer), who is equally fulsome in his praise
of Ryan's command of No 18 Casualty Clearing Station during the Battle of
Loos in September 1915: 'His record of work during the battle is something
to be proud of ... there is never a word against our medical service. They are
really magnificent – and there is no other word – in their efficiency'. Ryan's at-
tachments to Haig's headquarters staff (I Corps, First Army, and GHQ) were
welcomed by Charteris: 'I am very glad, for he ... is the best of companions'
and by Duncan (Haig's chaplain) who refers to Ryan as 'an invaluable member of our GHQ fraternity' and notes 'his robust and cheerful attitude to life
and his unfailing commonsense'. Ryan's cheerfulness is also remarked upon
by Lieutenant General Charles Burchaell (Director General Medical Services
in France 1919): 'his professional knowledge, tact and cheery disposition has
been invaluable in maintaining the health of many Staff Officers serving at
GHQ.' Ryan's medical attention to his military colleagues and their families
extended far beyond the years of the Great War. After a period of ill health
for Dorothy Haig in 1926, during which Ryan was on hand to advise, Haig
wrote 'I can't tell you all I feel about your care & kindness & can only say I
thank you a thousand times'. In a similar vein, in 1921 Field Marshal Claud
Jacob wrote: 'I cannot tell you how grateful I am to you for all you have done
for my wife. ... You have been a perfect brick.' Ryan was at ease in all strata
of the military and social worlds. This may be partly attributable to his Irish
background and upbringing, which freed him from the strictures of the British

class system of the late-Victorian/Edwardian age with its attendant deference to rank and status. 'Micky' Ryan appears to have taken his colleagues (and they him) at face value. This is epitomized by his advice to Major Ivor Hedley, who, on taking command of Haig's cavalry escort, was beset with self doubt:
   'He's all right if ye only treat him as a man & not as a bloody Field Marshal.'

Acknowledgements

First and foremost, I thank my wife, Frances, for her tireless transcription of Ryan's letters and diaries. The diaries, in particular, required many hours to decipher. Ryan's use of pencil and his unusually small handwriting conspired to render the task highly non-trivial: the 1918 diary, for example, is truly pocketsize – measuring only 7cm by 5cm. I am greatly indebted to Gerolama, 2nd Countess Haig, for her consent to my reproducing – and quoting from – correspondence between the 1st Earl & Countess Haig and Ryan & his wife Sadie, for her permission to quote from Haig's papers, and for her approval of the inclusion of a letter to Ryan from her late husband, written on the occasion of the 2nd Earl's eleventh birthday. As custodians of The Haig Papers (NLS Acc. 3155), thanks are due to the Trustees and staff of the National Library of Scotland for the assistance offered in accessing this collection. It is a particular pleasure to acknowledge the advice, encouragement, corrections and encyclopaedic knowledge of John Hussey OBE: to him I am especially thankful for generously sharing his extensive library, papers and other material pertaining to Haig. The War Diaries written by Ryan whilst in command of No 18 Casualty Clearing Station, Lapugnoy, also feature in the text: I am grateful for access to these (reference TNA WO 95/344) at The National Archives, Kew.

   Initially, I embarked on the task of editing my grandfather's papers with only immediate family in mind. I thank Professor Gary Sheffield for suggesting that the material might be of interest to a wider audience: to him I am deeply indebted for consenting to write the Foreword to this book. Since our first meeting, Professor Sheffield's authoritative biography *The Chief: Douglas Haig and the British Army* has appeared: his permission to quote from that book is greatly appreciated. I am grateful to Lieutenant Colonel John A Charteris MBE, MC for granting permission to reproduce material from Brigadier General John Charteris's works *At G.H.Q.* and *Field-Marshal Earl Haig*. My thanks also to Kathy Stevenson, copyright holder of the late John Terraine's book *Douglas Haig : The Educated Soldier*, for her permission to quote from that masterfully crafted work. Likewise, I am indebted to Dr John Bourne, Dr J P Harris, Professor Mark Harrison and Walter Reid for permitting the use of excerpts from their respective works *Who's Who in World War One*, *Douglas Haig and the First World War*, *The Medical War* and *Douglas Haig – Architect of Victory*. Unsuccessful efforts were made to determine the copyright holder of Duncan's book *Douglas Haig As I Knew Him* and Davidson's book *Haig: Master of the Field*. If copyright has been unwittingly infringed by quoting from those books, I apologize.

Except where otherwise indicated and acknowledged, maps, photographs and other images reproduced in the book are works by the author, or items from Ryan's personal collection, or from publications with lapsed copyright. The advice of the National Portrait Gallery, London, on copyright is gratefully acknowledged.

Family & friends have contributed to this book through their encouragement, provision of material, and suggestions on early drafts: it is a pleasure to thank Sarah & David Revill, Terry Kavanagh, Deirdre O'Donovan, Fiona Ryan, Brian O'Mahony, Columba Johnson, Howard Nicholson, Jill Parker, and John Toland.

Finally, my thanks to the publishers, Pen & Sword, and, in particular, to Brigadier Henry Wilson and Matt Jones for their advice, assistance and patience throughout the production process.

Eugene P Ryan
Bath, August 2013

1
The Early Years: 1901 – 1914

'E. Ryan, Gent.', was commissioned into the Royal Army Medical Corps (RAMC), as Lieutenant, on 29 January 1901.

First commission 1901.   ©Author's collection

Within months, active service in the Second Anglo-Boer War followed: he embarked for South Africa in August 1901.

The Second Anglo Boer War 1899 – 1902

South Africa in the 1890s was a volatile amalgam of the British colonies of Natal and Cape Colony and the independent states of the Transvaal and the Orange Free State occupied by the Boers (or Afrikaners), descendants of Dutch and French settlers. The discovery of gold in the Transvaal in the 1880s had precipitated an influx of foreigners (uitlanders), mainly British, whose number eventually exceeded that of the Boers, leading inevitably to confrontation. Against a backdrop of escalating tensions, in 1899 negotiations took place to reach a compromise – ostensibly on the issue of the rights of the uitlanders (but de facto on the issue of control of the gold mining industry). Following the failure of these negotiations, the British issued an ultimatum demanding equal rights for the uitlanders in the Transvaal; the Boers responded with an ultimatum of their own, demanding withdrawal of British troops from the borders of the Transvaal. The rejection of both ultimata led to the outbreak of war on 11 October 1899.

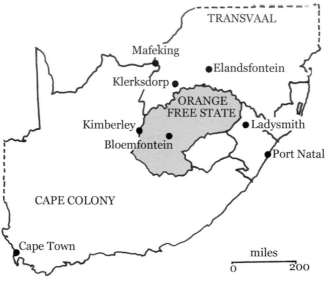

©Author's collection

During the initial phase of the war, the British – fighting over difficult terrain with long lines of communication – were severely stretched. In what became known as the 'Black Week' (10–15 December 1899), the Boers inflicted a number of defeats on the British and besieged the strategic towns of Ladysmith, Mafeking, and Kimberley. With the arrival of large numbers of reinforcements, the tide slowly turned in favour of the British: the besieged towns were relieved, Bloemfontein fell to the British in February 1900, and Johannesburg was taken in May. At this juncture, the Boers changed tactics and embarked on guerrilla warfare. The British responded with a scorched-earth policy. Boer farms were destroyed and their inhabitants were held in concentration camps. This was far from Britain's finest hour: the plight of women and children in the camps provoked international outrage. The Boers capitulated and lost their independence at the Peace Treaty of Vereeniging on 31 May 1902. It is estimated that more that 20,000 Boers died in the concentration camps, and approximately 7,000 were killed in combat. British losses amounted to 22,000, of whom approximately 8,000 died in combat; the remainder succumbed to illness and disease (typhoid being particularly prevalent).

South Africa service

Lieutenant Ryan embarked for South Africa in August 1901. On arrival at Cape Town, he was ordered to join the Field Ambulance attached to 9 Brigade at Klerksdorp. He contracted enteric (typhoid) fever in January 1902 and was transferred to the Simmer & Jack Hospital at Elandsfontein (a suburb of modern-day Johannesburg). Ryan was invalided home: he left Port Natal on a hospital ship, *Nubia*, and arrived at Plymouth on 17 March 1902.

Ryan wearing the Queen's South Africa Medal with five clasps:
South Africa 1902, South Africa 1901, Transvaal, Orange Free State, Cape Colony.
©Author's collection

Cork, Malta, Edinburgh, Millbank, Plymouth

On returning home from South Africa, Ryan appeared before a Medical Board and was given six months' sick leave, on termination of which he was posted to the Cork Military Hospital in September 1902. He remained in that post until ordered for service in Malta in February 1903.

Ryan arrived in Malta in March 1903, and served there (in the Military Hospitals at Valletta and Cottonera) until February 1908. On returning to England, Captain Ryan was posted by the War Office to the Scottish Command, Edinburgh Castle, where he served until January 1909. He then received orders to join the Royal Army Medical College, Millbank, for the Senior Officers Course (specialism – Gynaecology) from January 1909 to August 1909. On completion of that course, he was ordered to join the Southern Command for duty as Medical Officer In Charge of The Citadel at Plymouth, where he served from September to October 1909. He then received orders to proceed to Aldershot for duty as specialist in charge of women & children. He was posted to Stanhope Lines (South Camp, Aldershot, reconstructed in 1890 and named after Edward Stanhope, Secretary of State for War 1886-92), where he was attached to the Louise Margaret Hospital (opened in 1898 and named after Princess Louise Margaret of Prussia, the wife of Prince Arthur, Duke of Connaught, the seventh child of Queen Victoria).

Louise Margaret Hospital, Aldershot, 1909 – 1914

In summer 1911, Sir Douglas Haig (who had been in India since 1909 as Chief of Staff to General Sir Garrett O'Moore Creagh) was offered and accepted the Aldershot Command. Lieutenant General Haig returned to England at the end of the year and took up his appointment in March 1912: among the personal staff he brought with him from India were Captains John Charteris and Harry Beauchamp Douglas Baird, two individuals who feature frequently in Ryan's diaries and letters. The Aldershot Command formed an Army Corps which was to become I Corps of the BEF at the outbreak of war in 1914.

Haig: the first contact

It was whilst attached to the Louise Margaret Hospital at Aldershot that Ryan met Douglas Haig. The precise circumstances of their meeting are unknown but, given that the function of the Louise Margaret Hospital was to care for the wives and children of military personnel, it seems likely that health issues for Haig's wife Dorothy (Doris) or their children Alexandra (Xandra) and Victoria (Doria) provided the catalyst. Among Haig's final duties before leaving India was his involvement, in December 1911, in the organization of the Imperial Durbar – a mass assembly at Coronation Park, Delhi, India, to mark the coronation of King George V. On 23 December Douglas and Dorothy Haig embarked for England; soon after, Dorothy fell ill with dysentery, believed to have been contracted through sleeping in damp tents at the Durbar. There were fears for her life, but by the time of their disembarkment in England in January 1912, those fears had lifted. It is plausible that, following Haig's arrival in Aldershot, the Louise Margaret Hospital had a role to play in Dorothy's recovery. A second point of contact may have been Haig's eldest daughter, Alexandra, who, during her parents' absence in India, had undergone surgery for a glandular condition: Ryan's familiarity with this chronic case is evident from the update on Alexandra's condition contained in a letter (20 December 1915) from Dorothy Haig to Ryan. Whatever the circumstances of their meeting, Haig first appears in Ryan's papers in the following reference to his (Haig's) taking the Aldershot Command in 1912.

'Douglas Haig took over from Smith-Dorrien[1] at Aldershot in 1912. Soon after this it was noticed and talked of in the messes that the training of both officers and soldiers became much more strenuous. Regimental exercises, Brigade and Division training with long route marches were the order of the day. The manner of training changed frequently, especially during the hot weather the men worked without wearing their tunics and in the long route marches the men when they did wear their tunics did so with open necks (unbuttoned). '

©Author's collection

In [21, page 51], Terraine comments on Haig's tenure at Aldershot and his ability to inspire loyalty thus: 'Within two years - all that remained of peace - he undoubtedly imbued the Army Corps with a formidable corporate spirit, and his officers with a particular loyalty to himself that lasted throughout the War. What was the foundation of that loyalty? What was the nature of the man, poised now on the very brink of the great business which, more than anything else, has determined the course of the twentieth century? A quality which emerges with special emphasis from this period of his life is repose. This had both its professional and personal aspects. Professionally, he knew what he was about, and where he was going: he was not distracted; he knew he was going to war, and against whom. This lent to his ideas and his actions a focus and a composure that was bound to come across to all his associates.' Terraine [21, page 55] elaborates further. '...Haig's personal relations, outside his family, were only developed warmly with men who were constantly around him, his juniors. To them he was unfailingly loyal, and they, without exception, to him. These men, who truly understood him, and what he was after, who could "interpret" him, admired him deeply ... In the space of two years I Corps had become a very remarkable military organization. It would not be too much to call it a "band of brothers".'

'Micky' Ryan must be counted among 'these men': he was a dedicated member of the 'band of brothers'. Writing to his wife on 4 November 1914,

---

[1]General Sir Horace Lockwood Smith-Dorrien (1858 – 1930).

after his return to the front (on 28 October – into the melée of 'First Ypres') following hospitalization in Paris caused by being thrown from his horse, Ryan says: 'I could have stayed in Hospital much longer but was quite well enough to join my Hd Qrs and look after my dear General.' In his tribute, written for the commemorative issue of The British Legion (vol. 7, March 1928) following Haig's death, Ryan has Haig's reciprocation of loyalty as a central theme:

The outstanding feature of his character was his great loyalty to the cause he held at heart, and loyalty to the men who had given him all that was in them to bring the struggle in which they were engaged to a successful conclusion.

In October 1912, Ryan was appointed Officer Commanding the Louise Margaret Hospital.

In May 1914, King George V and Queen Mary visited Aldershot.

Dictated.

ROYAL PAVILION,
ALDERSHOT CAMP.

20th May 1914.

Dear Major Ryan,

I am commanded by The Queen to thank you very much for so kindly looking after Her Majesty's Dresser and at the same time I am to send you the enclosed little Souvenir of Her Majesty's visits to Aldershot.

Believe me,
Yours very truly,

Master of the Household.

Major E.Ryan,R.A.M.C.
Louise Margaret Hospital,
Stanhope Lines,
ALDERSHOT.

©Author's collection

20th May 1914

Dear Major Ryan,

I am commanded by the Queen to thank you very much for so kindly looking after Her Majesty's Dresser and at the same time I am to send you the enclosed little Souvenir of Her Majesty's visits to Aldershot.

Believe me,

Yours very truly,
Derek Keppel
Master of the Household.

Sir Derek William George Keppel (1863 – 1944), Master of the Household, was the second son of the 7th Earl of Albemarle. His sister-in-law, the Hon Mrs Alice Keppel, was a mistress of King Edward VII. Alice Keppel had two daughters: Violet, chiefly remembered for her affair with Vita Sackville-West, and Sonia, grandmother of Camilla, Duchess of Cornwall.

Ryan's command of the Louise Margaret Hospital continued until 9 August 1914, when he proceeded on Active Service as Medical Officer to Headquarters Staff, I Corps, British Expeditionary Force (BEF).

2
First World War: 1914

Last week I stated that we were working for peace not only for this country, but to pre-serve the peace of Europe. Today events move so rapidly that it is exceedingly difficult to state with technical accuracy the actual state of affairs, but it is clear that the peace of Europe cannot be preserved.

The above is an excerpt from a speech made in the House of Commons by Foreign Secretary Sir Edward Grey on 3 August 1914. On the evening of the same day, Grey is believed to have coined the following evocative phrase.

The lamps are going out all over Europe.
We shall not see them lit again in our time.

Outbreak of war, August 1914

Imperialistic foreign policies and ambitions of the dominant western powers – the British Empire, the German Empire, the Austro-Hungarian Empire, the Ottoman Empire, the Russian Empire, and France – contributed to a volatile pre-war situation. The touchpaper was lit by the assassination of Archduke Franz Ferdinand of Austria, the heir to the throne of the Austro-Hungarian Empire, by a Serb radical on 28 June 1914. Alliances formed over the previous decades were invoked. On 28 July 1914, Austria declared war on Serbia. Five days later, the British Foreign Secretary (Sir Edward Grey) announced to the House of Commons that, as a consequence of a German ultimatum to Belgium, a British ultimatum had been issued to Germany. Within 24 hours, on 4 August came the declaration of war. Transportation of the British Expeditionary Force (BEF, under the command of Field Marshal Sir John French) from England to France commenced on 12 August. Initially consisting of about 100,000 men, the BEF was divided into two Army Corps, the First commanded by Lieutenant General Sir Douglas Haig, the Second by Lieutenant General Sir James Grierson. In each Corps there were two Divisions. The First and Second Division belonged to the First Army Corps (I Corps) and were, respectively, commanded by Major General Samuel Lomax and Major General Charles Monro. Haig's principal staff officer was Brigadier General John ('Johnnie') Gough VC; his quartermaster was Brigadier General Percy E F Hobbs; artillery was the remit of Brigadier General Henry Horne and engineering that of Brigadier General Spring Rice; his ADCs included Captains Harry Baird and John Charteris. 'It is of interest to note that Haig had his own Medical Officer, a jolly Irishman, Colonel "Micky" Ryan. Ryan was indeed a personality. A regular officer in the Royal Army Medical Corps, he crossed to France with Haig in 1914; and his services during the Retreat from Mons and the First Battle of Ypres had been so meritorious that Haig in 1915 got him attached to the HQ Staff of the First Army.' [11, pages 32-33]

Dolphin Hotel, Southampton, 9–14 August 1914

Prior to crossing from Southampton to Le Havre (where they disembarked on 15 August), Haig and his Headquarters Staff, with Ryan as Medical Officer, stayed at the Dolphin Hotel in Southampton.

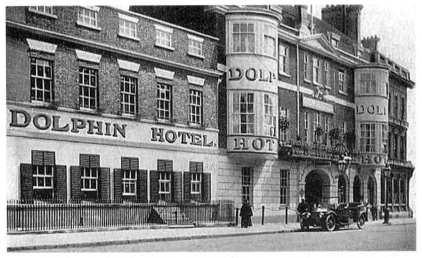

1914 postcard featuring the Dolphin Hotel. © Copyright expired

Ryan had arrived at the Dolphin on the previous Sunday (9 August). There, he initiated what was to become a lengthy series of letters to his wife Sarah (known as 'Sadie' or 'Sall'), with frequent references to the 'kiddies' (at this time, Ryan had three sons and a daughter: a fourth son was born in 1917 and a fifth in 1919).

Dolphin Hotel, Southampton
Sunday 5pm.
[9 August 1914]

My dear little one.

I have just checked my medical equipment and seen my horse which is a very nice one. Sir Douglas, Lady Haig, Baird, Charteris have returned to Aldershot as there is nothing definitely known as to when we will embark. Some say not before Friday and if Charteris' wife comes off in the meantime don't be surprised if you see me again within the next few days, or I might run up anyway but say nothing as we H.Q. people must keep things very quiet. You were very good and made things very easy for me at the right moment. I wonder if you could open that safe containing besides other things my watch & if it does not cost too much have it repaired & send it on to me at once as this rotten thing I have got is not keeping proper time. If you get the other done send the strap attached to the gold watch with it. Kiss my darling kiddies for me & with tons of love to self. Lady Haig stated she was going to call & see you some day next week. Cheerio be brave & will try & mind myself for your sake & kids as well as my own. Your loving Jane

The above letter makes reference to the imminent arrival of Charteris's first child: John Douglas Charteris was born shortly after Haig and his staff had crossed to France; Charteris did not see his son until January 1915, when Ryan sent him home for a week to recover from an attack of bronchitis.

The Dolphin Hotel, Southampton
Tuesday. 4.30pm
[11 August 1914]

My darling Sall,
I got your first letter about an hour ago. ... After a good deal of dodging about I have got my horse & saddlery & medical equipment checked and completed.
We don't know yet definitely when we embark. Colonel Sargent[1] is coming with us. Colonel Boyce[2] & Surgeon General Woodhouse[3] left on Sunday night. I went down to the ship but did not see others. I had a line from Fee this morning & fully expected one from you & was disappointed at not receiving it. I have met quite a number of chaps I know. This place is full of soldiers & officers of every description. Henniker[4] also sailed on Sunday. I will write again tomorrow.
Kiss the kiddies for me & with tons of love from Jane.

©Author's collection

---

[1] Colonel Percy W G Sargent RAMC.
[2] Colonel William G B Boyce.
[3] Surgeon General Thomas Percy Woodhouse RAMC.
[4] Major Alan M Henniker.

The Dolphin Hotel, Southampton
Thursday morning 9.30am *[13 August 1914]*

My darling little one,

I received your 3 letters last evening & one this morning and was delighted to hear you are so fit also the kiddies. You can please yourself about staying in Aldershot but if so I hope you won't let yourself be done by that landlady & I think if you stay on she ought to reduce the rent.

... I am very fit, have everything ready & expect to move tomorrow, but be certain & write to me frequently. I will on every available opportunity. The P.O. has not yet decided whether a penny or $2\frac{1}{2}$ stamp is to be put on. Hd. Qrs. 1st Army Corps will find me.

... Lochrin & a lot of chaps passed through here yesterday & embarked but I did not see any of them. I am just going to inoculate some men at 10 so I must close with ever so much love to you & kiddies.   ...   Your loving Jane.

The above letter makes reference to Captain Michael Joseph Lochrin RAMC, whose time in France & Flanders was to be tragically short. Lochrin was killed in action at Pilken near Ypres on 23 October 1914, aged 31 years.

The Southampton Constitutional Club,
14th August 1914

My own darling Sall,

Here is the last for sometime from the shores of old England. Sir Douglas & all his crowd are here and we start this evening. All full of courage and hope. Personally I am feeling splendid.

... Take care of yourself & our kiddies & with God's help ye will see me back safe & sound.

... Sir Douglas, Baird, Charteris, Gen Gough, Gen Grierson arrived last night. This place is full of soldiers one day & practically empty the next. Nearly or all the Aldershot regiments have gone though I saw very few of them. I have a nice horse and have been out on her several mornings trying what she was like. I put her over some jumps on the common. You might as well get rid of the trap & brougham otherwise the wheels if not covered with wet sacks will give away. You might pay if you think right the bill at the brewery. I can't remember any other outstanding. I will write to you on every possible chance and hope you will do the same even if only a line or two or a p.c. All letters have to pass the censor so we must be very careful of things put in ink. As I have already said I am in the best of spirits and think it is a great chance for me. Trusting everything will work out O.K.   ...   Your loving old man Jane

Embarkation of Headquarters Staff: I & II Corps

In the early hours of 15 August, I & II Corps Headquarters Staff boarded the *Comrie Castle* bound for Le Havre. The *Comrie Castle* was built in 1903 in Glasgow and operated as a troopship during the First World War. In the Second

World War she was again requisitioned by the Admiralty and met an igno-
minious end – sunk as a block ship in Folkstone Harbour.

Comrie Castle   ©http://www.clydeside.co.uk (Joe McMillan Collection)

Diary Friday 14 August 1914. Embarked *Comrie Castle* at 1am *[15 August]*.
Rained all night. No accommodation. Ship overloaded.

In his diary entry for 14 August, Haig comments on the unsuitability of the
ship. 'I understand that it was a mistake our being put on board such a small
uncomfortable steamer. The one intended for us has been delayed by fog.'

Saturday 15 August 1914. Disembarked at 3pm. Raining all day. After 3 hours
waiting in shed was billeted at Tortoni Hotel.

©Author's collection

The Tortoni Hotel, Le Havre, was destroyed in the Second World War.

Before disembarking, Ryan wrote to his wife:

My darling little one.
    Here we are just about to get on shore after a hell of a night. They packed
over 2000 troops & 100 officers & 43 nursing sisters on board a ship which
accommodates 5 officers & 130 at other times. Sir Douglas Haig & Grierson
are on board. Col Sargent, Charteris, Baird & about 90 officers had to sleep or
try to on deck down came the rain about 12. I stuck it for an hour but was
drowned out so I upped & scouted & got what shelter I could. It is raining all
day & looks as if it will continue. ...

In [4, page 83], Charteris describes the crossing.
'On August 14th the two Corps Commanders and their Staffs crossed from Southampton to Le Havre in a small Union liner - the *Comrie Castle*. It was an unpretentious introduction for the future Commander-in-Chief to the theatre of war, for the *Comrie Castle* had no passenger accommodation. The ship's officers gave up their cabins to the two Generals and their Chiefs of Staff - the remainder of the Staffs of the Army Corps bivouacking on deck. The ship could not provide meals; the only food that most of the officers could obtain for the thirteen hours of the voyage were some "picnic" provisions, hastily collected at Southampton prior to embarkation. Haig himself was more fortunate, for Lady Haig with practical forethought had provided him with a well-stocked luncheon basket.'

In his diary entry for 15 August, Haig also records the crossing.
'Saturday, August 15. I was roused about 2 a.m. by a heavy downpour of rain blowing into the ports. We were going down Southampton Water and the search lights were very bright. Our decks are crowded with men and a good many officers had also to sleep on deck. All get very wet except our servants and grooms who are with the horses under cover. I get breakfast about 8 a.m. ... Coffee and milk, sandwiches from last night's and marmalade and cake. The steamer goes very slow, about 10 knots.'

Ryan's account of the crossing follows.

©Author's collection

War declared on 4th Aug. Most of the units had already made preliminary preparations for mobilisation. The Headquarters of 1st and 2nd Corps (Grierson) left Southampton on 14th August. Reached Havre on 3pm of 15th, crossing in a ship *Comrie Castle* having very little accommodation. Only 4 bunks for officers. On arrival we were loudly cheered 'Vivez les Anglais' the inhabitants got wildly excited. The two Headquarters put up at the Tortoni Hotel, departed about midnight on 16th for Amiens in a train which was nearly wrecked before we left the station as the engine which was to take our train hit it hard causing several small injuries.

The advance to Mons: 17–23 August 1914

Death of Lieutenant General Sir James Grierson

The two Army Corps Commanders (Haig and Grierson) were proceeding on 17 August by train from Le Havre to Amiens, when Haig was called to the telephone at the station of Serqueux to be told that Grierson had died suddenly (of an aneurysm of the heart) in the train immediately following his own.

Ryan noted this incident as follows: 'DH ... ordered me over to see General Grierson (who was in the train following us) ... He had died of apoplexy'.

In [12, page 37], Sir John French (Commander-in-Chief, BEF) provides the following pen-picture of Grierson.

'I had known him for many years, but since 1906 had been quite closely associated with him; for he had taken a leading part in the preparation of the Army for war throughout that time. ... He had been British Military Attaché in Berlin for some years, and had thus acquired an intimate knowledge of the German Army. An excellent linguist, he spoke French with ease and fluency ... His military acquirements were brilliant, and in every respect thoroughly up-to-date. ... I regarded his loss as a great calamity in the conduct of the campaign.'

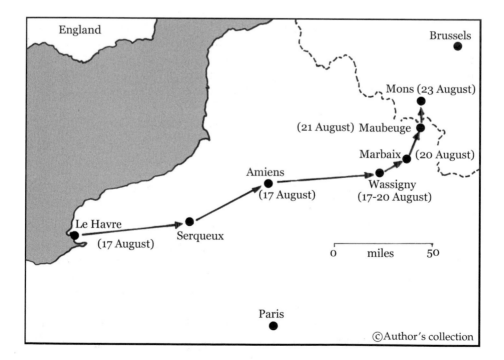

©Author's collection

On 19 August, Lieutenant General Sir Horace Smith-Dorrien was appointed Commander II Corps, in succession to Lieutenant General Grierson.

The Battle of Mons

On Monday 17 August, I Corps detrained at Amiens and established its first HQ at Wassigny. To counter the German advance through Belgium, on 20 August GHQ issued the order to advance northwards: the BEF advance (together with the French Fifth Army) into Belgium began on 21 August in the Bavai-Mons direction. From the outset, Haig had misgivings which Charteris [5, page 13] records thus: 'D.H. is much concerned about the general plan. He has heard reports that the Germans are advancing in strength right round our left flank and have forestalled our own movement. ... The country in front of us is very difficult, and we could be held up by comparatively few troops while the Germans worked round our flank.' On Saturday 22 August, II Corps held Mons and a line to the west along the Mons-Condé canal; I Corps took up its position to the right of II Corps, south-east of Mons, with the French Fifth Army, under General Charles Lanrezac, on its right. In [12, page 36], Sir John French paints an unflattering portrait of Lanrezac. 'Having heard such eulogies of him at French G.H.Q., my first impressions of General Lanrezac were probably coloured and modified in his favour; but, looking back, I remember that his personality did not convey to me the idea of a great leader. He was a big man with a loud voice, and his manner did not strike me as being very courteous.'

At 9am on Sunday 23 August, a German attack was launched – mainly concentrated on the line held by II Corps, which fell back under the pressure to a new line two miles to the south; on the other hand, I Corps sustained only minor attacks. Following intelligence reports of superior enemy numbers, the French Fifth Army was ordered to retreat: this precipitated the British decision to withdraw. Early on 24 August, the BEF was ordered to fall back to a line through Bavai – thus began the Retreat from Mons.

When contrasted with the enormous losses suffered in later battles of the war, the casualties at Mons were relatively light: German casualties are estimated at 5,000, whereas the British, who inflicted disproportionate losses on the numerically superior Germans, sustained approximately 1,700 casualties.

Early on the morning of the battle, 23 August, 'Jane' wrote to Sadie.

My sweet little one

Here we are just waiting for a pitched battle. The Germans are within 5 miles and some fighting has taken place already. I attended the first man shot in an aeroplane yesterday. He was shot through the hip at a height of 4000 feet. He is doing very well. There are about 250,000 Germans in a radius of 5 miles so we expect plenty of work today or tomorrow. Our cavalry have already taken some of the German cavalry prisoner besides killing a certain no. of them. The Germans are burning all before them in Belgium. The more I see of this country the more horrible it is to think of war. It is really a beautiful country. I am just scribbling this as there is a post going out. How I should love to see you & our dear little ones. Will write again as soon as possible.

With tons of love to you & kiddies.   Your loving Jane

"A" Form.

Army Form C. 2121

MESSAGES AND SIGNALS.

No. of Message _____

Prefix _____ Code _____ m. | Words | Charge

Office of Origin and Service Instructions.

This message is on a/c of :

Recd. at _____ m.

Sent _____ m.

Service.

Date _____

From _____

To _____

By _____ (Signature of "Franking Officer.") By _____

TO {

My sweet little one

Here we are just waiting for a pitched battle. the Germans are within 5 miles and some fighting

Sender's Number | Day of Month | In reply to Number

* has taken place already. I attended the first man shot in **AAA**
an aeroplane yesterday. he was shot through the hip at a
height of 4000 feet. he is doing very well. There are about
250,000 germans in a radius of 5 miles. as we expect
plenty of work to day & to morrow. Our cavalry have already
taken some of the German Cavalry prisoners beside tallying a
certain no of them. The Germans are burning all before them
in Belgium. The more I see of this country the more
horrible it is to think of war. it is really a beautiful
country. I am just scribbling this as there is a post going
out. How I should love to see you & our dear little ones
write again as soon as possible.
with love & love to you & kiddies
your loving Jack

From

Place

Time

©Author's collection

I attended the first man shot in an aeroplane yesterday. It is generally believed that the first British shot of the war was fired near the Belgian village of Casteau early on 22 August 1914 – preceding the Battle of Mons by only 24 hours – in an engagement with a German Cavalry unit involving the 4th Dragoon Guards on a reconnaissance mission ahead of the BEF. In the above letter,

Ryan records treating a Royal Flying Corps (RFC) casualty on the same day. In his 'Short Record of Service in France', Ryan again refers to the event: '21st found us at Maubeuge where I attended [on 22 September] a Sgt Major RFC shot through buttock & belly'.

This casualty was Sergeant Major David S Jillings of No. 2 Squadron, based at Maubeuge, who was indeed the first British airman 'shot in an aeroplane'. The circumstances of Jillings's wounding are described in *The War in the Air* by W Raleigh (The Clarendon Press, Oxford, 1922). 'On the 22nd there were twelve reconnaissances which revealed the presence of large bodies of troops moving in the direction of the British front, and did much to dissipate the fog of war. The first machine to return came in soon after eleven. This was piloted by Captain G. S. Shephard, with Lieutenant I. M. Bonham-Carter as observer. They had landed at Beaumont (about twelve miles east of Maubeuge) for petrol. Here they were informed that French cavalry had encountered German infantry north of the Sambre canal on the previous afternoon, and had had to fall back. The next machine to return came in at 11.50 a.m. with a wounded observer, Sergeant-Major D. S. Jillings of No. 2 Squadron. He was the first British soldier to be wounded in an aeroplane, and this casualty seemed to bring the German armies nearer than a dozen unmolested reconnaissances could have done. The machine, piloted by Lieutenant M. W. Noel, had come under heavy rifle fire first of all at Ollignies, south-east of Lessines, and then, after passing over a cavalry regiment just south-west of Ghislenghien, had been met with rifle and machine-gun fire. Frequent rifle fire was encountered all the way back to Ath, and just south-east of Ath, over Maffle, Sergeant-Major Jillings had been wounded in the leg by a rifle bullet.' In the Second World War, Jillings attained the rank of Group Captain. He died in 1953.

Mons: Ryan's account up to 24 August

Arrived at Amiens ... DI I sent for me and ordered me over to see General Grierson (who was in the train following us) who he heard was very ill. He had died from apoplexy. Our Hd Qrs temp. was at Wassigny 5pm on the 17th to 9am on the 20th. Marbaix 20, 3pm collecting his Corps. Friday 21st Maubeuge and Saturday the 1st and 2nd Div (1st Corps) marching through Maubeuge all the afternoon, evening and night to take up their position round Mons. The 2nd Corps now under SD [Smith-Dorrien] took up their position along the Condé Canal N.W. of Mons. There were several small engagements on Friday and Saturday between our advanced cavalry and the Uhlans. Before our

Corps had time to dig any entrenchments they were peppered with shells, machine gun and rifle fire. There was a heavy frontal attack early on Sunday am, our right wing was supposed to be in touch with the French on our South who had taken a nasty knock on Friday at Charleroi, leaving our right wing in the air until DH put in some cavalry to find and keep in touch with the French on our South. About 3am on the 24th we got orders to retreat to Bavai where I found the place filled with ambulances full of wounded which I got transferred to the French Hospital. I notified Amiens Line of Communication asking them to send an ambulance train at once.

©Author's collection

The retreat from Mons: 24 August – 5 September 1914

By the afternoon of 24 August, I Corps held a line to the east of Bavai: Haig set up his HQ in an 'indifferent farm' near Vieux Mesnil. In his diary entry on that day, Haig wrote: *When I got to my room I turned v. sick, diarrhoea – and continued for two hours, then went to sleep.*
This incident is also recorded by Charteris [5, page 17]:
'... was awakened by Secrett [*Haig's personal servant*] to say that D.H. was very ill; had shut himself up in his room, and given orders that he would see no-body. I got hold of Micky Ryan and went in to D.H. and insisted that he must see Ryan. D.H. was at his worst, very rude but eventually did see Ryan, who dosed him with what must have been something designed for elephants, for the result was immediate and volcanic! But it was effective, for D.H. ulti-mately got some sleep, and in the morning was better but very chewed up,

and ghastly to look at. He wanted to ride as usual, but Ryan insisted on his going in a car that day.'

In a letter to his wife on 4 October, Haig identifies a possible cause of his illness.

As to that sickness, it was stupid of me to have written it in the Diary. ... I have been v. fit ever since. I think I was poisoned by some powder which is dusted onto grapes to kill the insects. It was a v. hot day I remember & I ate a couple of bunches of grapes.

On the morning of 25 August, the retreat was resumed, with I Corps to the east of the Forest of Mormal and II Corps to the west: this separation of the two Corps hampered communications.

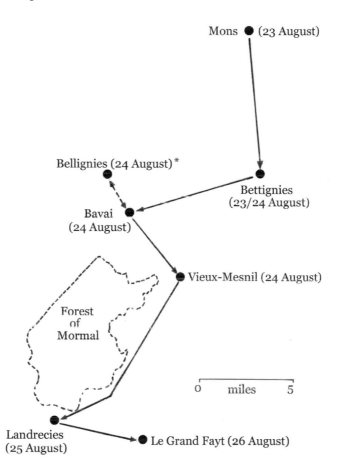

Initial Phase of I Corp's Retreat from Mons
* On 24 August, Ryan took a wounded officer from Bavai to a temporary hospital in Prince de Croÿ's Château at Bellignies. ©Author's collection

Landrecies

In the afternoon of 25 August, Haig established his HQ at Landrecies, leaving a gap of several miles between I Corps and II Corps with its HQ at Le Cateau. During the evening and night, German sorties into Landrecies (with attendant confusion and rumour) alarmed Haig: in unusually melodramatic language, he is reported to have said

If we are caught, by God, we'll sell our lives dearly.

His uncharacteristic behaviour at Landrecies is often interpreted as evidence that Haig was 'rattled' or 'caught off balance': a more prosaic explanation is that he was in poor physical condition, debilitated by the severe nausea and diarrhoea of the previous night. (By 27 August, Haig had regained his health and composure: on that date, Ryan observed that 'the contrast between DH & others was very striking, he calm & like Kipling's If.')

In any event, late in the evening of 25 August, Haig decided to move his HQ to Le Grand Fayt, about 3 miles to the south-east of Landrecies. In [13, page 75], Harris notes that: 'Haig decided to evacuate his headquarters to Le Grand Fayt, several miles to the south. He, Gough and Charteris left Landrecies by staff car at around 11.30 p.m. It was pitch dark. The surrounding countryside was thought to be alive with marauding Germans. Though Haig and his entourage were in a hurry to be gone, they did not want to draw fire by using the car's lights. Inevitably it was a hair-raising ride. This part of the great retreat seems to have been a still more alarming experience for Major Ryan, Haig's medical officer, Captain Baird, one of his ADCs, and his soldier servant, Secrett, all of whom are reported to have followed on horseback, bringing Haig's horse with them.'

The journey is also recorded by Charteris [5, page 95]. 'The only roads available were village tracks with many turnings; the night was misty, and neither headlights nor sidelights could be used. A Staff Officer memorized the map and directed the car, but no one had much hope that the venture would succeed. At one point indeed, the car was challenged, but no shot was fired, and by 1 a.m. Haig had rejoined the main body of his force and resumed command of the Corps. The incident at Landrecies was not the only occasion when Haig's personal safety had been seriously threatened. On the early morning of the first day of the retreat, a Staff Officer directing his car mistook his road, and for a mile motored straight towards the enemy, only discovering the error in time to avert the disaster of Haig's capture.'

Haig's servant, Sergeant Thomas Secrett [17, pages 83-84], records the retreat from Landrecies thus: 'It was eleven o'clock at night when Sir Douglas consented to leave, and the firing between our own troops and the Germans in the streets was plainly audible. He left in the staff car, and I rode the horse I generally used and led his and another. I was accompanied by Colonel Ryan, the medical chief at headquarters, and Captain Baird, one of Sir Douglas's aides. ... Behind us the sound of battle was never far distant. ... It was a murderous ride.'

Ryan's account is more low key. 'DII left Landrecies about 10pm in a car with Johnny Gough and Charteris: Baird and I mounted, arrived Le Grand Fayt about 2 am.'

The latter stages of the retreat

While II Corps (under Smith-Dorrien) engaged the enemy – some 8 miles west of Le Grand Fayt – in a skilful defensive action that became known as the Battle of Le Cateau, I Corps continued its retreat on 26 August, arriving in the evening at Etreux. On 27 August, the retreat was resumed, through Guise to Mont d'Origny, the German pursuit having been delayed by an engagement with the 2nd Battalion Royal Munster Fusiliers, which suffered very heavy casualties. After a march in intense heat, the night of 28 August found I Corps positioned between La Frère and the Forest of St Gobain.

In [5, page 93], Charteris makes the following observation. 'Throughout the whole of the Retreat, Haig shared the hardships of the troops. He took no longer hours of rest than he could afford to allow the men. From dawn till nightfall he was in the saddle. His Headquarters moved at the rear of the main columns in close touch with the rearguards, but each day he himself rode along the whole length of the line.' This observation resonates with Ryan's letter of 29 August in which he states that 'I saw ... any amount of old pals as I rode with Sir Douglas all around his army, and although I did 45 miles I felt fresh as a daisy last night'.

On 28 August, RFC air reconnaissance reported a vulnerable gap between the German I and II armies. Haig instructed one of General Lanrezac's Staff Officers, Captain Jacques Helbronner, to pass on this information to the General and to inform him that the enemy was exposing his left flank and that he (Haig) was anxious to cooperate in an attack. In seeking the sanction of the Commander-in-Chief, Sir John French, for I Corps participation in an attack, Haig received the following response. 'Commander-in-Chief does not approve of any active operations on the part of our First Corps tomorrow and has already ordered a halt for one day's rest.' This exchange was symptomatic of a deteriorating relationship between Haig and Sir John French, whom Haig was to replace as Commander-in-Chief in December 1915. The following query from GHQ, received by Haig early on 29 August, did little to paper over the cracks: 'Please be good enough to inform C-in-C how it was that any confidential promise of support by First Corps was made to General Lanrezac or why any official exchange of ideas was initiated without authority from Headquarters'. Against this background, 29 August was a day of rest for I Corps, whilst the French Fifth Army were engaged nearby in what became known as the Battle of Guise. The latter helped in slowing the German advance, which was being stretched logistically. (In his diary entry for 13 August, a prescient Haig had remarked: 'I gather that there are 6 or 7 [German] Corps in the area Namur-Liege-Bastogne. It is doubtful how this mass could cross the R. Meuse & operate upon the French left and be supplied!')

The retreat continued on 30 August; that night, I Corps HQ was in a château two miles to the south-west of Soissons. On 31 August, I Corps crossed the Aisne and HQ was set up at Villers-Cotterêts, where a rear-guard action, with heavy casualties, was fought on 1 September. On the following day, I Corps HQ was at Meaux, from where Ryan wrote to Sadie:

My own darling
Just a scrawl to let you know that I am alive and kicking ... I have just got in after 15 hrs in the saddle & am scrawling this to catch a post. Will write again tomorrow.

On 3 September, HQ was at La Fringale. In *Everyman at War: Sixty Personal Narratives of the War* (edited by C B Purdom, Dutton, New York, 1930), Corporal John Bernard Denore, 6 Brigade, 2nd Division, I Corps, vividly depicts the plight of the 'Tommies' on 2–3 September.

We bivouacked outside Meaux. ... I was rounding up stragglers most of the night until 1 a.m., and at 3 a.m. we moved off again. ... It was the most terrible march I have ever done. Men were falling down like nine-pins. They would fall flat on their faces on the road, while the rest of us staggered round them, as we couldn't raise our feet high enough to step over them, and, as for picking them up, that was impossible, as to bend meant to fall. What happened to them, God only knows. An aeroplane was following us most of the time dropping iron darts; we fired at it a couple of times, but soon lost the strength required for that.

In persistent heat, the retreat continued on 4 September, on the night of which I Corps HQ was in a château at Faremoutiers. At 3am on the morning of 5 September, I Corps resumed their march south in the direction of Melun. At the village of Marles, Haig received orders from GHQ: the Germans had ceased their pursuit and I Corps should be prepared to assume the offensive on 6 September.

In effect, the Retreat from Mons was over. In the 12 days of the retreat, I Corps had marched approximately 160 miles.

In [12, page 139], Sir John French comments on the rapid reversal of fortune for the Allies. 'Splendidly, however, as the Allied Armies fought, skilfully as each of the various corps and armies which were engaged supported one another; it was the Germans themselves who deliberately threw away whatever chance they ever had of securing a decisive victory. We have seen that so late as the morning of September 6th, Joffre[5] and I were still so certain that the German thrust was in full career ... Yet at that time von Kluck's[6] great "advance" had for some hours become a counter-march in hurried "retreat." Why this sudden change? Because he then discovered that his communications were about to be threatened on the Ourcq. Surely the most inexperienced of generals might have anticipated some such threat ... The fact probably is that von

---

[5]Marshal Joseph Joffre (1852 – 1931), Commander-in-Chief of the French Armies.
[6]General Alexander von Kluck (1846 – 1934), Commander of the German 1st Army.

Kluck and his Staff never really liked the role which was forced upon them by the Great General Staff, and that they undertook their part in the battle with wavering minds and with their heads half turned round.'

The retreat from Mons: Ryan's account

Sir J French & Archy Murray[7] were met by DH at Bavai about 11 am on 24th. We trekked S.W. & spent the night at a farm house which was filthy & full of flies. About 11pm DH was taken violently ill as if he had been poisoned & vomiting was intense. Stomach was washed out with Sodium Bicarbonate solution which gave him instant relief. He was OK at 4 am when we left for Landrecies. The route was blocked by retiring French Cavalry, each riding one & guiding another, the horses looking very badly kept & most of them suffered from huge saddle galls. I went to the hospital [illegible] which I found full of wounded, many of whom I dressed. Went to the Stn, saw the R.T.O. [Railway Transport Officer] ordered him to get up an ambulance train: eventually I got 136 wounded officers and men away about 5pm. The Germans were still on our heels. Troops arriving in motor buses & lorries. There was a general action about 8 pm. the Guards doing great execution. DH left Landrecies about 10pm in a car with Johnny Gough and Charteris: Baird and I mounted, arrived Le Grand Fayt about 2 am. DH, Gough & Charteris stayed in motor car. The night was cold & wet, the morning very sultry. ... At this place the troops looked tired & weary and a big number of them left their overcoats and pack behind.

[7]Major General Sir Archibald Murray (1860 – 1945), Chief of the General Staff.

DH gave instructions that country carts should be got to collect th
bring them along. He was very observant, saw things that others i.
always gave his orders in such a quiet & intelligent manner as if he .
thorough grasp of the situation even in the most trying circumstances. S
trekking S.E. thro 26th Hannappes to Guise. 27th having frequent scraps wit.
the Bosh and then getting away. Our rear guard actions getting it hot by Germans brought up in buses. On arrival at Guise about 11 pm we were met by
our Camp Commander who informed us that he had good billets for us. We
"dined" at a public house & like John Jorrocks, where we dined we slept. DH
and John G. *[Gough]* in two small rooms upstairs the rest of us helter skelter
in the Salle a Manger. About 2 am J.G. came down stairs and into the dining
room. I was awake. He seemed rather excited and asked me where were the
other officers? I said we are nearly all here. He said tell them to get up & get a
move on. At that moment DH came down stairs, calm & collected. He asked
me to get General Horne to come to see him, to whom he explained the latest
reports & the situation in general & told him to get in touch with General Al-
lenby & asked him to cover us while he intended to get his troops away down
a rather narrow winding road - double banked formation on our way to St
Gobain. The contrast between DH & others was very striking, he calm & like
Kipling's 'If'.

©Author's collection

From Gobain to Terin *[probably Terny]*, which some of us reached at midnight,
others long after. We again trekked from here at 4 am, reached Vauxbuin about
2 pm, troops not arriving till next morning.

Villers-Cotterêts Monday 31st. The Irish Guards put up a great show here,
killing a lot of enemy & captured some field guns that had been rushed up.
DH looking very well. Johnny *[Gough]* ill with pharyngitis, temp 102. Left at
2am for Mareuil.

1st Sept - Mareuil sur Ourcq.

2nd Meaux, everybody tired but ready always to fight.

3rd Sept. Left Meaux at 7am & bivouacked in a wood at La Fringale.

4th Faremoutiers. Got a car and went to GHQ. Saw Col O'Donnell[8] and advised him to put a Medical Officer in each rail head to look after the wounded
pending the arrival of ambulance trains to pick them up. This he promised
to do though he was very hard pressed for M.O.s as a big number had been
taken prisoners.

---

[8]Colonel Thomas Joseph O'Donnell RAMC.

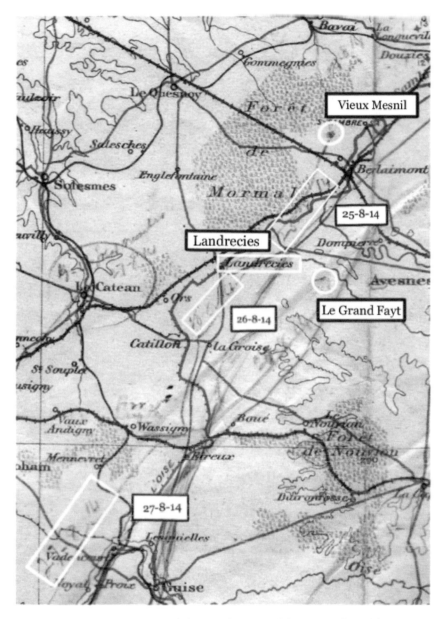

Ryan's annotated map of the initial stages of the retreat from Mons:
dates (25-8-14, 26-8-14, 27-8-14) are discernible but other annotations are illegible.
©Author's collection

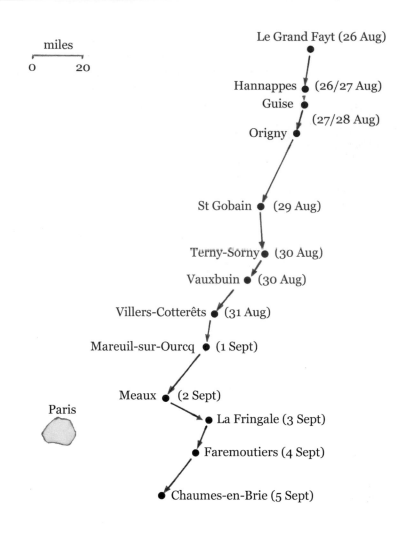

miles

0   20

Le Grand Fayt (26 Aug)

Hannappes (26/27 Aug)

Guise

(27/28 Aug)

Origny

St Gobain (29 Aug)

Terny-Sorny (30 Aug)

Vauxbuin (30 Aug)

Villers-Cotterêts (31 Aug)

Mareuil-sur-Ourcq (1 Sept)

Meaux (2 Sept)

Paris

La Fringale (3 Sept)

Faremoutiers (4 Sept)

Chaumes-en-Brie (5 Sept)

Ryan's itinerary in the latter stage of the Retreat from Mons.
©Author's collection

Ryan's diary and his letters to Sadie provide further insights into the retreat.

Diary Sunday 23 August. ... Got to Château at Bettignies at 4 o.c. ...

Monday 24 August. Moved from above at 3 am to Bavai. Shelling going on. Took wounded officer to Prince de Croÿ's Château at Bellignies. Shrapnel wounds. Left at 6 pm for Vieux Mesnil. I crossed the Belgian frontier yesterday. Shells bursting all round Le Bonnet.

took wounded officer to Prince de Croÿ's Château at Bollignies. Prince Reginald de Croÿ (1878-1961) was a Belgian aristocrat whose family home, Château de Bellignies, is situated south west of Mons near the Franco–Belgian border. During the Retreat from Mons, in addition to the wounded left behind in field hospitals, many troops, both British and French, became separated from their units. De Croÿ and his sister, Princess Marie de Croÿ (1875 – 1968), were part of an underground network which hid and assisted the escape of an estimated 200 soldiers, some of whom passed through Bellignies.

Château de Bellignies.   ©Author's collection

In the event of threat of detection, fugitives at Bellignies took refuge in a stairway hidden within the walls of the mediaeval tower on the left of the château – the stairway entrance was concealed behind the wainscot on the ground floor. (The author is indebted to Princess Diane de Croÿ, daughter of Prince Reginald, niece of Princess Marie, and current châtelaine of Bellignies, for her warm hospitality in allowing access to the château in July 2010.) A key figure in the network was Nurse Edith Cavell who was matron at the Berkendael Medical Institute in Brussels, which had become a Red Cross Hospital at the outbreak of the war. The network was compromised in July 1915: Reginald evaded arrest and escaped to neutral Holland; Marie, Cavell and several others were charged with espionage, Cavell was sentenced to death and executed by firing squad on 12 October 1915, and Marie was sentenced to 10 years imprisonment and held at Siegburg in Germany until her release in 1918.

In her book *War Memories* [8, pages 11-12], Marie de Croÿ records the following, which resonates with Ryan's diary entry for 24 August ('Took wounded officer to Prince de Croÿ's Château at Bellignies'): it is probable that the 'doctor' referred to below was Ryan.

August 24. Soon we heard that wounded and sick men were lying in farm-houses and on the roadside, so my brother and the chauffeur started out to bring them in. ... The first wounded that came in were so exhausted from want of food that I had jugs of milk and glasses ready by the door to give them before they were lifted down from the cars or horses which brought them in. .... About this time a car brought in a superior officer accompanied by a doctor. He was a Major of the Gordon Highlanders, who had a bullet in his shoulder which could not be extracted at once. He had lost much blood, and must have a night's rest and be sent by special train to the English base at Amiens next day, the doctor told us.

Ryan's diary entries continue.

Tuesday 25 August. Started at 4 am next morning for Landrecies. Dispatched 36 wounded officers and men from French hospital to Amiens. Place attacked at 8 pm. Left for Le Grand Fayt - concentration of No 1 A. Corps. Lost 123 at Landrecies: 6 killed, 2 officers.

Wednesday 26 August. Engaged with enemy. Went on to Hannapes where I enjoyed a good nights rest in a bed. 4 RAMC officers[9] of No 19 FA *[Field Ambulance]* stayed to attend wounded at Landrecies.

Thursday 27 August. Left at 8 am for Guise/Origny. Fought a rear guard action all day. The Munsters losing very heavily ... The enemy holding ground from Cateau to St Quentin. Dug *[Major William F B R Dugmore]* & I bivouacked at Guise.

On 27 August, he also wrote to Sadie.

My darling Sall
      We have been so hard at it for the last three days and nights that I have not had time to write you. Last night I had a good sleep and wanted it as I had not 3 hrs during the last 4 days + nil for 48 hrs. ... The Germans shelled our place the other night and things were very hot for some hours but again we gave them more than they gave us. ... Poor little me had only 2 biscuits yesterday as we lost our baggage for 36 hrs. Write and tell me all about everything as we are like savages here. I have not seen a paper for 10 days. ... I am going to write to Lady Haig today if I have time. Sir Douglas is splendid - merry & bright. You should see Baird and me sharing a small waterproof sheet for a bed the night before last under the canopy of heaven. Still it is a grand life and most exciting, very much so at times. Charteris is very bucked on the arrival of the son. I am scrawling this during a halt and as we are just going to move to the music of shot & shell I will close with lots of love & kisses to you & our darling kiddies.   Your loving Jane.

Friday 28 August. Left at 3 am for La Fère. The enemy marching in a parallel road. The men tired but cheery. *[Illegible]* reached Gobain. The men doing 20 miles. Went on to St Gobain. General Gough ill. Pharyngitis, temp 101.

Saturday 29 August. The F *[The French, under General Lanrezac, in the Battle of Guise]* engage the enemy along the Oise, the Germans being on the St Quentin-Omissy line, the F on eastern side. Very heavy cannonade. Our men rested. All sick & wounded evacuated. Left St Gobain at 11 pm. Arrived Terny *[Terny-Sorny]* at 2 am. Left Terny at 4 am. Reached Vauxbuin at 1 pm. Troops arriving till midnight.

---

[9]Major Walter B Fry, Major James C Furness, Captain Winfred K Beaman & Lieutenant Arthur B Preston. All four were taken prisoner; Fry died in March 1915 in the typhus-stricken camp at Wittenberg in Saxony.

On 29 August 'Jane' again wrote to Sadie.

My darling Sadie,

Ever the old old tale only two letters from you. What of this and why? I hear there are great accounts of our achievements in the papers at home. They can have very little idea of the work and fighting our chaps are doing, really they are splendid. The mortality amongst some regiments is high but it is nothing in comparison with the losses on the German side.

I saw J.S. Bostock the night before last – we had not time to talk only just a passing word. Our chaps are having a fairly quiet time today but tomorrow or after will see another bloody battle in which I hope the enemy will be wiped out. I saw Betsy[10] yesterday, also Hinge,[11] Capt *[Herbert C.]* Potter of the Liverpools, *[Henry C.]* Stanley-Clarke (Gunners), *[Bowcher C. S.]* Clarke (Worcs), in fact any amount of old pals as I rode with Sir Douglas all around his army, and although I did 45 miles I felt as fresh as a daisy last night.

©Author's collection

A great number of our chaps are missing. They are being taken by the Germans when attending the wounded and if rumour is true some of them have been shot in cold blood. It is stated that Leahy (the champion boxer) was shot while dressing some wounded cavalry in a house. I left 4 of our officers to attend some wounded about 4 days ago - and have not seen or heard of them since. Those damn Germans stop at nothing. They came into one town here - dressed up as British soldiers - having stripped the dead. They have broken every rule of the game and won't get much quarter from our chaps in future.

I trust you and the kiddies are splendid. ...   Your loving Jane.

I saw J.S. Bostock the night before last – we had not time to talk ...
Major John Southey Bostock RAMC (1875 – 1930) is mentioned frequently in Ryan's papers: also referred to as 'J.S.' or 'J.S.B.'. Bostock gained his first commission on the same day as Ryan. The RAMC appears to have been a closely-knit Corps and relatively small in number: the British Medical Journal (Jan 2, 1915, p.18) records the Active List for December 1914 as comprising 1099 officers. The career paths of Bostock and Ryan were to converge again in 1930 when Colonel Ryan was Officer Commanding the Queen Alexandra

---

[10]Major Maurice Guy Winder RAMC (1876 – 1932): his sobriquet 'Betsy' is unexplained.
[11]Major Harry Alexander Hinge RAMC (1868 – 1948).

Military Hospital, Millbank, London, and Colonel Bostock was Commandant of the adjacent Royal Army Medical College. Bostock was one of six brothers, three of whom were killed in action on the Western Front. In the Second World War, Bostock's elder son, Flight Lieutenant John Oliver Bostock (serving in the RAF Volunteer Reserves), was killed in action over the Netherlands in 1943.

It is stated that Leahy (the champion boxer) was shot ...
Captain Michael Patrick Leahy RAMC. In 1899, Leahy commenced his studies in medicine at Trinity College, Dublin. Introduced to the sport of rowing by Bram Stoker (author of *Dracula*), Leahy joined the Boat Club and was in the eight that lifted the Thames Cup at the 1903 Henley Royal Regatta.

Leahy, second from right, at Henley 1903.
[By kind permission of the ©Dublin University Boat Club.]

Having excelled at rowing, Leahy turned his attention to boxing, becoming Irish amateur heavyweight champion in 1908 and 1909. On graduation in 1906, Leahy had joined the RAMC. On Saturday 5 April 1913, The Times records that, in the light heavyweight semi-final bouts of the Army Championships, 'Captain M.P. Leahy (R.A.M.C.) beat Lieutenant H.J.S. Shields (R.A.M.C.)'. Lieutenant Hugh John Sladen Shields was killed in action

near Ypres on 26 October 1914. During the retreat from Mons in September 1914, Leahy was wounded and captured. The severity of his wounds necessitated the amputation of his right leg. He was released and repatriated in July 1915. The loss of a leg deterred neither his serving with the RAMC nor his sporting endeavours. In 1953, Leahy returned to Henley and sculled the course to commemorate his role in winning the Thames Cup fifty years before. Leahy died in 1965.

[Photograph from the article 'Oarsman, pugilist, doctor and war hero',

©Peter Henry, Trinity News, November 2007.]

Sunday 30 August. Vauxbuin. The Field Ambulance shacked at Château, very kindly treated by Mme de Mestre. A big engagement at Guise. Went to mass with Dugmore. Villers-Cotterêts.

The name 'Dugmore' (or 'Dug') occurs often in Ryan's papers. This probably refers to **Major William Francis Brougham Radclyffe Dugmore (1869 – 1917)**. Dugmore's association within I Corps Headquarters Staff is unclear. In his diary entry of 3 December 1914, Ryan records that Dugmore was 'farewell' dined. It is likely that Dugmore then rejoined his regiment, the North Staffordshires. Acting Lieutenant Colonel Dugmore was killed in action on 12 June 1917 during the Messines-Wytschaete Ridge offensive, whilst in command of 1st Battalion North Staffordshire Regiment. The plausibility of Dugmore's identification is supported by a somewhat esoteric source. An entry in the quaintly-titled *Converts to Rome: a Biographical List of the More Notable Converts to the Catholic Church in the United Kingdom during the Last Sixty Years* (compiled & edited by W Gordon Gorman, published by Sands & Co., London, 1910) reads: 'Dugmore, Captain Francis Sandys (1846-1898) ... father of Captain William Francis Brougham Radclyffe Dugmore D.S.O., of the North Staffordshire Regiment'. Amidst the anxiety of the retreat and with the Germans in close pursuit, the Catholic Dugmore and Ryan found time to seek out mass!

Monday 31 August. Day very hot. Went to Villers-Cotterêts and slept at Dolphin Hotel [*Hôtel du Dauphin, Place du Marché*]. Left at 2 am for Mareuil. Rode about 15 miles to Marolles.
Tuesday 1 September. Started for Mareuil sur Ourcq.
Wednesday 2 September. Meaux.
Thursday 3 September. Left Meaux at 7 am & entrained sick. Bivouacked at La Fringale in a wood (shooting box). [*Haig's diary entry for the same day, 3 September, includes: 'I have my H.Q. at La Fringale a shooting box evidently owned by a syndicate.'*]
Friday 4 September. Went to Mormant and saw about 100 sick. Collected them in Station. Slept at Faremoutiers. [*Haig's diary entry for the same day, 4 September, includes: 'I have my H.Q. at the Château of Faremoutiers for the night.'*] Wrote Sadie.

Sept 4th 1914. 7pm.

My darling Sadie.

We have just called a halt after a trying and strenuous day and am writing this in the grounds of a beautiful château [*Faremoutiers*]. Our times are very strenuous but I am pleased to say our casualties for the last few days have been slight. I saw Hinge & Lochrin & Easton[12] today. I saw Bostock yesterday. I am pleased to say they are all well but tired. We scarcely get any sleep. I am afraid a lot of our chaps have fallen but one hears such a lot of rumours

---

[12]Major Philip George Easton RAMC (1879 – 1960).

that one is doubtful about believing all one hears. I got a letter from you this morning dated Aug 23rd. On reading one of your letters I see you mention some forage bill. I don't owe anything for forage so please don't pay. We have been over a huge portion of France and it is a most delightful & prosperous country and it is a sorry sight to see the people old & young - even babies a few days old leaving as they are terrified of the Germans. In a village we were in yesterday I was called to see a woman who had a baby the day before ... I put her right & you cannot imagine how grateful the people were. The people are very kind & supply the troops with fruit cider & wine. I have never seen anything like the fruit trees they are drooping with peaches, pears, apples, even the trees along the road side. I wrote you the evening before last & had not time to finish it so I closed it and sent it off. I trust you & the kiddies are splendid - kiss them all for me. It is getting dark. We had breakfast at 3am and shortly expect a bit of dinner. I am full of dust & thirst so I must go & have a wash & get something into little Mary. I am splendid. I had a bit of trots yesterday but am OK today.

With tons of love to you & kiddies. You did not mention anything about them. Is Jack saying his lessons?   Your devoted Jane.

Saturday 5 September. Left at 6am for Marles with Dugmore. Arrived at 8.15. Went to HdQrs & saw O'Donnell. Got M.O. appointed to Railheads. Billet in a nice château at Chaumes where I had a good dinner and a bed. *[In Haig's diary entry for the same day, 5 September, he records: 'I spent the night near Chaumes in a fine (newish) Château de Crénille owned by a Baron Léonino. I had a fine suite - bedroom writing dressing room with bath in it. The others were well accommodated downstairs.']*

Sunday 6 September. Left at 7am on Sunday, rode cross country to Chaubuisson Farm . Heavy cannonade about 2 miles on our east by our cavalry Brigade. A great pow-wow of generals at 11am. An aeroplane has just reported that the Germans are retiring.

'On the early morning of the 6th Sir John French gave verbal instructions that the Royal Flying Corps were to send aeroplanes to report for reconnaissance direct to the First and Second Corps. The officer commanding No. 5 Squadron, with three machines, was to report for tactical reconnaissance direct to Sir Douglas Haig at Chaubuisson farm ... '

(Excerpt from *The War in the Air* by W Raleigh, Clarendon Press, Oxford, 1922.)

The Marne & the Aisne: Autumn 1914

The Marne: 6–12 September 1914

With the end of the retreat from Mons, the situation had quickly reversed. After only one day of rest, I Corps was on the move again on 6 September, under orders from GHQ to be in position on a line at Rozay-en-Brie-Fontenay, from which position it was to attack the German First Army as part of an offensive known as the Battle of the Marne (c.f. Ryan's letter of 6 September: '... we are just off and expect to be heavily engaged before many hours ...'). On 7 September, I Corps crossed the Grand Morin river without opposition. The Petit Morin was crossed on 8 September, where the advance troops engaged with the German rearguard. During this encounter, Haig and his staff went forward to some high ground to observe: they came under machine-gun fire, taking shelter behind the tombstones in a churchyard. On 9 September, I Corps crossed the Marne unopposed. The next day, Thursday 10 September, the advance was resumed, with orders 'to continue the pursuit and attack the enemy wherever met' (vide Ryan's letter of 10 September: 'We have given hell to the Germans during the last 4 days & have them on the run'). Abandoned equipment provided evidence of enemy disarray: nevertheless, the Germans successfully retreated across the Aisne on 11–12 September and entrenched on the northern bank at the Chemin des Dames, an east-west ridge road (originally a carriageway renovated in the 18th century by Louis XV to facilitate the frequent journeys of his daughters – les Dames de France – from Paris to the Château de la Bove, home of his former mistress Françoise de Châlus, Countess of Narbonne-Lara).

The Marne: Ryan's account

©Author's collection

6 September. Choisy. [*This probably should read Chaumes. Haig's diary entry for 6 September states: 'We stay tonight at a newly built Château about $\frac{1}{2}$ mile from Chaubuisson Farm, where we had our Head Quarters all day.' Chaubuisson Farm is close to Chaumes and is some 12 miles south west of Choisy.*] A pow-wow of Generals French and British. They state the Germans are retiring. Our troops have about turned, reinvigorated at the idea of no longer running away. Pushing N.E. a good deal of gunning and some heavy fighting.

Sunday Sept 6th 1914, 7am

My darling Sadie.

I am writing this in a beautiful château [*the 'newly built château' near Chaubuisson Farm, referred to in Haig's diary entry of 6 September*] where I got this bit of paper and am writing early as we are just off and expect to be heavily engaged before many hours. I am fit & well and so are all the chaps I am in charge of. The fall in has gone so I must be up & going. ...   Your own Jane

7 September. Fighting continued right through the night. The Bosh retreating now and their rear guard actions severely punished.

8 September. Rebais, still pushing on, some pretty severe scrapping, collecting some hundred of prisoners and some guns.

9 September. Pushed on thro Tretoire, Belle Idée and Charly sur Marne. 800 prisoners.

10 September. Hautevesnes, a sharp fight taking 400 prisoners.

Sept 10th 1914

My darling little one,

Here I am as fit as ever thank God. we have given hell to the Germans during the last 4 days & have them on the run. Poor Scotchard got killed by a Shell the day before yesterday. it is very Sad & I am very sorry for his wife & children. I saw I.B.B. this morning at 5. he too is very fit. Col Thompson & Major Irvine were snuffed by the enemy. Col Dobbie has just joined here to do Col Thompsons job. I have pushed John B's claim as D.A.D.M.S. Sclton told me he would get J.S. if he cannot get Davidson. Our troops have done wonderfully well. they marched 320 miles in 16 days under a broiling Sun. during that time sleep was at a discount as well as other things. we have not had any letters for 9 days. so I cannot blame you as even Sir D. has not got any. I have a show on for us. so I am dropping you these epistles. I sent M9 cards the last opportunity. I got in cluding one to I.D. oc. It is rotten that we don't get any letters or news. Our casualties have been heavy but nothing in comparison with the Germans. we got 180 prisoners yesterday & 7 guns. Love to my darling & my sweet kiddies whom I hope to see soon. write often as they may turn up some day—

Your loving Jane

16

Sept 10th 1914

My darling little one,

Here I am as fit as ever thank God. We have given hell to the Germans during the last 4 days & have them on the run. Poor Scatchard got killed by a shell the day before yesterday. It is very sad and I am very sorry for his wife & children. I saw J.S.B. *[John Bostock]* this morning at 5. He too is very fit. Col Thompson & Major Irvine were snaffled by the enemy. Col Dalton has just joined here to do Col Thompson's job. I have pushed John B's *[Bostock]* claim as D.A.D.M.S. Dalton told me he would get J.S. if he cannot get Davidson.[13] Our troops have done wonderfully well. They marched 320 miles in 16 days under a boiling sun. During that time sleep was at a discount as well as other things. We have not had any letters for 9 days so I cannot blame you as even Sir D. has not got any. I have a spare half hour so I am dropping you this epistle. I sent off 9 cards the last opportunity I got including one to J.D.O'C *[John D O'Connor, Ryan's father-in-law]*. It is rotten that we don't get any letters or news. Our casualties have been heavy but nothing in comparison with the Germans. We got 180 prisoners yesterday & 7 guns.

Love to my darling & my sweet kiddies whom I hope to see soon. Write often as they may turn up some day.　　　　　Your loving Jane.

Poor Scatchard got killed by a shell the day before yesterday.
Captain Thomas Scatchard RAMC was killed in action on 8 September 1914 near Sablonnières. He is buried nearby in Bellot Communal Cemetery. Before crossing to France, Scatchard was attached to the Connaught Hospital, Aldershot, while Ryan was Officer Commanding the Louise Margaret Hospital.
[Photograph from *The Bond of Sacrifice, Vol 1,* L A Clutterbuck, W T Dooner & C A Dennison, The Anglo-African Publishing Contractors, London, 1917.]

ⓒ Copyright expired

Colonel Thompson and Major Irvine were snaffled by the enemy.
Colonel Henry Neville Thompson RAMC was captured at Prisches on 26 August 1914. He was taken south to Etreux, where he assisted the German No 47 Field Hospital at the Mairie. Thereafter, he was sent to Ulm in southern Germany and thence to Ingolstadt where he remained until his release and repatriation in early 1915. In his letter of 30 January 1915, Ryan remarks: 'I hear Col Thompson RAMC who was taken prisoner is home'.
Major Francis Stephen Irvine RAMC was captured at Maroilles on 27 August 1914. He was marched east to Landrecies where he met up with **Captain Percy Dwyer RAMC.** Irvine and Dwyer, together with many other captured RAMC personnel, were marched to Bavai on 29 August. There, Irvine and Dwyer were left to assist the French Red Cross Hospital. On 10 September, whilst the BEF was advancing to the Aisne, Irvine and Dwyer slipped out of

---

[13]Major Percival Davidson RAMC (1874 – 1930).

Bavai and made their way to Dunkirk. Both officers were back with the BEF by October. In his letter of 24 September, Ryan comments: 'I see that Irvine and Dwyer have turned up'.

The re-appearance of these two officers was also noted in the British Medical Journal (26 September, 1914, p.556):

Officers Reported Missing who have now Reported Themselves.
Dwyer, Captain P., R.A.M.C.
Irvine, Major F.S., R.A.M.C.

11 September. Breny. DH left at 6am in a car, Baird and I rode about 25 miles, heavy gun fire all round. 2nd. Div. held up owing to bridge across the Marne having been blown up. Raining nearly all day. To Jouaignes.

September 12th 1914

My darling Sadie

Here we are pushing the Germans back & giving them a pretty bad time. Today we again accounted for 500 of them between killed, wounded and prisoners in addition to the 1000 we took 2 days ago. I got the Duke of Westminster[14] to take a letter on the 10th which I hope you got pretty quick as they on French's staff get their letters through in about 2 days & I hope to get this off pretty quick too. It has been raining like blazes during the last 48 hours. I want you to send me out a large size oil coat & oil pull on trousers like fishermen wear. You will get them at the Aldershot Stores opposite the Arcade. There has been an awful battle raging for miles all round us today.

We are on the German's heels, picking them up every hour. I saw Bostock this morning - he is now D.A.D.M.S to Col Dalton. I suppose you heard that Col Thompson & Major Irvine - I believe I told you - were taken as well as a huge number of our chaps. I also saw S. Hickson.[15] He is very well.

We are having a very strenuous time but all are very keen in getting a hit back as the enemy gave us a rotten time for the 1st 20 days - in numbers they were simply overwhelming. I hear the Crown Prince is at the head of an army about 10 miles from us. Everybody is keen on catching him. The Hd. Qrs of 1st Army [Corps] are all OK, merry & bright. The last letter I got from you was headed "Saturday" - no other date. You know Saturday means anything as frequently we don't know which day of the week it is. How are you & our darling kiddies? I hope splendid. Kiss them all for me. It was I [who] put Dalton on to J.S.B. If he cannot get Davidson J.S.B will have it permanently. Mrs B. [Bostock] will be pleased so you might let her know. ... They have started at a bit of dinner. I am quite ready for it as we had breakfast at 5 am.

With lots of love and kisses.   Your loving Jane

----

[14]Hugh Richard Arthur Grosvenor, 2nd Duke of Westminster.
[15]Colonel Samuel Hickson RAMC.

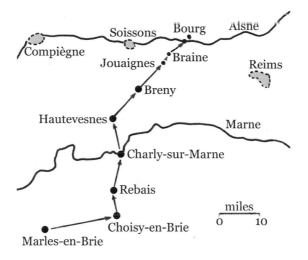

Ryan's itinerary 5–13 September 1914.   ©Author's collection

Ryan's itinerary 5–13 September 1914 – from end of Retreat from Mons to crossing of the Aisne.
5 September: Marles-en-Brie.
6 September: Choisy-en-Brie [*Possibly inaccurate – probably Chaubuisson Farm*].
8 September: Rebais.
9 September: Charly-sur-Marne.
10 September: Hautevesnes.
11 September: Breny.
12 September: Jouaignes.
13 September: Crossed the Aisne at Pont Arcy/Bourg-et-Comin.

HD[16] Saturday 12 September 1914. 'In accordance with ... general plan we continued our march N.E. with orders to reach the line of the Aisne and seize the crossings – my Corps was to occupy those at Pont Arcy and Bourg. ... The day was showery in the morning & turned into a ... wet afternoon & evening. ... Owing to the wet it was difficult to get any air reconnaissance. ... The 3rd Division on my left was also somewhat behind us. On the right was the 18th French Corps – an uncertain quantity! So I ordered the Divisions not to proceed as far as the Aisne today ... '

On 13 September, I Corps reached and crossed the Aisne.

The Aisne: 13 September – 19 October 1914

In Haig's diary entry for 13 September, he makes the following observations. 'For today I order Divisions to reconnoitre at daylight up to the Aisne bridges. ... If enemy in position orders for attack will be issued by Corps HQ. If enemy

---

[16]Throughout, the abbreviation HD is used to indicate an excerpt from Haig's Diaries.

is continuing his retreat, they will cross at once & follow enemy with patrols. ... All the bridges over the R. Aisne are reported as having been blown up. The 1st Divn. was to cross at Bourg. Here the "Oise & Aisne Canal" joins the Aisne Canal and since the latter is on the south side of the R. Aisne it (the Oise & Aisne Canal) is carried over the R. Aisne by a bridge. This latter had not been destroyed. This was most lucky as it is the only means we have of getting our heavy artillery & motor vehicles across to the north bank of the Aisne. At Arcy ... the main bridge, an iron girder, had been broken at 2 points ... Along side of this bridge a pontoon bridge was being constructed. This was finished at 4.30 p.m. - a good performance. I ordered Lomax [1st Division] to cross the whole of his command at Bourg, and Munro [2nd Division] to do his best at the pontoon bridge. His heavy guns and any other heavy vehicles which the pontoon bridge would not carry, were to cross after the 1st Divn. at Bourg.'

The pontoon bridge used by 2nd Division to cross the Aisne.
© Crown Copyright (Imperial War Museum Ref Q 054988)

Thus, on 13 September, troops from I Corps crossed the Aisne at Pont-Arcy and Bourg-et-Comin but did not advance further: unbeknown to Haig, the section of the Chemin des Dames (an east-west ridge approximately 4 miles north of the Aisne) facing I Corps was weakly defended – by not advancing on that day, a valuable opportunity was lost; German reserves were in position on the next day. The BEF advance towards the Chemin des Dames began on 14 September under GHQ orders to 'continue the pursuit' and to 'act vigorously against the retreating enemy'. The Germans stood their ground and the offensive was halted. On 15 September, GHQ issued the following order: 'The Commander-in-Chief wishes the line now held by the Army to be strongly entrenched, and it is his intention to assume a general offensive at the first opportunity.' Thus began trench warfare.

On 13 September, Haig had set up his HQ at the Château de Courcelles.

Château de Courcelles. ©Author's collection

His Advanced Reporting Centre was initially located at Bourg and later moved to Moulin de Bas at Viel-Arcy, referred to by Ryan as the 'Mill'.

With the advantage of high ground and artillery, the Germans inflicted heavy losses on the BEF over the period 13 September to 3 October (the Battle of the Aisne). In [12, page 144], Sir John French observed that 'The first surprise came when the "Jack Johnsons" began to fall. This was a nickname given by the men ("Black Marias" was another) to a high-explosive shell fired from 8-in. howitzers, which had been brought down from the fortress of Maubeuge to support the German defensive position on the Aisne. They were our first experience of an artillery much heavier than our own. Although these guns caused considerable damage and many bad casualties, they never had any very demoralising effect upon the troops.'

The BEF started to withdraw from the Aisne on 2 October, to be replaced by French troops (c.f. Ryan's letter of 12 October in which he optimistically states: 'We have them beaten to a frazzle here and our services are required at a more important point [Flanders]'). I Corps had withdrawn south of the Aisne by 16 October and entrained for Hazebrouck on 19 October; Haig established his HQ at Poperinge, west of Ypres.

The Aisne: Ryan's account

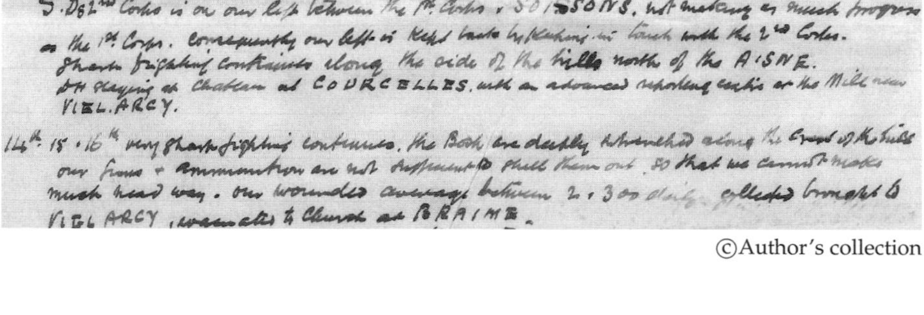

[handwritten diary entries:]

13th The 1st Corps Crosses the AISNE at BOURG *[Viel.Arcy]* after repairing the bridge which had been blown up.

S.D. 62nd Corps is on our left between the 1st Corps & SOISSONS. not making so much progress as the 1st Corps. consequently our left is kept back by Kluck in touch with the 2nd Corps. Sharp fighting continues along the side of the hills north of the AISNE. 4H staying at Chateau at COURCELLES. with an advanced reporting centre or the Mill near VIEL.ARCY.

14th 15 & 16th very sharp fighting continues. the Boch are deeply entrenched along the crest of the hills our guns & ammunition are not sufficient to shell them out. so that we cannot make much head way. our wounded average between 2 & 3 on daily collected brought to VIEL ARCY, evacuated to Church at BRAINE.

©Author's collection

13 September. The 1st Corps crossed the Aisne at Bourg/Viel-Arcy after repairing the bridge which had been blown up. S.D.'s [Smith-Dorrien's] 2nd Corps is on our left between the 1st Corps and Soissons, not making as much progress as the 1st Corps. Consequently our left is kept back by keeping in touch with the 2nd Corps. Sharp fighting continues along the side of the hills north of the Aisne. DH staying at château at Courcelles with an advanced reporting centre at the Mill near Viel-Arcy.

14, 15, 16 September. Very sharp fighting continues. The Bosh are deeply entrenched along the crest of the hill [Chemin des Dames]. Our guns and ammunition are not sufficient to shell them out so that we cannot make much head way. Our wounded average between 2 & 300 daily, collected, brought to Viel-Arcy, evacuated to church at Braine [Abbey Church of St Yved].

Ryan's diary elaborates further.

Sunday 13 September 1914. Arrived at Château at Courcelles. Moved HdQrs on to Bourg [Bourg-et-Comin]. A very hot engagement is taking place along the slope of hill on the other side of Aisne.

©Author's collection

Monday 14 September 1914. Black Maria *[German heavy howitzer]* spitting shells all over the place. HdQrs shelled from bridges beyond Bourg. Also some dropped about Bourg. About 400 German prisoners taken. 70 wounded. I removed a bullet from forearm of one & dressed about 20.

Tuesday 15 September 1914. Still at Courcelles riding up to reporting centre each morning. Battle still raging for miles around. Wounded coming in.

Wednesday 16 September 1914. As above. A great cannonade between 5 & 6pm on the enemy lines. No reply from them. Lt.Col Ferguson[17] reported his arrival, also saw Davidson DADMS.

> Monday 14th Sept.
> About 70 miles from Paris

My own darling.

I have just met the King's Messenger[18] who has promised to take this letter so I am writing it with our guns blazing away within 100 yards of us. We have the Germans on the run, have taken about 2500 prisoners during the last 4 days so we are commencing to get a bit of our own back. We have pushed them back 40 *[miles]* in 4 days. This is our 25*[th]* day's continuous trek. I saw J.S.B. this morning - he is D.A.D.M.S. to Col Dalton - feels very well. I also saw Betsy *[Major Maurice Guy Winder RAMC]* in a cave where he slept last night. Tell Lady Haig Sir Douglas & the rest of our Hd. Qrs are splendid. We have only lost two men by ordinary sickness. I write you nearly every day. I gave the Duke of Westminster one to post on 9th, another to a Frenchman who was going to Paris who said you would get it in 3 days. This one will probably be posted in London so I am not afraid of the censor. Our troops are in great form & doing splendid work. Tell Mrs B. all about John. He said he has not had a letter for a fortnight. Get me a large oil coat & oil trousers (like fishermen wear) & send them along. Also an oil hat (southwester if you can) as it has been raining like blazes for days & nights. I enclose a prescription for Lady Haig. She can get it dispensed at the Cambridge H*[ospital]*. The Germans have blown up all the bridges round about. We captured 40 officers & 600 prisoners yesterday.

Kiss the kiddies for me. I must finish as the K. messenger is off.

> Your loving Jane.

> Sept 17th 1914
> Hd.Qrs. 1st Army Corps

My darling Sall

I received your exceedingly welcome letter dated Sept 1st last night & was glad to hear ye are all so well and taking things so well. As I told you in my letter of the 15th things have taken a turn and we are killing the damned Germans by the thousand and have taken about 5000 prisoners during the last week (that is Sir Douglas's army alone). I am writing Lady Haig. It is still

[17] Lieutenant Colonel Nicholas Charles Ferguson RAMC.
[18] The King's Messengers: a corps of couriers who relayed, by hand, sensitive documents.

raining.

I sincerely hope this infernal war will come to a speedy and glorious finish. All my crowd are OK and I am very fit DV *[Deo volente]*. I am being called so I must finish ...

Kiss my darling kiddies from me and with tons of love to self.

Your loving Jane

Thursday 17 September 1914. Condition of affairs unchanged. Wounded collected at Viel-Arcy and evacuated to Braine. Col Dalton hit by shell. Saw Bostock.

Friday 18 September 1914. Still at Mill & at Courcelles. Went with Sir D to see the wounded at Braine. 700 sent up by ambulance train. Col Holt came as DDMS 2nd Div. Battle still raging and wounded being collected at Viel-Arcy & Villers *[Villers-en-Prayères]*.

©Author's collection

HD Friday 18 September 1914. ... I visited some of the wounded. The ambulance personnel have been much overworked. ... The situation is quite unlike what the reg[ulatio]ns anticipated! To collect wounded at dressing stations only means that they will get shelled and a number of slightly wounded men will be killed along with the Drs.! Shell wounds are either very severe or slight. The flesh is lacerated & difficult to dress. If left for 2 or 3 days (as happens sometimes here) the wounds get into bad state.

Saturday 19 September 1914. As above. Buried poor Dalton at cemetery at Viel-Arcy. Holt , Ferguson , J.S. [Bostock], Baird, Betsy [Winder], Potter & I present. Shells bursting all round the hospital & cemetery, also near mill, also at Bourg & Pont-Arcy. Went with Col Ferguson to Villers where we saw 170 wounded evacuated to Braine and 200 from Viel-Arcy. A severe attack by enemy last night between 11 & 12. Also between 5 & 7 this evening which we repulsed. Evacuated wounded in new motor ambulances.

Hd. Qrs. 1st Army, 19-9-14

My own darling

... I have just been present at a very sad ceremony and that was burying poor Col Dalton who only joined here about 8 days ago to take Col Thompson's place. Col Holt has now come up to take Col Dalton's place. I hope he will have better luck. Col Holt, J.S. Bostock, Davidson, Winder and I as well as a few others were at the funeral. ... We are still having a pretty tough time but are giving the Germans far more than they give us. They are frightened of our infantry and nearly altogether depend on big gun fire which we have styled Black Maria as it flicks up such a cloud of dust and muck. ... My Hd Qr staff are fine which is a great pleasure to me. ... I am writing this to the boom of guns and feel very happy although poor Dalton's grave made me sad. He was attended by Fr. Dey,[19] got last sacraments etc. We put a cross and some flowers on his grave and I suggested that a photo be taken and sent to his poor mother. ...

Kiss my darlings for me and with lots of love to you. I have kissed this letter as you suggest.   Your own loving Jane.

Death of Lieutenant Colonel Charles Dalton RAMC.

Excerpt from [3, page 218].
'When the British Expeditionary Force sailed to France, Colonel H.N. Thompson, D.S.O., was A.D.M.S. of the division [2nd Division, I Corps], and it is to his notes that we are indebted for the information we have with regard to the Mons fighting. Then his diary comes to a sudden end, for he was captured ... and indeed remained a prisoner for some months before the Germans released him. He was succeeded during the remainder of the retreat by Lieut.-Colonel R.J. Copeland of the 5th Field Ambulance, and on the 8th September by Lieut.-

---

[19]Rev Major James Dey, Roman Catholic chaplain.

Colonel C. Dalton, who was sent up from No. 1 General Hospital to fill the vacant position. That same shell-fire which troubled the bearers so much and had already accounted for some of the R.A.M.C. now struck down this promising officer: a high-explosive shell bursting near him as he was carrying wounded into Verneuil Château and wounding him severely. Eyewitnesses of the occurrence say that immediately after receiving his wound Lieut.-Colonel Dalton was further injured by a gun limber, the horses attached to which bolted when the shell burst. In any case his injuries were of a grave nature. That fact and continuous shelling of Verneuil made it impossible to move him, and at night he was taken to L'Hôpital, where the end came. It was under heavy shell-fire again that his brothers of the R.A.M.C. laid him to rest in the village churchyard at Viel-Arcy. A cross marks the grave of this very gallant Irish officer.'

Château de Moussy-Verneuil where Dalton was mortally wounded.
©Author's collection

©Author's collection   © Copyright expired

Dalton is buried in the communal cemetery at Viel-Arcy. His is the sole Commonwealth War Grave in the cemetery. In the photograph on the left, the Chemin des Dames runs along the ridge in the distance.

Dalton's portrait is from *The Bond of Sacrifice, Vol 1*, L A Clutterbuck, W T Dooner & C A Dennison, The Anglo-African Publishing Contractors, London, 1917.

Sunday Sept 20th 1914.

My own Darling

I sent you a card this morning at 5 a.m. also a long letter which I gave to Bostock to post as he was on his way to the base for stores etc. as owing to the heavy fighting we are nearly short of dressings etc. Col Holt, J.S., Carter, Winder and I attended poor Col Dalton's funeral yesterday. He was hit by one of those infernal shells. This fight still continues, this is the 8th day and we are still at it as hard as ever. This battle extends over a frontage of 120 miles, thus

©Author's collection

We are gradually driving them back. I thought I would get yesterday's letter off by Westminster but did not see him after writing it so I sent it on by J.S. However, I hope to get this off by the Duke as I saw him about 2 hours ago and hope to see him again. Already this morning I have seen Smallman,[20] Greenwood, Easton is OK but I did not see him, Major Mitchell, Carter, Betsy [Winder] giving Chloroform, Holt and Davidson, these are all up at the front in Sir D's army. I am splendid and so is my Hd Qr. staff.

Poor Tanner of the Liverpools was sent down by train very badly wounded. I scarcely expect him to live as he has several bad wounds. The wounds from shell are dreadful but those from bullets are slight. Our infantry can knock spots out of the Germans if they can get near them, it's the same with our cavalry but those infernal German shells do our poor chaps a lot of harm. The weather has been cold and wet but now the sun has made a welcome appearance. The wounded are being got away very well and, now that we have got a certain number of motor ambulances and hope to get more directly, we can get them to ambulance trains quickly which is a great thing for them.

I told you in yesterday's letter how Col Holt came up to take Dalton's place. It was sad to see him rolled in his blanket and put into the cold clay. He was such a fine chap, R.I.P. I trust you are keeping fit and well also our darling kiddies. Tell them Daddy will take them home something nice when he returns, please God. As I write this there is Boom - Boom - rattle and bang, but you get quite accustomed to the sound of them. It is pitiable to see the wounds some poor chaps get. The hill over which we are fighting is strewn with Germans dying and dead. We collect a certain number of them and they all state they are sick of this war. I don't believe they have much more left in them. Our Tommies and officers are the bravest fellows in the world, scarcely a man or officer going sick, all sticking it like bricks.

I am wanted so must finish. ...   Your loving Jane

_____

[20] Major Arthur Briton Smallman RAMC.

Sunday 20 September 1914. 8th day of Aisne battle. Shells still bursting all round & a sharp attack at 4am again repulsed. Our guns playing on enemy's position. Very few reported wounded the result of last night attack.

Monday 21 September 1914. Battle still on. Wounded evacuated daily to Braine. Shells bursting all round Viel-Arcy & our hospital.

Head Qrs. 1st Army   21.9.14

My own darling,

I wrote you yesterday and same the day before. I also sent you a card each day so you see if you don't receive any letters it is not my fault. I got yesterday's taken by Westminster and I am writing this as I have just seen the King's Messenger by whom I hope to get this off. I am splendid. This is the 9th day of a pitched battle and I am pleased to say we are doing very well.

Bostock is OK and was sent down to the base two days ago by Col Holt to gather and fetch some stores. We are a regular Aldershot crowd here Holt, Bostock, Carter, Lloyd-Jones, Mitchell, Greenwood, Easton, Betsy and all are well. I am sorry a lot of our chaps are getting killed or wounded. O'Connell, that poor chap who married in Aldershot recently was killed last night. Capt Potter, Tanner (very seriously) and Feneran of the Liverpools are also wounded. They come in all night long as owing to the intensity of the shell fire the ambulance wagons cannot move during the day. ...

Thank God the sun is out again today. The enemy made a fierce attack on us during the last 48 hrs but they were driven off with tremendous loss. ... I don't think I have felt fitter for years though the hours of sleep are scanty. ... The wounds inflicted on our chaps by shells are dreadful. ...

          Your own loving Jane

We are a regular Aldershot crowd here: Colonel Maurice Percy Holt RAMC, Major John Southey Bostock RAMC, Major James Edward Carter RAMC, Captain Percy Arnold Lloyd-Jones RAMC [killed in action on 22 December 1916], Major Arthur Henry McNeill Mitchell RAMC, Major Arthur Rowland Greenwood RAMC, Major Philip George Easton RAMC, Major Maurice Guy ('Betsy') Winder RAMC.

I am sorry a lot of our chaps are getting killed or wounded. O'Connell, that poor chap who married in Aldershot recently was killed last night. Capt Potter, Tanner (very seriously) and Feneran of the Liverpools are also wounded.

Lieutenant John Forbes O'Connell RAMC. Killed in action on 20 September 1914, aged 25. He is buried in Vendresse British Cemetery. O'Connell was Medical Officer with the Highland Light Infantry. His commanding officer, Colonel Wolfe Murray, wrote to O'Connell's wife (of a few months): 'He was shot dead in the trenches while attending Lieutenant Fergusson, H.L.I., who had been very seriously wounded, and who himself died later in the day. We all feel his loss most acutely. ... I have never seen any one pluckier; he was just as cool under fire as he was at any other time, and the act which cost him his life was characteristic of him.'

Captain Herbert Cecil Potter. In a letter to his mother, Potter reported that he was 'temporarily out of action, slightly wounded thro' both legs'. He recovered from his wounds.

Captain Ralph Eyre Tanner. Mortally wounded on 14 September, Tanner died on 23 September 1914 at the Base Hospital in Versailles, aged 29. On 13 September, the day before his mortal wounding, Tanner's only son was born. Tanner is buried in Les Gonards Cemetery, Versailles. [Photograph from *The Bond of Sacrifice, Vol 1*, L A Clutterbuck, W T Dooner & C A Dennison, The Anglo-African Publishing Contractors, London, 1917. Ⓒ Copyright expired]

Captain Frank Edward Feneran. Wounded in September 1914 and repatriated. On recovery, he returned to the Western Front in December 1914. Feneran was killed in action at Neuve Chapelle on 10 March 1915, aged 33. Feneran has no known grave: he is commemorated on the Memorial at Le Touret Military Cemetery, Richebourg-l'Avoue. [Photograph from *The Bond of Sacrifice, Vol 2*, L A Clutterbuck, W T Dooner & C A Dennison, The Anglo-African Publishing Contractors, London, 1917. Ⓒ Copyright expired]

Tuesday 22 September. As above. Wounded about daily. All being well cleared out by supply columns & motor ambulances.

23 September 1914

My own darling,

I have written you so many letters lately giving you all the news that I have nothing new to say in this one except that after ten day's battle we have again routed the enemy from his positions. ... We were never within 35 miles of Paris. ... I regret to say that our casualty list in this pitched battle during the last ten days is a heavy one - but don't say anything about it. However, there is one consolation, that the German loss is at least 5 times heavier. ... J.S.B. has gone to the base to fetch some things rather badly wanted. Write and tell Mrs B. he is fit, also Holt, Betsy, Greenwood, Mitchell, Carter, Easton, Fr. Moloney are all fit. I saw them all today. Lloyd-Jones had a bad time with the L[iver]pools - he has been relieved and brought into a field ambulance.

Sir Douglas, Baird and I had a long ride yesterday - he is very fit and so are we all, thank God. ..   Your loving Jane

Sir Douglas Baird & I had a long ride yesterday - he is very fit & so are we all Thank God -

Wednesday 23 September. As above. Dentist came & extracted tooth for me & put a filling in for Sir D. One shell went clean over Mill & burst about 100 yds from us.

Dentist came ... & put a filling in for Sir D. On 26 September, Haig wrote to his wife: 'By the way, I had a tooth pulled out y'day. ... A dentist was brought out here from Paris, quite a good man. He put some stuff into it for 2 days, and then ... advised taking it out. But he had to give a good pull! Ryan holding on to my head and the dentist tugging at the tooth.' The dentist was Auguste Charles Valadier who was to become a pioneer in the treatment of maxillo-facial trauma suffered by troops during the war. In August 1914, no dental surgeons had accompanied the BEF to France: the unavailability of a British dentist to treat Haig generated a request to the War Office for dental surgeons; by 1918, there were 850 RAMC dental officers serving in France.

Thursday 24 September. Things are quieter. Number of wounded few. No rifle fire but Black Maria bursting all round us not doing much harm. Wrote Sadie ...

Hd Qrs 1st Army Corps, Sept 24th 14.
My darling Sall,
  ... The battle still rages and the enemy is being gradually beaten off. The weather is delightful for the last two days. We love the sun after the continuous drenching. Bostock has not yet returned from the base and I think I have managed to get him to our Head Quarters - it is not finally fixed but I think it will be OK. The casualty list amongst our poor chaps has been very high. I see Irvine and Dwyer have turned up. I cannot make out who is the Major L. you refer to. I hope it is not John Langstaff,[21] the last time I saw Surg Hickson about ten days ago Langstaff was OK. ...
  We are all OK thank God. Did you send that prescription to Lady H?, I was sorry to hear about her. ... Charteris has just got 5 photos of his son - he is showing them to everybody and quite proud of him. ...   Your loving Jane.

Friday 25 September. Artillery duel still on. Shells flying over our reporting centre. Infantry resting. ... Not so many wounded.
Saturday 26 September. Still at Courcelles & at Mill near Viel-Arcy. Shelled continuously & night attacks the order of the day. J.S.B *[Bostock]* joined our FA *[Field Ambulance]* yesterday & slept at Courcelles – we both under the same roof. ... Went to Vidris with Col Sargent. Black Maria dropping all round the place.
Sunday 27 September. Sir J.F & Winston *[Churchill]* present. This is the 1st day without being shelled for some time. Rothwell[22] sent down wounded by Black Maria the same shell killing poor Ball ... A sharp night attack was repulsed.
Monday 28 September. Several shrapnel shells burst close to Mill which is

---

[21]Major James William Langstaff RAMC (1876-1948).
[22]Captain William E Rothwell (Royal Inniskillling Fusiliers).

getting very insanitary. Moving to farm close by. A night attack from 10.30 to 2 all along our line. Heavy artillery & rifle fire. Poor Ball killed by shell. Rothwell wounded in leg.

Lieutenant William Ormsby Wyndham Ball RAMC. Medical Officer to the 2nd Battalion, South Staffordshire Regiment. Ball was killed by a shell while attending to the wounded at Soupir, north-west of Viel-Arcy, on 26 September 1914, the eve of his 25th birthday. Ball is commemorated on the Memorial at La Ferte-sous-Jouarre. [Photograph from *The Bond of Sacrifice, Vol 1*, L A Clutterbuck, W T Dooner & C A Dennison, The Anglo-African Publishing Contractors, London, 1917. © Copyright expired]

Moving to farm close by. On 28 September, Haig moved his HQ to Monthussart Farm. In his diary entry for that day, Haig records: 'Reached our new H.Q. about 6pm. It seems a good farm with large barn, big enough for a whole Battalion! Also plenty of water. The place stands high and seems healthy.'

Tuesday 29 September. Black Maria spitting shells all over the place. Our new reporting *[centre]* coming in for some attention. In afternoon I motored to Mount Notre Dame with Col Sargent. Wounded still coming in but in decreasing number.

Excerpt from letter to Sadie on 29 September 1914: 'You need not send me the Daily Mail as Sir Douglas often gives me a paper which Westminster brings to him. He is a brick. He tells me more about the general situation than anybody else, which makes some of them quite jealous.'

Wednesday 30 September. Things are not much changed. Sporadic night attacks are everywhere repulsed. The enemy usually losing heavily.
Thursday 1 October. Lovely morning. Nights getting cold. The men are given a blanket. Some cases of suspected enteric reported. 6 from No 1 Company 2nd Battalion Cold Stream Guards. Poor Studd hit in both knees with a shell.

Major Herbert William Studd (1870 – 1947) was John Charteris's predecessor as Intelligence Officer on Haig's staff. In his diary entry for 17 September 1914, Haig remarks: 'The Guards being short of officers Major Studd, my Intelligence Officer, left on return to reg[imenta]l duty. Captain Charteris has taken over from him.' Charteris's replacement as ADC was Lieutenant Guy Straker, whose arrival at HQ on 18 October was noted by Haig in his diary. 'Lt. Straker 15th Hussars joined to take Charteris' place as A.D.C. ... Straker came to my notice at Landrecies where he had a piquet on a bridge near the town when it was attacked.'

Oct. 1st 1914.

My own darling,

I got yours of the 21st written from Woolwich and was pleased to hear you are eating better and hope you will shortly get alright. There was a sharp frost last night but this is simply a glorious morning and it is a treat. Last night was the first night for 18 nights that we were not troubled with the cracks of rifle and the boom of heavy guns, and so far this morning things have been fairly peaceful though our chaps are just commencing to blaze away at them. From the evidence of prisoners and diaries of wounded it appears that the enemy in front of us are becoming demoralised and that the German officers order their men to attack and stay behind themselves. They admit very heavy losses and are terrified of our cavalry and infantry. They are very mean, up to every form of deceit and frequently raise the white flag and open fire on our chaps who cease fire. It will not be recognised in future as our chaps have learned their lesson dearly.

I hear we are in future to have a five day post from England. I don't know how long letters will take to go home. I am writing this early and will give it to my P. master if I see him. He is a very fine chap and one of the best of fellows (Westminster). He now has a quick firing gun mounted in his Rolls Royce. ...

I am glad to say our wounded have been much slighter both in character and number during the last week. Black Maria is a dirty thing, she has a range of 10,000 yards, makes a hole about 10-15 feet deep and about 30ft in diameter where she strikes, so it is a case of God help you if she coughs near you. Saw some 'Tommies' playing football within a few hundred yards of where she was bursting; they are a brave lot of fellows. Another name is 'Jack Johnson' or 'Old cough drops'. I am really of [the] opinion that we have broken the spirit of the Germans. I may be premature in saying so but I hope not. ...

He now has a quick firing gun mounted in his Rolls Royce. Westminster had a Hotchkiss machine gun mounted on his car: this *ad hoc* modification became the prototype of the Rolls-Royce Armoured Car.

On 3 October he again wrote to Sadie:

My darling Sadie

... I got the waterproof outfit last evening. The trousers are big enough for Finn MacCool *[a giant in Irish mythology]* and I don't know why you want to make a German of me, for a certainty if I dared to put that cap on I would be taken for one and be peppered not alone by our chaps but by the French as well. ... We are still here. Our chaps are entrenched within very few yards of the Germans who attacked again last night with the usual results, driven back like rabble with great loss. ... J.S and I rode out yesterday to all the Cavalry field ambulances. I saw John Langstaff and Lewis. They are very well but looking slightly thin. All the Aldershot crowd are very fit but a very nice youngster of ours named Ball (an excellent boy) got killed by a shell. The same shell took a bite off Rothwell's leg - that good looking chap who was ADC to General Murray. I saw him off the other morning quite happy. He said he was going to do Piccadilly shortly with his battered legging on.

Capt Potter is at that home where Lady Haig is (Princess Eugénie). I hope he is doing very well - give him if you see him and Mrs P. my best wishes.

The weather is nice, sunny in the day and cold at night but I don't mind personally as I have a good bed but I pity the poor Tommies and officers who are in the trenches, one blanket per man given to them. Yesterday was a very quiet day as there was a thick fog. ...   Your loving Jane

Capt Potter is at that home where Lady Haig is (Princess Eugénie). Captain Herbert Cecil Potter, rendered 'temporarily out of action, slightly wounded thro' both legs' a few weeks earlier was recuperating at Farnborough Hill, the Hampshire home of Empress Eugénie, wife of Napoleon III. She had volunteered part of the house for use as a hospital for wounded officers and, in this venture, was aided by Dorothy Haig.

Friday 2 October. The new reporting centre is not very suitable from a sanitary point of view as Black Maria is dropping some of her excreta round about. One portion of shell came to door of the house & several past the gates.

Saturday 3 October. Charteris & I sought out a new reporting centre, a beautiful Château Bellème in the centre of a wood quite near our heavy battery of guns 300 yards away. The place very filthy, occupied by a signalling company who were ordered out. The usual signs of the enemy were visible - clothes presses broken also doors etc.

In his diary entry for 4 October, Haig records the change of HQ location:
'I then rode to the Château de LaRoche also called Château de Bellème about $1\frac{1}{2}$ miles from Mont Hussart Farm. I changed because the farm did not seem very sanitary – a "midden" (or dunghill) in the middle of the square opposite the front door!'

Sunday 4 October. Day passed off quietly but a vigorous night attack was again repulsed.

Monday 5 October. Conditions unchanged. Firing by day & sniping at night Very few wounded daily.

Tuesday 6 October. There is a rumour of a change of climate. Nothing new to relate. Went shooting with J.S. *[Bostock]* & Dugmore. Shot the first partridge.

Shot the first partridge. Charteris [5, pages 42-43] records: 'Following the example of Wellington's officers at Torres Vedras some of the Staff who can find time, go out and shoot partridges with shot-guns borrowed from the inhabitants - it provides a welcome change of diet and the sportsman has the excitement, additional to that of shooting little feathered birds, of having shrapnel dropped near him every now and then.'

On 7 October, 'Jane' wrote to Sadie.

My darling Sadie,
... We are still at that battle and have given the Germans a thorough hiding - their number of killed & wounded must be immense. An officers' patrol went out a short distance the night before last and counted 150 dead Germans in front of his lines. The others are demoralized & refuse to attack us. ... J.S. *[Bo-*

stock] has not got that ship but Sam [Colonel Samuel Hickson RAMC] said he would see about it for him. As I told you I would gladly take one were it not for Sir D. I must try and mind him. ... Send me on some soap also soap for washing shorts etc it cannot be got in this country. ...   Your loving Jane.

Thursday 8 October. Chassemy was heavily shelled, also Bourg & Villers.

HD Thursday 8 October. Arthur Lee M.P. arr[ive]d to see me, stating that he has been sent by Lord Kitchener to enquire into medical arrang[emen]ts. He has the rank of Colonel & wears staff tabs! ... I attached Major Ryan to show him around.

Arthur Hamilton Lee, later 1st Viscount Lee of Fareham, was a British politician and diplomat. In [14, page 25], Harrison comments '[t]hat Lee was sent to France on such a mission is hugely significant because it shows that Kitchener was sensitive to public criticism of the War Office on medical grounds. Having been blamed for the breakdown of medical arrangements in the Sudan and in South Africa, Kitchener was acutely aware of the importance of medical provisions in sustaining public morale.' Lee is probably best remembered for donating, to the nation, the country house of Chequers in Buckinghamshire: in 1917, Lee and his wife gave the 1,000-acre estate, and the entire contents of the house, in trust to the nation to be used as official residence and retreat of British Prime Ministers.

Friday 9 October. The usual shelling. Craone taken by us.

On 12 October, Ryan wrote to Sadie:
... We are just after a very good dinner & are moving out of this place in a day or two & going on a long trek. We have beaten the Germans in front of us here & are going to have a go at them at a more important point in Belgium [Ypres] so if you don't hear from me very regularly don't be surprised though I will write whenever I can. ... We are very busy at present. There was another night attack last night which we absolutely pulverised. We have them beaten to a frazzle here & our services are required at a more important point. ...

Our services are required at a more important point. This signals the imminent transfer of I Corps from the Aisne to Flanders.

Paris: Hotel Astoria 15–27 October 1914

Oct. 13th while riding with Sir D. the horse reared up, fell back on me, bursting up my right hip joint; necessitating my going to Hotel Astoria Hotel, Paris on the 15th

©Author's collection

'Oct 13th while riding with Sir D, the horse reared up and fell back on me, bursting up my right hip joint, necessitating my going to hospital Astoria Hotel, Paris on the 15th.'

Hotel Astoria, Paris, was used as an Auxiliary Hospital (administered by No 1 British Red Cross Base Hospital, Le Touquet) from September 1914 to February 1915. Base Hospitals were part of the casualty evacuation chain, further back from the front line than the 'Clearing Hospitals' (later to be termed Casualty Clearing Stations).

Diary Tuesday 13 October 1914. Going out riding with C *[Chief]* & B *[Baird]* my horse reared & fell on me hurting the old hip. Rode on to Longueval after but returned alone. Hip painful on dismounting at Courcelles.

Thursday 15 October 1914. Came to Astoria in Rolls Royce.

Saturday 17 October 1914. Saw Mrs Studd whose husband is on the 2nd floor badly wounded, formerly one of our staff. *[Major Herbert William Studd, wounded by a shell on 1 October.]*

Hotel Astoria, Avenue des Champs Elysées,
Place de l'Etoile Paris, 17.10.14

My darling Sall,

I sent you a p.c. from above hotel last evening which is used as an Auxiliary to No 1 Red Cross Hospital. I am one of the biggest frauds in creation to be here at all as I could quite easily have stuck it but had to comply with orders. ... There are a lot of old trouts here who bring your meals etc. They fancy themselves in the Red Cross badge & uniform, also some real English nurses ...

Major Cochrane[23] is staying here and came to my room about 9pm last night when we had a long chat. I hear Sir A. Sloggett[24] is out here and that Sir A. Keogh[25] has taken over the Director Generalship.

[Harrison [14, page 19] describes the respective roles of the latter two individuals as follows. 'Sloggett effectively ruled the roost in France and Belgium while Keogh, based at the War Office, took a strategic overview of the medical services as a whole.']

I am longing to get back to my old crowd & hope to do so in about a week.

... It was sad about Antwerp but the unfortunate Belgians are all having a pretty bad time - I hope our chaps will hunt these intruders from that part of the country. ... Your old man Jane

It was sad about Antwerp ...

The Fall of Antwerp, 6 October 1914. In the third week of August 1914 and unable to counter the German offensive, the core of the Belgian army had fallen back to a line around the fortified city of Antwerp. Following the halting of the German advance into France at the Battle of the Marne and their subsequent entrenchment at the Aisne, the Germans refocussed on Belgium and

---

[23]Major Edward Warren Webber Cochrane RAMC (1872 – 1933).

[24]Lieutenant General Sir Arthur Thomas Sloggett RAMC (1857 – 1929), Director General of Medical Services for the BEF.

[25]General Sir Alfred Henry Keogh RAMC (1857 – 1936), Director General of Army Medical Services.

laid siege to Antwerp. Using heavy artillery (including the infamous 420mm howitzer known as 'Big Bertha'), the city's outermost fortifications had been destroyed by 1 October 1914. In one of the more foolhardy episodes of the war, on 2 October, Winston Churchill – then First Lord of the Admiralty – crossed the channel to assess the situation in Antwerp personally. On 4 October, the defence of Antwerp was briefly bolstered by the arrival of a brigade of marines from the British Naval Division. However, the situation was hopeless and, on 6 October, the decision was made to evacuate: some two thirds of the Belgian army effected an escape along the coast to the south west. They took up a new defensive position along the river Yser, thereby forming the extreme left of the Allied front line which now stretched from the North Sea to Switzerland.

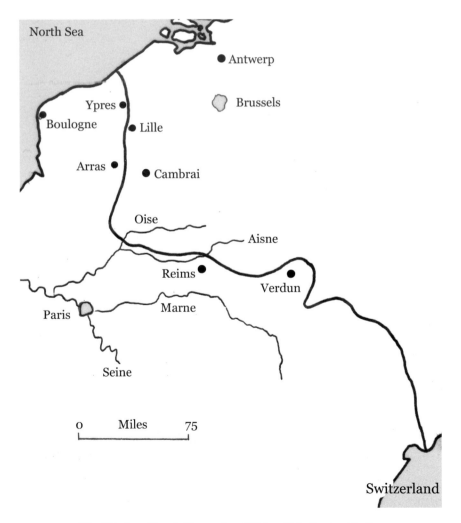

The Western Front, November 1914.   ©Author's collection

Diary Sunday 18 October 1914. A visit is hourly expected from Monsieur Taube *[German aircraft]* by French. Il n'est pas arrivé.

Rumpler–Taubes served only about six months' active duty in the front lines of the First World War, but since these early monoplanes comprised about half Germany's available aircraft strength at the opening of hostilities, they saw considerable duty in many roles. One became notorious as the 'five o'clock Taube', a regular visitor over Paris in 1914, dropping three-kilogram bombs and leaflets demanding the city's immediate surrender.

Tuesday 20 October 1914. Saw my name in dispatches *[First Mention: Field Marshal Sir John French's Dispatch of 8 October 1914]* in Daily Mail, also Gen French's narrative of fighting from 6th Sept tells me about Sir D on the Aisne.

Hotel Astoria, Avenue des Champs Elysées, Paris
20th Oct 1914

My darling,

Since coming into above I have not got any scrawl from you so I have taken to reading your last containing Jack's, Eugene's & Nell's epistles 3 or 4 times a day. You will be glad to hear the old leg is O.K. again but I will probably have to wait until this weekend when I expect my Rolls Royce man back to take me back to my old job again. I see my name appearing unexpectedly in this day's Daily Mail - 20th October amongst the number of those 'mentioned in dispatches'. I was pleased to see Major Henniker's name also there, & what do you think of Sir Douglas? He saved the situation on the Aisne on numerous occasions & wound up by not leaving a kick in the enemy there, so we took our departure for a place where a lot of fighting is taking place ... and I am very anxious to get back there. Col Sargent & Col Boyce & Col Hickson & poor Col Dalton are also amongst the names. I want you to keep all copies of paper containing description of the fighting in Sir John's dispatches. I have been petted a lot here and made stay in bed, but to-day I have been up since my massage man came at 11 o'c Cochrane has just been in to see me - he is off to join No 6 General *[Hospital]* at St Nazaire this evening by the 5.15 train. I have sent him out to get me some stamps as I cannot find a Censor's stamp by anybody here. As far as I can see from my window Paris is still pretty quiet. I have a lovely view of the Eiffel Tower from my window – it is only a few hundred yards away.

The French people are extremely kind. A dear old Countess has volunteered to take me round in her car as soon as I like. This place is partly financed by a dear white-haired Baroness who brings me the Daily Mail and a pear at 7.30, it sounds like home does it not? The pity of it is that it is not Nell who brings the paper to poor Dads. I hope you said nothing to anybody about my being in here and that you & the dear kiddies are in every way in the pink. Cochrane is rather disappointed that his name is not in the list. I could see by his face. I have no more news so I will close with lots of kisses & love to you & the kiddies. Your loving Jane

Ryan's *Rolls Royce man* was Monsieur Lazare, a French interpreter attached to Haig's staff, of whom Haig noted: 'a financier of standing, with a splendid car' [13, page 201].

Wednesday 21 October 1914. Feeling better having massage done. Still in bed. Start of Battle of Ypres. 1st Div Langemarck to Poelcappelle.

Hotel Astoria, Paris, 22.10.14

My dearest Sall,

... The leg is OK again & am now only waiting for my chauffeur to roll up & take me back to Hd Qrs. He usually comes in for the weekend & goes back about Monday or Tuesday so I hope to get back about Monday or Tuesday. Consequently address my letters as of old. ...

An old Colonel of ours who is doing duty round about here came to my room this morning & brought me about 500 letters to read & censor. Some of them were the funniest productions imaginable & were very amusing.

Miss Dalton *[sister of Lieutenant Colonel Charles Dalton RAMC who was mortally wounded on 17 September 1914. Dalton had three younger sisters, Adelaide, Florence and Maude: it is not evident which of these is the 'Miss Dalton' or 'Miss D' frequently referred to by Ryan.]* is trying hard to get out & see her brother's grave & usually turns in here for me to help her over her difficulties which are many. She is trying to join the Red Cross here, but so far she has not been successful in either. I have been up all day (now 3pm) in my room. The weather is dull. The sun is just trying to show himself through the clouds and a ray has just fallen on my paper. I have not seen it for days & appreciate it though it is a mere flicker. I have not any news. ...   Your loving Jane

Friday 23 October 1914. Feeling much better. Still being massaged. French attack in direction of Klerken. Was repulsed & retired in disorder towards Dixmude-Bruges road.
Saturday 24 October 1914. Went to see Notre Dame church with Miss Dalton & went to see L'Hôpital in afternoon. Saw Napoleon's tomb & captured German plays a beautiful militaire. 600 prisoners were taken by us on yesterday & 1500 killed near Pilken.

Astoria Hotel
25.10.14 Sunday 2pm

My own darling,

... What bunkum putting my photo in the Cork Examiner. What did it say or how many Cork photos appeared there? My Rolls Royce man has not yet turned up nor have I heard from anyone there except a p.c. from J.S. *[Bostock]* this morning dated 17.10.14. ... I will probably send you a wire as soon as I know I am going. I fully expected to return on next Tuesday as the leg is practically itself again. ...

Miss Dalton cannot get up to see the grave at present and I am trying to do all I can to get her in here as a red cross nurse. She is very nice and really angelic. I think she spends most of her time in church. I don't believe I have ever seen a person think so much of a brother – she is perpetually talking about poor Charlie.

I have not any news from the front but as far as I can learn by the papers things are doing well – as the Germans have again massed a huge number of troops against us on our left flank between Dunkirk & Arras. No more to say little one but best love & kisses to you & kiddies. ...   Your loving Jane

[By kind permission of ©The Irish Examiner]

'Surgeon-Major Eugene Ryan, youngest son of the late Mr. Thomas Ryan, Temple Hill, Cloghroe, who has been mentioned in Sir John French's dispatch for distinguished bravery.' [Cork Examiner, 21 October 1914.]

First Ypres: October – November 1914

During Ryan's sojourn in Paris, I Corps had withdrawn from the Aisne and entrained for Flanders. On 20 October 1914, Haig had established his HQ at Poperinge, west of Ypres, with his Advanced HQ/Reporting Centre variously located at the Hôtel de la Châtelaine in Ypres, at Château Hooge (on the Menin Road about 3 miles east of Ypres), at the White Château (near the Menin Road, about one mile east of Ypres), and at Château des Trois Tours (about one mile west of Ypres).

Under GHQ orders to capture Bruges, I Corps began an eastward advance on 21 October – the opening of the first Battle of Ypres ('First Ypres'). On reaching the Langemarck-Zonnebeke road, I Corps came under heavy fire: at 3pm, Haig called a halt to the attack and issued orders for 'the Corps to content itself with strengthening its position on the line which it held, and to prepare for the attacks which there could be little doubt would be made upon us'. The Germans counter-attacked on 22 October: west of Langemarck, the centre of the line was forced back – but Haig mustered sufficient reinforcements to close the gap. On the following day, 23 October, the French attempted a counter-attack, which also failed. On the same day, the Germans attacked once again but were forced back with heavy losses. During the Langemarck conflict, there had been no respite, the fighting had been practically continuous, and such short intervals as occurred were occupied in digging and preparing to resist the next attack. Ryan left Paris on the morning of 27 October and rejoined the Corps HQ at Ypres on 28 October.

Tuesday 27 October 1914. Left Astoria at 8.30am. Lunched at Abbeville. Saw Fell, Fawcus & Barefoot there.[26] Arrived at 5pm at Poperinge our HdQrs. 1st Eschelon at Ypres. Reporting Centre at White House [*White Château*] near Halte [*railway level crossing*].

White Château, Ypres.
[By kind permission of ©The Archives Office, Stedelijke Musea, Ieper.]

Wednesday 28 October 1914. Pushed on to Ypres this morning, a big battle taking place along the East & SE side of Ypres. Terrific cannonade & rifle fire.

Head Quarters 1st Army Corps.
28.10.14

My darling Sall,

... I left Paris yesterday morning at 8.30am journeyed on via Abbeville where we stopped for lunch and where I met Fell & Fawcus. After lunch we continued on our journey and arrived here in Belgium about 5.30pm having done about 180 miles. They all seemed pleased to see me back. There has been some very heavy fighting round here and from what one hears the enemy must have lost close on 1500 here during the last week. Our 1st division killed 1500 one day & took 800 prisoners and at another spot which was shelled by our artillery 700 dead Germans were found. We are gradually pushing them back and if only the French troops on our flank did as well we would have them absolutely on the run - but if our neighbours can't keep up we cannot

---
[26]Major Matthew Henry Fell RAMC, Major Harold Ben Fawcus RAMC & Lieutenant Colonel George Henry Barefoot RAMC.

expose our splendid valiant fellows to a flank fire on either side as well as a heavy frontal one. I am very fit thank God and so are all the others except one whom you don't know and he was sent to hospital two days ago. Things were never looking better than at present as not alone have we stopped the rush to Calais but have again beaten & demoralized the flower of the German army who were especially ordered up here with a view of getting along the coast towards Dunkirk & Calais. Our chaps are all in the best of spirits and every-body even in Paris is talking about the good work done by Sir Douglas' army. No doubt the country ought to be proud of him & I have never seen him look better. Lady Haig sent out a box of Egyptian cigs & a dozen boxes of matches to each member of the Head Qr staff, but she sent me two boxes of cigs. After finishing this if I have time I will write and thank her. ...

We are a good way into Belgium and hope to be further before long. Prince Maurice of Battenberg *[grandson of Queen Victoria]* - 60th Rifles was killed last night. It is a pity as he was a very good chap. I sent you a card the moment I got back last night. J.S. *[Bostock]* was delighted to see me - he is still trying to get that ship. I hear Morgan[27] is in charge of Hd Qrs of the 4th Corps. ...

Your loving Jane.

They all seemed pleased to see me back. In a letter to his wife on 1 November, Haig noted Ryan's return. 'Ryan is back I am glad to say. He hurt himself getting onto his horse ... dragged his horse over.'

On 28 October, information was received that a major German attack on the British line was to take place on the following day. This offensive began early on 29 October, under the scrutiny of the Kaiser who, for the following five days, was based at Thielt (22 miles north east of Ypres) from where he intended to make a triumphal entry into Ypres. The attack was focussed on a crossroads east of Gheluvelt. In a letter to Sadie on that day, Ryan remarks: 'From 4 am this morning the most severe engagement of the war so far has taken place. We again succeeded in driving back the Germans & we reckon their losses for the 12hrs cannot be much short of 7000 and I am sorry to say our losses must be pretty heavy too. It is now 6.30pm and the battle has not yet ceased though it is not as fierce just at present. I have just come in from our reporting centre *[White Château]* and am scrawling this to you before having a bite of dinner.'

In his diary entry of the same day, 29 September 1914, Haig records: 'Move reporting centre back to White house near level crossing to enable Lomax to make himself comfortable in Hooge Château.' The latter was shelled on 31 October, mortally wounding Lomax; the White Château was shelled on 2 November.

Thursday 29 October 1914. Attack along our line very violent. Casualties fairly heavy averaging 1500. Billeted at Rue des Chiens at Ypres. Several shells

---

[27]Major Claude K Morgan RAMC.

burst in town of Ypres, one going through the French Hospital. Battle started at 5.30 am.

©Author's collection

Friday 30 October 1914. The battle is more severe. Cannonading being continuous & deafening and on the slight intervals the perpetual rattle of musketry can be heard. Ypres shelled again, one dropping on either side of Chief's house. 1320 wounded evacuated.

©Author's collection

Saturday 31 October was a critical day. At 06:00 near Gheluvelt, the Germans again mounted a major assault on I Corps, which was repulsed. The assault was followed by a bombardment of the area. Charteris [5, pages 52-3] elaborates: 'A Staff officer was sent out to get news and we could only wait. ... Then about 11 the Staff officer returned with the news that the 1st Division had been almost overwhelmed by the bombardment, but that our artillery had retrieved the situation and the line still held. A few minutes later came a definite report that Gheluvelt had fallen and the 1st Division line had been broken. D.H. sent me forward to find out what the situation was. ... The road was full of troops retreating, stragglers, wounded men, artillery and wagons, a horrible sight. It was impossible to get any clear idea of the situation. Nobody knew anything except what was happening on his immediate front and

that was always the same story 'The Germans were attacking in overwhelming strength and our men were being driven back but fighting every inch of
the way. ... When I got back to our own H.Q. (at the White Château) I found
that D.H. had ridden forward himself...'.

Charteris's account tallies with Haig's diary entry for 31 October: '2.30.
Gen. Lomax reported that 1st Div. had broken and he was trying to reform
on the line east of Hooge. Soon after this 4 big shells fell into Hooge Château
into a room which H.Q. 2nd Div. occupied and killed Col. Kerr senior g..s.o.
[Colonel Frederic Walter Kerr, senior general staff officer] 1st Div., Lt-Col. Paley
g.s.o.2 *[Lieutenant Colonel George Paley, general staff officer grade 2]* 1st Div, Col.
Percival g.s.o.1 *[Colonel Arthur J Percival, general staff officer, grade 1]* 2nd Div.,
wounded Gen. Lomax and stunned Gen. Monro. About 3p.m. Sir J. French
arrive to see me. He was most pleasant but had no reinforcements to send me.
I got on my horse & rode forward to see if I could do anything to organise the
stragglers & push them forward to check enemy.'

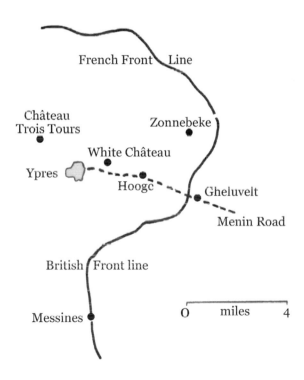

Situation at Ypres on 31 October 1914. I Corps Advanced HQ at White Château
(moved to Château Trois Tours on 5 November). ©Author's collection

Churchill [6, page 792] noted the latter incident. 'At the desperate crisis
of the First Battle of Ypres, British battalions and batteries, wearied, outnum-
bered and retreating, had been inspired by the spectacle of the Corps Com-

mander riding slowly forward at the head of his whole staff along the shell swept Menin Road into close contact with the actual fighting line.' Terraine [21, pages 113-4] also comments on the ride. 'He could see the confusion for himself: he could not see much else. As a gesture, this ride had its value; as a source of information, it only underlines what has been said above'. Reid [16, page 196] reaches a similar conclusion. 'The heroic image of this ride became one of the few celebrated cameos of Haig to emerge from the war. It is doubtful whether he saw more than confusion around him, but he certainly put heart into his troops.' In a similar vein and somewhat melodramatically, the New York Times, in an article of 15 September 1918, relates: 'On the darkest day, when all seemed lost, down the Menin road galloped Sir Douglas Haig and his smart escort of the 17th Lancers, shells falling thick about them, to encourage the faltering troops – for no other reason, the General's place being behind the line.' Sheffield [18, page 95] attaches a more strategic tag to the ride: 'Haig did not undertake a joyride, nor did he go towards the front line just to stiffen the morale of whatever soldiers happened to see him. The commander of I Corps went forward to assess the situation for himself, to speak to commanders on the spot ...'. Whatever the rationale for the ride, the mounted figure of Haig on the Menin Road was to become an iconic image of his command.

Haig's diary entry for 31 October continues: 'I ride to Veldhoek and see Gens. Landon, Capper & FitzClarence, and find that Gheluvelt has been re-taken by the Worcesters and the situation has been restored'.

Following the shelling of Hooge, Major General Herman James Landon took (acting) command of 1st Division in place of the wounded Lomax. The other two generals mentioned by Haig were subsequently killed: on 26 September 1915, at the Battle of Loos, Major General Sir Thompson Capper (7th Division) was struck by a sniper's bullet and died on 27 September 1915; Brigadier General Charles FitzClarence VC (1st Battalion, Irish Guards) was killed in action on 14 November 1914 near Zonnebeke.

Ryan's Diary 31 October 1914. Intense attack again repulsed, the Guards, the Worcesters & London Scottish doing great execution ... The wounded are quickly evacuated. Gen Lomax hit by shell in Château Hooge.

Head Quarters 1st Army Corps,   31.10.14

My darling,

... That fight I told you of in my last still continues, it was fiercer than ever yesterday. A mighty German onslaught, which seems to have fizzled out and today we are putting in a strong counter-attack & I hope we will succeed in driving them back. They are making this fight the 'battle of the war' massing troops in huge numbers against us with a view of breaking through to Calais. It seems extraordinary where they are getting all their troops from. As you are very anxious to know where we are I will run the risk and tell you that we are fighting round YPRES in Belgium in about a line from Dunkirk - now keep this quiet. ... I saw Easton, Cree, Irvine, (J.S. I see every day) Hinge - in fact nearly all the Aldershot crowd to-day. They are all having a very busy time attending & evacuating wounded. ... Prince Maurice of Battenberg is being buried this afternoon at 3pm if I am not busy I may go to the funeral. ... Charteris wants me to go off with him so I will close ...   Your loving Jane.

Ryan's account of events at end of October 1914.

©Author's collection

The things that struck me during this prolonged battle was the fine resistance our troops had. We were losing heavily in killed and wounded. Scarcely any reinforcements came except the London Scottish which came up on the 31st October from the L.O.C. numbering about 900. Went straight into the lines and pulled out within 36 hours having lost more than 50%.

©Author's collection

Owing to lack of reinforcements his body guard including cooks were ordered up to fill some breaches on 31st Oct and as breaches and holes in the line occurred he ordered companies which frequently numbered under 20 from other portions of the line to fill gaps. The weather was cold, rainy and wretched. The sub soil water so near the surface that trenches were useless.

Diary Monday 2 November 1914. Our reporting centre [*White Château*] shelled.

The shell-damaged White Château, Ypres
[By kind permission of ©The Archives Office, Stedelijke Musea, Ieper.]

On 2 November, Ryan wrote to Sadie.

This infernal battle still continues. The bombarding of guns is almost deafening. I saw Capt Nimmo today for the first time since Aldershot. I am glad to say he is very well - as the regiment he is with had a rather bad time. I am sorry poor Lochrin & Nolan were killed. Our poor chaps are at it night & day collecting, dressing & getting wounded away. Sir D. is keeping splendid, though this battle is a high strain on him especially.

Captain W C Nimmo RAMC was Medical Officer, 1st Batallion, Loyal North Lancashire Regiment.

Captain Michael Joseph Lochrin RAMC was killed in action at Pilken near Ypres on 23 October 1914, aged 31 years.

Captain Rupert Henry Nolan RAMC was killed in action near Ypres on 21 October 1914, aged 33 years.

Tuesday 3 November 1914. Ypres continually shelled one going through Chief's house.

Wednesday 4 November 1914. For last 5 days, 5218 evacuated from Ypres. Now free of wounded at 10.30am. At 5pm our reporting centre shelled killing 4 wounding 5. Lt Banning killed. Col Marker seriously wounded. Leg amputated at Clearing Hospital Poperinge.

Ryan's account continues:

Sir Douglas had his HQrs at the white house near the Halte where the railway crosses the road to the East of YPRES. which was severely shelled at 10.30 .AM on 2nd Nov The chandelier in the room in which DH was working was blown to dust by a shell which killed 3 in the Kitchen. we left this place . came back to a house near the Menin Gate which again was flattened on the 4th Several being killed . & wounded . Col Marker was thrown on to the top of me. when I found I saw his leg was shattered above the Knees. then moved to the Chateau of TROIS TOURS about a mile west of YPRES.

©Author's collection

'Sir Douglas had his HdQrs at the white house [*White Château*] near the Halte where the railway crossed the road to the east of Ypres, which was severely shelled at 10.30am on 2nd Nov. The chandelier in the room in which DH was working was blown to dust by a shell which killed 3 in the kitchen. We left this place and came back to a house near the Menin Gate which again was flattened on the 4th, several being killed and wounded. Col Marker was thrown on to the top of me, when I got up I saw his leg was shattered above the knee. Then moved to the Château of TROIS TOURS about a mile west of YPRES.'

The shelling of his HQ in three different locations on successive days elicited the following comment in Haig's diary entry for 4 November. 'But enemy had evidently some spies about to help him to direct his fire so accurately. This is the third place my H.Qs. have been shelled in the last few days.'

In [5, page 56], Charteris also records the shelling on 4 November – which he (incorrectly) dates 5 November. 'On Thursday, poor Marker was hit. You will have heard of his death. Four of us had established our Report Centre in an inn at a cross roads. Horne, Marker, Banning and Myself. The Germans were shelling down one of the roads, gradually getting nearer – but none of us thought it would come right up to us. Then one shell struck the building. Horne and I went out by one door in case the building should collapse, and Marker and Banning went out by another. Horne and I got away scot-free. Marker and Banning walked straight into another shell; Banning was killed outright, Marker badly wounded in the leg. Ryan was near by and was splendid. He went straight to Marker, although shells were now falling pretty thick, and tried to dress the wound. He was thrown right across Marker by the burst of a shell – but still went on with his work. Marker was taken to hospital and seemed to be getting on all right. He sent a wire home that "he had had a quarrel with a shell" and was quite cheery. Then gas gangrene set in and he died a few hours later.' (Gas gangrene (clostridial myonecrosis) is a bacterial infection that produces gas in tissues at the site of a trauma or a surgical wound.)

Marker   Banning

Portraits from *The Bond of Sacrifice, Vol 1*, L A Clutterbuck, W T Dooner & C A Dennison, The Anglo-African Publishing Contractors, London, 1917. © Copyright expired

Colonel Raymond John Marker, Quartermaster I Corps, died of his wounds in hospital at Boulogne on 13 November 1914, with his wife at his bedside. His body was repatriated and buried at Gittisham in Devon. In view of mounting losses, the practice of repatriation was stopped shortly afterwards.

Lieutenant Percy Stuart Banning, Royal Munster Fusiliers, was killed on 4 November 1914, aged 29 years. Banning is buried in Ypres Town Cemetery.

Excerpt from Ryan's letter to Sadie of 4 November 1914:

We have already taken on & beaten over ten different German Army Corps each of which was stronger than ours. This battle is still raging but the attack is getting weaker. I don't know how our splendid chaps stand perpetual shelling - each & every one of them deserves the V.C. My crowd are all fit. Sir D. is simply splendid & is the talk of the country. Major Bostock is doing very good work here, he fully deserves 'a mention in dispatches'. I could have stayed in Hospital much longer but was quite well enough to join my Hd Qrs and look after my dear General. You need not be afraid of Calais as we have already driven them back & burst up their plans of invading ye, though I honestly think it would be the best thing for England to see what war at home is. There would not be much opposition to conscription then, if they only saw the poor unfortunate people fleeing from them in a terrified state. They are the most savage and low down race in the world. Only two days ago did they come up to our lines dressed as Highlanders, but the trick failed them with disastrous results. Col. Guise Moores[28] has now joined our 1st Division. I see him nearly every day. Holt, Winder, Carter, Lloyd Jones, Smallman are all well. I think things are looking well for our cause, but I wish K.o.K. *[Kitchener]* sent us out more re-inforcements as we badly need a fresh division or two. It is marvellous how our first army has fought without rest night or day since August 23rd. Nobody who has not been with them can believe what they have endured.

Château des Trois Tours, Brielen, near Ypres.
[By kind permission of ©The Archives Office, Stedelijke Musea, Ieper.]

Diary Thursday 5 Nov 1914. We shifted our reporting centre to Château Trois Tours. The usual bombardment very heavy 3-6. Ypres bombarded from 11pm to 4am. 4 Munsters killed. ... Marker doing well. Wrote to his wife.

[28]Lieutenant Colonel Samuel Guise-Moores RAMC.

Marker doing well Wrote to his wife. Notes in Ryan's diary include the following poignant message – dictated by the mortally wounded Marker to be sent to his wife, Beatrice Minnie Shrieve Marker (née Jackson):

©Author's collection

Marker. Stansted H[ouse] Stansted Essex.
Rather battered but getting on splendidly. Shall soon be with you.   Raymond

Friday 6 Nov 1914. Rumour of relief by 2nd Corps - report from GHQ of a great Russian victory on Vistula. Getting Col Marker away to base by No 1 Ambulance Train. Day fine & sunny. Black Marias and shrapnel dropping near reporting centre.

At this time, Beatrice Marker and her son Richard were staying at Stansted House in Essex – the home of her father, Sir Thomas Jackson. In a letter[29] of 7 November, to his sister, Sir Thomas records receipt of the news from France.

My dear Mary
    We have had distressing news about Raymond Marker. First came a telegram from him through the War Office as follows: "Battered a bit will be with you soon " ... A further message "Leg had to be amputated" bore operation well. ... A telegram since says he is at Boulogne.
    A thousand pities,   Loving brother,   Tom

Beatrice crossed to Boulogne, where Marker died on 13 November. In the meantime, Ryan's correspondence with Sadie continued.

                                            Head Qrs 1st Corps   Nov 6th '14
My darling wife,
    ... I suppose you have seen where the Germans were ordered by the "Bully" to take the place I mentioned in my last letter by Oct 30th [Ypres], and William [Kaiser Wilhelm II] who is near us here was to be feted in a beautiful town hall here, not alone have they not succeeded but they are further off it and during the last 3 days & nights they, feeling they could not take it, have shelled it night & day.

---

[29]Quoted from the website *www.thesilverbowl.com*, with the kind permission of S Oddie Brown.

You will be glad to hear that at last our Corps is about to be relieved for a few days. We have been at it without a moment's rest since Aug 22nd so God knows it is quite time they got a stand easy - keep this to yourself - we are going back about 20 miles behind the firing line. Personally I am fitter than ever D.V. though the continuous strain is commencing to tell on some of the staff. Sir D. I am pleased to say is very fit. ...

We have just got a message from the Tzar of Russia announcing a great victory on the Vistula, so that is bound to relieve some of the tension here as they are still massing troops against us but our chaps absolutely refuse to budge. They hate us more & more every day & do everything mean under the sun to obtain their point only to be check-mated by our small but gallant crowd. Some of the things one sees are heart breaking, and they as a nation will have a day of reckoning. As I am scribing this I see some more prisoners being brought in. They have long since ceased to interest me as I sometimes feel like kicking them. I had a long rigmarole from Miss D yesterday. She is still in Paris making futile attempts to get into one of Red Cross hospitals. ...

Your own loving old thing   Jane

Diary Saturday 7 Nov 1914. Ypres in flames again today. Attack at night time very severe. The French on our left gave away a lot of ground which our cavalry retook for them at great loss. Specially officers. Major Dawnay was killed. Day is fine. Intense fog at 5pm last evening when attack was started.

In *A History of the Great War* (Volume 1, Thomas Nelson, London, 1922), John Buchan wrote: '**Major the Hon. Hugh Dawnay**, who had come from the Headquarters Staff to command the 2nd Life Guards, led his men to the charge, and inflicted heavy losses upon the foe. In this action Hugh Dawnay fell, but not before his advance had saved the position. In him Britain lost one of the most brilliant of her younger soldiers, most masterful both in character and in brain, who, had he lived, would without doubt have risen to the highest place.'

© Copyright expired

[Portrait from *The Bond of Sacrifice, Vol 1*, L A Clutterbuck, W T Dooner & C A Dennison, The Anglo-African Publishing Contractors, London, 1917.]
Hugh Dawnay was the son of Major General Hugh Richard Dawnay, 8th Viscount Downe.

November 9–14 1914.   Ryan wrote daily to his wife.
9 November. We have succeeded in keeping the Germans out of Ypres, though we have paid heavily for it. Still our casualties are small in comparison with the enemy's. Poor Lochrin was killed round here just before I returned. I cannot give you any more information about him as everybody seems so busy. If I hear anything more I will let you know. The attacks for the last two days have been much weaker and personally I think we have again beaten the enemy in front of us. God knows our poor chaps could do with a rest. I hope they

will get it soon. They are daily shelling the town, also dropping inflammatory bombs on it. The Town Hall is one of historic interest. Gothic in design of the 12th century. It is now crippled. The populace has fled. Our chaps are busy putting out fires etc.

10 November. I pity the poor chaps who have been at it night & day, more especially those in the trenches. Our Hd.Qrs. staff though very hard worked are sticking it like the bricks they are.

11 November. Just a scrawl to let you know that I am doing well. Capt. C. of the Worcester Regt. that you asked about I hear was killed 3 weeks ago[30] but I am not certain as some chaps turn up after having been reported killed or missing. Major Fawcus has come up as DADMS instead of Smallman to the 1st division. Col. G. Moores is his ADMS. The number of wounded is gradually decreasing for the last few days. I shall indeed be glad when this war is finished but we are all doing our utmost to bring it to a successful finish. I have just heard that the Emden[31] has been sunk. This ought to cheer the spirits of ye cold footed Britons at home.

12 November. This battle is still raging. I don't know how they can stick it.

13 November. I have just seen Lt.Col. *[Webb]* Gillman from French's Hd Qrs and he has given me the very welcome news that they are starting to relieve us tomorrow, but it will probably take 5 days to do completely. Who knows that one might get a trip home for two days as I have heard a faint rumour to that effect. But one hears so many rumours that I don't pay much attention to them nowadays. There is no doubt that our little 1st Corps deserves it. The French people call it the Ironsides & worship it and all are anxious to get next to our Corps in the fighting line. Sir Douglas is idolized by them. The battle still continues at times in a most severe & deafening manner. Again I repeat I don't know how they stick it. It is not so bad for the enemy as when we wipe out one of their corps another takes its place. The result being that we are very nearly wiped out by the continual attacks of fresh corps, but we refuse to let them take this place. The trenches are full of water and it is pouring rain. But I am writing this in a coach house with my toes to the fire. Capt. Charteris is a few feet from me crying for a cigarette which I refuse to let him have as he smokes too much. He says I am a very hard master. I wish to God ye people in England woke up & send us out some re-inforcements. If we had even 10,000 fresh troops here now we would walk through the enemy. Col. Cree *[Lieutenant Colonel Gerald Cree RAMC]* was very ill & was sent home to pick up after doing magnificant work here. He was splendid.

14 November. I feel very happy today as not alone did our poor drenched chaps last night again kill any number of the enemy & beat off another severe attack but I have really got definite information that we are to be relieved on Monday the 16th. The weather is beastly raining, raining and making the roads worse

---

[30]This may refer to Lieutenant Frederick G Curtler (2nd Battalion, Worcester Regiment), who was killed in action at St Julien near Ypres on 21 October 1914.

[31]The German light cruiser Emden was beached and burnt on 9 November 1914 after an engagement with the Australian navy in the Indian Ocean.

than ever which really seems impossible. Those blighters are still trying all they can for that spot but they have absolutely failed to move us, though they have pushed the French back here & there. A bit of give & take.

Diary Saturday 14 November 1914. A severe attack yesterday again repulsed. Col Marker died last night. ... Heard today we are going to be relieved tomorrow night. No ambulance trains for last two days - evacuation done by 90 motor ambulances to Hazebrouck. Lord Roberts died at GHQ, St Omer.
[Field Marshal Frederick Roberts, 1st Earl Roberts, died of pneumonia, aged 82.]

Col Marker died last night. On the following day, 14 November, Marker's father-in-law, Sir Thomas Jackson, wrote[32] to his sister.

My dear Mary
    We are a sad party here. We heard last night that Raymond had a relapse, no cause was assigned. We got a telegram this morning "Raymond died last night, immediate cause of death heart failure. Will bring his body to London". And thus ends the life of one of the noblest men I ever knew. ... Little Richard is playing about outside my window – we will not tell him anything. We will leave that to his mother when she arrives.
    Your loving brother,   Tom

15 & 17 November 1914. Excerpts from Ryan's letters to Sadie.
15 November. We have again beaten our crowd in our front here and some of our poor fellows are being relieved tonight, others tomorrow & in 3 days we hope to march back some miles for our well deserved rest. It snowed like billyo this morning and has been raining for hours. I feel so much for those poor chaps in their sodden trenches & clothes.
17 November. Things are as usual here. The enemy is still trying to take that spot. I saw in one of the papers that Ypres was taken by the Germans – such is another lie. I am astonished that such papers are allowed to be printed. The weather and roads are on a par – wretched scarcely describes them. However in 3 days from now we hope to get clear of this place for a few days rest. I saw Fawcus, Easton & Irvine yesterday, they are all very well. It appears the Irvine was again reported as wounded. I also saw Percy Dwyer, who is running a fleet of Motor Ambulances and is doing some very excellent work. He asked about you and wished me to send his very best wishes. J.S. *[Bostock]* did also. He is now DADMS to our Hd.Qrs. Colds & stomach aches are common at present but thank God I never felt better. This is Tuesday and I am simply counting the days to see those chaps out of their trenches.

    The third week in November effectively marked the end of the First Battle of Ypres. The German attempt at a decisive victory had failed; the British success had been in defence rather than offence. In [21, page 122], Terraine comments: 'The cost had been terribly high ... Whole battalions had vanished; of those that remained, their trained drafts already absorbed and used up, many

---

[32]Quoted from the website *www.thesilverbowl.com*, with the kind permission of S Oddie Brown.

were reduced to less than a company strength. And it was not as though these handfuls of invaluable men could now be taken out of the line and sent home to do the work that they should have done - the stiffening of the new battalions that would take their place ... the survivors of the Expeditionary Force had to stay in the field.'

Diary Sunday 22 November 1914. Left Hazebrouck at 7.30am for Boulogne on 9 day leave. Boat stopped in mid channel owing to a floating mine. Arrived Aldershot at 6.30pm.

Sunday 29 November 1914. Went with Sadie to Empress Eugénie's place where I saw Lady Haig & several patients in Hospital. [*A wing of Empress Eugénie's home, Farnborough Hill, was in use as a hospital for wounded officers.*]

Tuesday 1 December 1914. Left Aldershot at 6.30 & Victoria at 8.30. Met General Rice. Reached Boulogne about 12.30.

From First Corps to First Army: December 1914

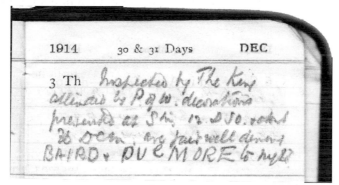

©Author's collection

Thursday 3 December 1914. Inspected by the King attended by the Prince of Wales. Decorations presented at Station. 12 DSO [*Distinguished Service Order*] & about 36 DCM [*Distinguished Conduct Medal*]. Are farewell dining Baird and Dugmore tonight.

Edward, Prince of Wales (1894 – 1972) was the eldest son of George V. He joined the Grenadier Guards in 1914. His serving at the front was vetoed by Kitchener, citing the harm that would occur if the heir to the throne were captured. He succeeded to the throne – as Edward VIII – in January 1936. His reign lasted less than a year: Edward abdicated in December 1936 in order to marry Wallis Simpson, an American divorcée.

Harry Beauchamp Douglas Baird was ADC to Haig from 5 August to 18 December 1914. He later gained the rank of Brigadier General and commanded 75 Infantry Brigade at Messines–Wytschaete in June 1917. Baird's replacement as ADC was Major Alan Francis Fletcher of the 17th Lancers.

William Francis Brougham Radclyffe Dugmore. It appears that Dugmore's period of attachment to I Corps Headquarters Staff ended in December 1914. Acting Lieutenant Colonel Dugmore was killed in action on 12 June 1917 at Messines–Wytschaete, whilst in command of 1st Battalion, North Staffordshire Regiment.

The King's visit is recorded in Haig's diary entry for Thursday 3 December. 'The King arrived at my H.Q. office at 9.35am. ... Then we went to the Railway Station as it was the only covered place here and the King presented D.S.O. and Distinguished Conduct Medals – some 30 to 40 ...'

Sunday 20 December 1914. Had a great game of football. Corps Headquarters versus Cavalry Headquarters. The Prince of Wales playing for Cavalry, who won 1-0 though we should have beaten them. Four Generals playing.

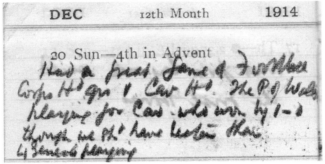

©Author's collection

This incongruous event was also noted by Charteris [5, page 64] who states that 'after lunch I turned out to play football for the Staff against a team of Cavalry. The Prince of Wales was playing' and by Haig (diary, December 20) 'First Corps Staff played 3rd Cav. Div. (Byng) at football at 2.45pm – about 6 generals playing! We were beaten by 1 goal. I did not play.'

Reorganization of the BEF

In December 1914, it was decided to restructure the British Expeditionary Force into two armies. First Army comprised I & IV Corps, with the Indian Corps as Army Reserve. Second Army comprised II & III Corps. The new organization came into effect on 25 December 1914, with Haig in command of the First Army and General Sir Horace Smith-Dorrien in command of the Second Army. On 27 December, First Army Headquarters moved to Lillers.

Saturday 26 December 1914. The Chief appointed to command First Army, 1-4 & Indian [Divisions].

Sunday 27 December 1914. Sir D, Gough, Hobbs, Charteris & ADCs left for Lillers.

Tuesday 29 December 1914. Straker better. Went to Lillers twice today. Hobbs also threatened with appendicitis.

Straker better. In his diary entry for 27 December 1914, Haig commented: 'Straker seemed ill at lunch so sent to bed temp. 104.7 – Sent for Ryan who said he had got a chill, administered physic and said temp. would be normal by 11 p.m.!'

Wednesday 30 December 1914. Hobbs better. Saw Sur Genl Macpherson.[33] Got orders to join 1st Army.

HD 30 December 1914. Some difficulty in getting suitable accommodation for me & my staff. ... a Château *[Château de Relingues]* at the N. end of Lillers has been chosen. Charteris says it is satisfactory, Alan F. says it is damp! Ryan now says I ought to turn the Maire out – he has a very fine house ... But then there is Mrs. Maire, who is full of determination.

On 30 December 1914, Ryan was appointed Medical Officer to Headquarters Staff, First Army. In [5, page 72], Charteris records:
'Ryan comes to us today as Medical Officer. We find we cannot do without him. The immediate cause was General Hobbs developing appendicitis. Whereupon D.H. - who believes that the medical profession comprises only Ryan and a few learners - telegraphed for Ryan and now will not let him go. I am very glad, for he is not only the best of companions, but has the quite invaluable faculty of making every patient fully convinced that there is nothing whatever the matter with him. He is also developing a tendency to bully D.H. - which is very salutary.'

Ryan's attachment to 1st Army is also mentioned by Haig in a letter to his wife on 2 January 1915: 'Ryan came along with me & is now on the 1st Army staff.'

'Micky' Ryan's 1914 diary finishes on a workmanlike note.
Thursday 31 December 1914. Sent General Hobbs home. Straker improved. Easton to relieve me at 1st Corps.

Here ends a terrible year

Under the heading 'Short record of service in France', Ryan summarized the period August – December 1914 as follows.

Left Southampton on 14th August 1914 on the ship *Comrie Castle*, reached Le Havre about 3 pm on Saturday 15th. Went with Sir D & others to Tortoni Hotel. Left Le Havre on Sunday night 16th at midnight & reach Wassigny at 5pm on 17th where we stayed till the 20th when we left at 9am & reached Marbaix. 21st found us at Maubeuge, where I attended a Sgt Major R.F.C. shot through buttock & belly. The 1st and 2nd Divisions marched through Maubeuge on 21st & 22 towards Mons-Condé canal.
23rd Aug. Battle of Mons. We stayed part of the night at the Château Bettignies leaving it toute de suite about 2am on 24th August & rode on to Bavai. 25th Landrecies shelled out & left at 11 pm, reached Le Grand Fayt.

---

[33]Major General William Grant Macpherson RAMC (1858–1927).

26th Hannapes. 27th Mont-d' Origny. 28th St Gobain. 29th Terny.
30th Vauxbuin through Soissons. 31st Villers-Cotterêts. 31st Marolles.
Sept 1st Mareuil-sur-Ourcq. 2nd Meaux. 3rd La Fringale. 4th Mormont, Faremoutiers. 5th Chaumes. 6th Choisy - we about turned. 7th Les Tarpins & Rebais. 9th through Trétoire & Belle Idée to Charly sur Marne.
Battle of Marne. 10th Hautevesnes, we took 800 prisoners. 11th Breny. 12th Jouaignes. 13 Courcelles & Bourg [Bourg-et-Comin] Bridge & Battle of Aisne starts. The Chief staying at Mill the others at Courcelles.
The Aisne battle continues till Oct 17th when the 1st & 2nd Divs left for Flanders. Oct 13th while riding with Sir D. the horse reared up & fell back on me, bursting up my right hip joint, necessitating my going to hospital Astoria Hotel, Paris on 15th.
20th Oct still in Hospital. Saw my name in Dispatches. 22nd Oct went to Versailles in a motor, very nice.
27th Left Hospital. Lazare's motor taking me to Poperinge. Battle of Ypres, 5th day, very hard fighting. 28th Joined Sir D at White Château, billeted in Ypres which is being shelled. 30th Ypres shelled fierce battle going on.
31st Things looking very black - troops retreating - the Guards, Worcs, London Scottish make a great counter attack. Situation saved. Nov 2nd. Shelled out of White House, some men being killed. Moved to Shelly Corner [also dubbed 'Hellfire Corner'] as reporting centre until we were again shelled out on Nov 4th killing several, Lt Banning. Col Marker badly wounded while walking with me. Nov 5th Reporting Centre at Château Trois Tours. 7th Ypres burning. Battle still fierce.
11th Battle fiercer than ever. Our 1st Brigade nearly wiped out but German Guard completely wiped out. 21st Finish of 1st battle of Ypres, our wounded during last 21 days = 15083. Left for Poperinge. Nov 22nd Hazebrouck. Left on leave with Sir D. Dec 1st Returned to Hazebrouck off leave. Dec 3rd Inspected by H.M. Weather very bad. Stayed Hazebrouck till Dec 22nd when we moved south to Hinges. Dec 27th Sir D appointed to 1st Army, left for Lillers.
Dec 30th Joined Head Quarters 1st Army.

31st December 1914. Here ends a terrible year. ©Author's collection

$$3$$

First World War: 1915

HQ First Army, Lillers: January 1915

On taking command of First Army, on his staff Haig kept a number of officers who had been with him in I Corps. He kept 'Johnny' Gough as Chief of Staff, Percy Hobbs as Quartermaster General, and John Charteris as Head of Intelligence – he also brought with him two ADCs, Alan Fletcher and Guy Straker, and 'Micky' Ryan as Medical Officer.

Diary Friday 1 January 1915. Joined 1st Army at 4 pm. Straker better but weak & slightly jaundiced.

Haig's letter to his wife, 2 January 1915: 'My ADC Straker ... has a touch of jaundice so Ryan is sending him off in the Hospital train today to England ... '

Head Qrs, 1st Army, 2-1-15

My own darling,

I joined Sir Douglas here yesterday & have been pretty busy ever since as I have been out all day motoring to the different Clearing Hospitals, and Field Ambulances with Surg Gen Macpherson as his DDMS pending the arrival of Major Morgan who is I am pleased to say about to come as his DDMS. Now as I said before I hope you are happy as I am not within even a donkey's roar of shells. I think I will get quite lonely without their boom. However I don't think I will. I saw Baird today, he wished me to thank you for your Xmas card. I sent Capt Straker A.D.C. into the hospital train passing through here this afternoon - not much wrong with him but Sir D wanted him to have a bit of a rest. It is dinner time & I don't know whether I can get this off this evening as our postal arrangements are not very good so far for this Army. I hope you and kids are splendid – kiss them all from their old Dads. ...   Jane

Sunday 3 January 1915. Raining all day. Sir D shifts into Château de Relingues.

Château de Relingues, Lillers.   ©Author's collection

HD Sunday 3 January 1915. We moved from the house in the town to Château near railway crossing on road to Aire. The house in bad repair but it has the advantage that there is nothing that our servants can spoil.

On the same day, Ryan wrote to Sadie.

Hd Qrs I Army, Sunday 3rd. 1.15

My own darling,

I have been busy for the last 3 days trying to put things right here. It is a difficult job as sanitation & WCs are the limit in this country. Flanders is a damp rainy low lying country and even the south of Ireland would not hold a candle to it for rain & mud. I have not heard from you for the last 3 days but it is probably due to our leaving our old crowd, and the postal arrangements here are in a rather elementary condition at present however till things settle down I will try & get mine away by the King's Messenger. I went to church this morning at 10 o'c and it is pitiable to see nothing but women in mourning and they are generally weeping specially during the sermon. I am scrawling this in my little room while it is raining cats and dogs and has been so all day. As far as I can hear the Russian news today is very good. Things are quiet in front of our lines but I am sorry to hear we lost another dreadnought with the majority of the crew. Also there is a rumour that Italy, Roumania and Bulgaria are coming in very soon so that taking it all round things are looking bright. We are all very fit thank God - hoping you & ours are ditto.

Kiss the kiddies for me & keep a plumper for yourself.   Your loving Jane

I am sorry to hear we lost another dreadnought: HMS Formidable, a battleship sunk by two torpedoes on 1 January 1915 in the English Channel with the loss of 550 crew.

Hd Qrs, 1st Army
8.1.15

My dear Scamp,

... Things are quiet - the poor devils have enough to do to live in water logged trenches without doing much fighting.
... Morgan *[Major Claude Morgan RAMC]* is expected here in a day or two. He, Macpherson and I are in the same mess. We have no less than 4 Generals in our mess. It is still raining but I have no cause for grousing as I can pretty well dodge it as whenever I go for any journey of any consequence I go in a closed motor & when Morgan turns up I need not even do that as I am doing his work at present. I hope you & the kiddies are very well. Give them a kiss from their Daddy. No more news.   Your loving old man, Jane

Thursday 14 January 1915. ... Was called to see Sir D. temp 102, pulse 118. Vomiting & diarrhoea.

Friday 15 January 1915. Still raining. Sir D. vomiting & diarrhoea, temp 101 - pulse 104. Feels a little easier.

Saturday 16 January 1915. Chief better. Had great difficulty in keeping him in bed. Put on light diet, Benger food etc.

Sunday 17 January 1915. Saw morning sick. Mass at 10 & went for a ride with Sir D., Lord Hythe *[Thomas Allnutt Brassey, Viscount Hythe]*, J. Gough & ADCs.

HD 17 January 1915. A fine day at last. All reported quiet and nothing to report. After lunch we all rode out by a disused railway track towards Rely. ... I put T.A.B. *[Lord Hythe]* on one of my horses known as 'His Lordship' because I got him (on the Aisne) from Lord Brooke. By mistake only a snaffle bridle had been put on him today! Consequently when I galloped, 'His Lordship' would not be denied but pushed to the front in spite of T.A.B.'s efforts to check him. I was riding a chestnut mare of some quality but easily kept in hand so I did not join in a race!

Head Qrs, 1st Army
18.1.15

My own darling,

... Sir D was not very well for a few days last week. He has promised me to take a week or ten day's holiday in the South of France as soon as things are fixed up properly here. He is going to get Lady H to meet him at Boulogne and motor through. He is quite OK again and I am very pleased. Don't mention this to a soul. ...   With kisses and much love from the old man.

Tuesday 19 January 1915. Selected some good billets at Aire - and a nice house for C *[Chief]*.

The 'nice house' referred to by Ryan is Moulin le Comte, close to Aire, whereto Haig moved his HQ on 1 February 1915.

Excerpts from Ryan's letters to Sadie 22–31 January 1915.

Friday 22 January. Charteris has been laid up with Bronchitis during the last few days. I am sending him home tomorrow for a week. Morgan is better. It is not raining today for a wonder. We are nicely billeted here and are all very happy. The Chief is OK and so are the rest of us. ... Everything is quiet but there is a rumour that a great number of Germans are congregating at Lille & Ypres.

In [5, page 73], Charteris records: 'My cold has developed into bronchitis, and Ryan has ordered me home for a couple of days' rest. I feel inclined to bless the word "bronchitis".'

Saturday 23 January - from Grand Hotel du Louvre et Terminus, Boulogne. I have just brought down Major Charteris. We have just had some coffee and rolls at this hotel. He is going off in 15 mins time and I am giving him this to post in London. He is not very bad and expects to call and see you some day next week, at least he says he will and that he will write and let you know. I am going to have a look at some of the hospitals, I also want to see ... Sebert[1] who is at the Pindi Hospital *[Rawalpindi British General Hospital, Wimereux]* about 4 miles from here. We had a severe frost last night. I return again after lunch in the motor that brought us down. Old John is waiting in anxiety telling me he will miss his boat. He is mad to be home to nurse his son. He is crazy about him. So must finish with love and kisses. I wish I was going across with him - but perhaps later on.

Monday 25 January. I also saw Sebert. It took him about an hour to show me all over the Pindi British Hospital of which he is in command at present. ... I don't think I stand a dog's chance of getting what you style a 'brevet'. Two of our generals here were promoted to the rank of Major Genl (Gen Gough and Hobbs) and a letter from the Army Council arrived putting them back in their former ranks of Brigadier Genls. Again I ask you to say not a word about this. It takes 3 hours good running to get from here to Boulogne. I got back at 5.30pm as the roads are very bad especially in the dark. The Germans are shelling all along the front and a wire has just come in stating that Béthune where the head quarters of the 1st Corps and 1st Div are was shelled early this morning. They also shelled a Clearing Hospital of ours there. I have not heard if they have done much damage. It is about 8 miles from us. Macpherson and Morgan are just gone off there with a view of shifting the Clearing Hospital further back. I often dream of you and was quite lonely on Saturday when I sent Charteris off. ...

[No 1 Casualty Clearing Station – situated in a Convent – was shelled out of Béthune on that day: the unit was relocated at Choques on 28 January 1915.]

Tuesday 26 January 1915. There was quite a lot of fighting yesterday and it

---

[1]Major Sebert Francis Green RAMC.

ended in our capturing quite a number of prisoners. I also heard that we downed a Cruiser of theirs.

[On 24 January 1915, the German cruiser Blücher was sunk in the Battle of Dogger Bank.]

Thursday 28 January 1915.

©Author's collection

There was a young lady of Ypres (Wipers)
Who was shot in the a... by some snipers
And the tunes that she played
Through the holes that they made
Beat the Argyle & Sutherland pipers.

Your old man Jane

Friday 29 January 1915. Our staff of the 1st Army is growing every day. We now number 35 officers, so we are shifting again on Feb 1st to a place more removed from the line of battle, not that they are gun shy but greater accommodation is required. In the attack of last Monday the Germans must have lost from 1200 to 1500 in killed and wounded. We had about 400 wounded.

©Author's collection

Saturday 30 January. I hope you did not show those papers I enclosed ... to anybody as Sir J. French sent round a circular yesterday stating that it had come to his knowledge that officers had sent home intelligence summaries etc in private letters and that any officer doing so in future would be severely dealt with. It shows how careful people ought to be.

You ask if there is any chance of my coming home. Well really I don't think there is, at least not for a few months. I have a nice soft billet and I mean to mind it. Sir D has not yet taken that bit of leave and now I scarcely think he will go for some time as the enemy are getting rather active of late.

Women are not allowed within a donkey's roar of this place. Millicent Duchess of Sutherland blew in near here the other day and she was promptly taken over by the Provost Marshal and sent down country ...

[Millicent Leveson-Gower, Duchess of Sutherland (1867–1955): British society hostess, social reformer, and playwright. She received the Croix de Guerre for her Red Cross work in the war.]

©Author's collection

... I hear Col Thompson RAMC who was taken prisoner is home.
[Colonel Henry Neville Thompson RAMC had been captured on 26 August 1914, during the Retreat from Mons.]

Sunday 31 January 1915. I am sorry we are leaving here as I had a beautiful room with electric light and fire etc. I am also lucky in having a very good servant, he is with me since the start and minds my things very well. We see very little of the other chaps nowadays. Charteris returns tomorrow. ...

HQ First Army, Moulin le Comte, February – March 1915

On 1 February 1915, Head Quarters, First Army, moved to Moulin le Comte, about one mile to the west of Aire-sur-la-Lys (Aire), with Advanced Head Quarters at Hinges.

Head Quarters, 1st Army, Moulin le Comte.   ©Author's collection

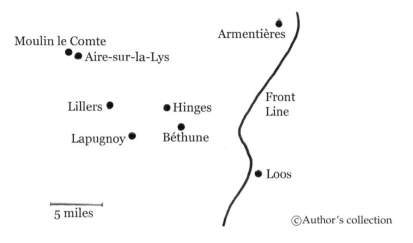

Moulin le Comte
Aire-sur-la-Lys
Armentières

Lillers
Hinges
Front Line

Lapugnoy
Béthune

Loos

5 miles

©Author's collection

Hd Qrs 1st Army, 5.2.15

My darling scamp,

Since you are such a good map reader and judge of our position to the proximity of the firing line, you might again refer to it and let me know if you think our present position "Aire" sufficiently safe. If you don't consider it so, I shall refer the matter to Sir D. and perhaps he will consider the advisability of putting you in amongst his staff and give you a red tab. ...

HD Thursday 11 February 1915. After lunch we rode through Mametz and Therouanne and home across country via Enguinegatte. I took Gen. Hobbs and Ryan along with me.

Haig's letter to his wife 11 February 1915. Gough has a big decision to come to today, as to whether he leaves me to take command of a Division or remain on. He asked my advice. I said that I thought it best for the Army & himself to go & take the Division.

Ryan's letter to Sadie 16 February 1915. There is a rumour that General Gough is going home to command a division.

There is a rumour that Genl Gough is going home to command a division.

©Author's collection

HD 17 February 1915. Gough in bed with a cold. Ryan says it is alright.

Thursday 18th [February] '15

My darling Sall,

I have just heard all the cross channel boats have been stopped so I don't expect letters will fly. .... Morgan and Hunter were lucky to have left yesterday. Some of the N.C.Os and men left here last night to catch the morning boat from Boulogne - they will be rather disappointed when they find they have to return. I have been fairly busy during the last fortnight or so as I am inoculating all my chaps against enteric. It is now 10.30am and I have already done 50 this morning. ... There has been some fighting in front of the 2nd Army not far from YPRES, but on our front things are fairly quiet. Poor Baird went to bury his brother yesterday who was killed near YPRES. The poor chap was in the Camerons. I knew him very well. I am very sorry for poor Baird as he is such a charming fellow. It is only about three days ago he and I were talking about his brother. I am glad to hear you are taking the pills. I don't know how long the channel packets will be stopped. I suppose the Irish boats will be also. I trust the kiddies are splendid and that you are really feeling as well as you state. I hear Genl. Sargent was to go home on leave on 23rd. I presume there will be a wave of disappointment on the part of the wives as well as the hubbies but anything is better than a cold and watery death. Lots of love and kisses to you and kiddies. Your loving Jane

Poor Baird went to bury his brother. Major Percy Thomas Baird was killed in action 15 February 1915.

Death of Brigadier General John Gough VC

HD Saturday 20 February 1915. ... Gough received a letter about breakfast time from Col. Stephens Commander 2/Rifle Bde asking him to go and lunch with his old brother Officers near Fauquissart ... I raised no objection but told him to be careful. ... I returned to Moulin le Comte for lunch. After lunch a message reached me ... saying 'General Gough dangerously wounded'. ...

Haig's letter to his wife 20 February 1915. Have just received a telegram from O.C. 2nd Rifle Brigade that Gough has been wounded. No details. He went off this morning to lunch with his Battalion of the Rifle Brigade which is in the 8th Division. I expect he went into the trenches which are really quite good there, but he will do foolish things! I have sent off Ryan & Charteris to find out all about him, and meantime I am waiting for news of the poor fellow. ...
P.S. I have just heard that Gough has been shot in the stomach. He is under morphia at present, but they have him in a house, and are keeping him quiet. It is very very hard and so unnecessary to have got hit like that.

Ryan's diary Saturday 20 February 1915. General Gough wounded today. Bullet through left hypochondriac region. No exit. Seen by Bowlby[2] a few minutes after being hit.

On 21 February, Ryan wrote to Sadie: 'Genl. Gough was accidently wounded yesterday – he struck up against a spent bullet – don't say anything about it. He went out to see his old regiment which is about 20 miles from here.'

HD Sunday 21 February 1915. Genl. Gough had a fair night. No material change in his condition. ... Sir A. Bowlby at his morning visit thought some

---

[2]Major General Sir Anthony Alfred Bowlby (1855 – 1929).

injury must have been done to the intestine by the bullet, so decided on an exploratory operation as soon as Moynihan[3] arrived – the latter arrived about 1 o'c. ... About 6 p.m. Sir A.Bowlby came here to see me, and reported that in the morning he saw things were not all right so had decided on exploratory operation. This was done by Moynihan and he (Bowlby) helped. The intestine below the stomach had been pierced. The wound had now been closed and although Gough's condition was ... serious, he had got over the operation well, and there was a good chance of recovery. ... About midnight telegram ... says 'Small but distinctly marked improvement'.

Ryan's diary Sunday 21 February 1915. General Gough operated on by Sir B Moynihan assisted by Bowlby. Jejunum severed and pancreas torn.

©Author's collection

Monday 22 February 1915. Gough died at 5 a.m. today. Buried this afternoon. Weather [*illegible*] cold – a full bevy of generals were present.

HD 22 February 1915. About 6 a.m. telegram was brought me that Gough had died at 5 a.m. from heart failure. 'End was painless and peaceful.' ... By Gough's death the Army loses a very capable soldier. Active in mind and body with a charming manner. He made everything go smoothly & ensured orders cheerfully obeyed.

Haig's letter to his wife 23 February 1915. Mrs Gough was at the funeral yesterday at Estaires [*Communal Cemetery*] and went back to England at night. She bore up wonderfully but I did not like to intrude upon her grief, so I did not speak to her.

---

[3] Major General Sir Berkeley Moynihan (1865 – 1936).

Reid [16, pages 203-4] observes that 'Haig was more affected by this casualty than any other single death in the course of the war. ... Gough had been with Haig since the beginning of the war and in addition to being a calm and efficient staff officer he formed a close friendship with Haig.'

Leave: 27 February – 8 March 1915

In a letter to his wife on 26 February 1915, Haig writes: 'Ryan had 'flu so I am sending him on leave to England soon – probably on Sunday.' In fact, Ryan went on leave on Saturday 27 February.

Saturday 27 February 1915. Left at 5 o'c for Boulogne on leave. Easton *[Major Philip Easton RAMC]* and I dined with Yates Ford *[Captain Carleton Yates Ford RAMC]* at Folkestone Hotel. Waited 4 hours for boat - rough crossing, arrived at Victoria about 9.45 pm.

©Author's collection

Wednesday 3 March 1915. Went to town with Sadie. Lunched. Went to Manor House also to see Mrs Banning at Earls Court about her late husband.
[On 4 November 1914, Ryan had been present at the shelling of I Corps' Reporting Centre at Ypres in which Lieutenant Percy Banning was killed.]

Monday 8 March 1915. Left Victoria at 6 pm for Boulogne where we arrived at 2.30 am. Reached Aire at 5 am.

Neuve Chapelle: March 1915

In February 1915, a joint attack on the German lines by the British and the French 10th Army was planned – to take place in early March.

To his wife on 5 March 1915, Haig wrote: 'I am just starting for Béthune, and stay the day there to make the enemy's spies imagine that my H.Q. are here.'

The attack was launched at 7.30am on Wednesday 10 March 1915. Terraine [21, pages 139-142] succinctly summarises the action.
'The British attack was entrusted to Haig's First Army; the objective selected was the so-called "Aubers Ridge", an almost indistinguishable feature of the flat land north of La Bassée ... Within it, however, lay an important prize - Lille.

The actual point of impact of Haig's attack was the German salient around the ruined village of Neuve Chapelle. At 7.30 a.m. on March 10th, the most strik-ing British artillery action of the war to date took place; at 8.05 the infantry of the IV and Indian Corps left their trenches and went into the attack, on a front of nearly 9000 yards. ... Forty-five minutes after zero hour Neuve Chapelle was captured; the first objective was gained along the whole centre of the attack, though setbacks had occurred on each flank. It was a most promising opening; but then, wrote Charteris on the 12th, "for some reason not yet explained, the whole machine clogged and stopped. It was maddening".'

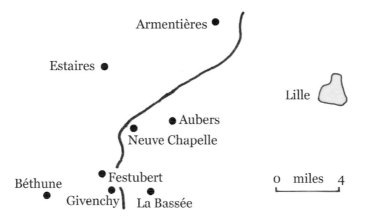

The Front Line at the opening of the Battle of Neuve Chapelle on 10 March 1915.
©Author's collection

Haig's letter to his wife 10 March 1915. One line to tell you that our plans have worked out well today. We have captured Neuve Chapelle & are pressing on to attack Bois de Biez and Aubers. Enemy quite surprised – so hope for large results.

In his letter to Dorothy on the following day, Haig was less optimistic:
'Today cloudy & so observation of Artillery fire difficult. However we are get-ting on through slowly. C.in C. called to say how delighted he was with the advance. Personally I am disappointed we did not get further!'

Terraine [21, page 142] continues: 'On the 13th, recognizing that the ad-vance had come to a full stop, and that ammunition was running low, Haig brought the battle to an end. The First Army had lost 583 officers and 12,309 other ranks ... The British had gained no more than their first objective, a pen-etration of some 1,200 yards on a front of 4,000 yards. ... It was not difficult to see that the breakdown stemmed from ... delays on the first morning and afternoon, which had given the weakened defenders at least five invaluable hours in which to reorganize their defence and begin the movement of their reserves.'

The delays (or as Ryan puts it 'some trouble about our re-enforcements not arriving in time') gave rise to recriminations largely centred on General

Sir Henry Rawlinson (Officer Commanding IV Corps) and Major General Sir
Francis Davies (Officer Commanding 8th Division). In his diary entry for 12
March [5, page 81], Charteris comments: 'D.H. was determined to find out
the cause of the delay and went today to both Corps and Divisional H.Q. to
investigate the matter personally. The breakdown was undoubtedly at Corps
H.Q. where D.H.'s orders stuck and were not transmitted to the division concerned for some hours. Corps H.Q. tried to put the blame on the division, and
there was a rather unpleasant incident, which leaves a very nasty taste in one's
mouth. It is no good finding scapegoats.'

On 13 March, Haig was in little doubt where to lay the blame (but changed
his mind on the following day, when it emerged that Davies held back the
reserves on Rawlinson's orders). In his letter to his wife on that day he comments: 'You will see that we have done fairly well, but not so well as we ought
to have. Instead of pressing on as ordered on the first day, Old Davies did
nothing after getting Neuve Chapelle: so he failed to profit by the surprise
which we had effected. Rawlinson has therefore recommended, and I agree,
that he will be better training a Division at home, than leading one in the field.'

Terraine [21, page 143] elaborates on the Rawlinson-Davies incident. 'Undoubtedly there had been command failures, in which the residual friction
of Rawlinson's earlier misunderstanding of the role of his own subordinates
played a part. He now tried to lay the blame for the failures of IV Corps on
General Davies of the 8th Division; on the strength of this, Haig considered
sending Davies home. The next day, however, he examined that officer's own
evidence: "This at once showed that Rawlinson felt himself to blame for the
delay and not Davies".'

Sheffield [18, page 110] comments further: '... Rawlinson attempted to
scapegoat ... Davies for the failure on 10 March. Davies fought back. Rawlinson confessed to Haig, and French and Haig decided, on balance, not to send
Rawlinson home. Over the next three years, Rawlinson became one of Haig's
most important lieutenants, with the Davies affair silently in the background.'

Haig's view of the events is described in his diary entry for 18 April.

HD Sunday 18 April 1915. I saw [Hubert] Gough at 9.30 and ordered him to
take over his new command [7th Division] at once. I also told him the facts
of the case in which Rawlinson had asked for M.Genl. F. Davies to be removed from command of 8th Division on account of his failure to carry out
orders at N. Chapelle but that, on Davies putting forward a statement of orders rec[eive]d & issued by him, Rawlinson had written in to say that he (R)
accepted all the blame for the delay which had occurred – I gave Gough this
information because Davies had told me privately that neither he nor his staff
had full confidence in Rawlinson because they felt that if his personal interests
required it, he (R) would throw over his subordinate commanders! and that
he would not hold to any order which he had given.

Neuve Chapelle: Ryan's account

The 1st Army was formed about X mas 1914. Their Command of which was given to DH. HD. Q~ were located at AYR. with advanced H? Q~ at HINGES nothing much doing till the battle of NEUVE.CHAPELLE on 10th of March 11. 12.13th at first we pushed the enemy back over 1000 yds on a frontage of over 3000. took a few hundred prisoners. Our loses were heavy. we evacuated during last 4 days 329 Officers .7872 other ranks. Mr. Asquith viewed the battle with DH from a windmill about a mile behind the firing line. There was some trouble about our re-inforcements not arriving in time. Some mistakes about the route between Rawley . Davies (Cold Streams). on 9/c of which the latter was degommed.

©Author's collection

'The 1st Army was formed about Xmas 1914, command of which was given to DH. Hd.Qrs were located at Aire with advanced Hd. Qrs at Hinges. Nothing much doing until the battle of NEUVE CHAPELLE on 10th March 11, 12 & 13th. At first we pushed the enemy back over 1000 yds on a frontage of over 3000 & took a few hundred prisoners. Our losses were heavy. We evacuated during last 4 days 329 officers & 7872 other ranks. Mr. Asquith viewed the battle with DH from a windmill about a mile behind the firing line. There was some trouble about our re-inforcements not arriving in time. Some mistakes about the route between Rawley [*Rawlinson*] & Davies (Cold Streams) on account of which the latter was degommed [*sacked – from the French* dégommer, *to dismiss*].'

As previously noted, the latter sacking did not take place. Following the shifting of blame (for the failure to exploit the early gains at Neuve Chapelle) from Davies to Rawlinson, Haig personally reassured Davies that his position was safe.

Wednesday 10 March 1915. A good day today. We have taken Neuve Chapelle. 3000 yards of trenches. 1000 yards in depth & over 900 prisoners.

Thursday 11 March 1915. Severe fighting continues. We have repulsed all counter attacks. Casualties pretty numerous. I sent down country in an improvised train 466 British & 230 Indians all lightly wounded also 12 Germans.

Friday 12 March 1915. Up to 9pm tonight we have evacuated 245 British Officers & 5995 other ranks, 12 German Officers & 258 other ranks. To-day we continued our progress & captured 4 maxims & 400 prisoners. Fighting still continues.

Saturday 13 March 1915. Number of casualties [*evacuated*] up to 9pm tonight is 327 British Officers & 7872 other ranks, 13 German Officers & 333 other ranks. A number of lightly wounded were sent down in improvised trains to Havre. These trains got their personnel locally instead of from the base. No cooking arrangements, rations, medical equipment & blankets were supplied to the train. Additional stretcher bearers were provided - the local French being used on Thursday & Friday.

©Author's collection

Deadlock: 14 March – 21 April 1915

From Neuve Chapelle to the beginning of the German offensive – known as 'Second Ypres' – on 22 April 1915, the situation was essentially deadlocked.

Sunday 14 March 1915. A heavy cannonade going on until late in the afternoon. The enemy got 10 trains of reinforcements yesterday. Our guns found them when massing.

Monday 15 March 1915. The enemy made a severe attack on 2nd Army capturing trenches & village of St Eloi south of Ypres. A counter attack recovered St Eloi & some of the trenches, the others being destroyed & no man's land. All quiet in front of 1st Army. Day cold.

Saturday 20 March 1915. An Aviatik dropped some bombs at Estaires damaging the gas works. *[The Aviatik was a German reconnaissance aircraft that carried 10kg bombs for light offensive missions.]*

Sunday 21 March 1915. An Aviatik dropped bombs at Lillers killing 3 women & wounding 6 others. Two Zeppelins reported over Paris last night. Motored to Hazebrouck.

Monday 22 March 1915. Sir D left for Boulogne on leave.

March 24th 1915

My own darling

... We are getting more confident day by day. Sir D now has 164,000 men in his army and it is daily increasing. Our losses in Officers in that last show was very heavy but not as bad as the Daily Mail states. Still our chaps are full of confidence. Things are quiet round about here. Occasional shelling and small attacks are the order of the day, but the German has all the attack knocked out of him. ... I hear Bostock is going home. I have not heard when or for what job, but there is a rumour he is getting some convalescent camp there.

... Kiss the darlings from Dads ...   Your loving Jane

I hear Bostock is going home. Bostock returned to England to take command of Summerdown Camp Military Convalescent Hospital, Eastbourne.

Saturday 27 March 1915. Sir D returned from leave to-day.

Monday 29 March 1915. Saw Sir D. looking much better for his leave.

Death of General Lomax, April 1915. Lieutenant General Samuel Lomax, wounded in the shelling of Château Hooge at Ypres on 31 October 1914, died on Saturday 10 April 1915. In a letter to his wife on 16 April 1915, Haig comments as follows. 'I was very sorry to hear of General Lomax' death. He wrote to me from Bath 5 weeks ago and seemed so much better, because he spoke of coming to join me again. It was very kind of you to go to his funeral.'

Saturday 17 April 1915. Fighting about Ypres. Hill 60 reported taken by us. A good number of casualties. *[Hill 60 was a strategically important low rise on the southern flank of the Ypres salient.]*

Monday 19 April 1915. Still severe fighting for Hill 60. The enemy making many severe counter attacks. Casualties on both sides heavy.

Tuesday 20 April 1915. Still battle raging S.E. of Ypres. Saw Yates Ford returning from Boulogne & dined with himself & Lumsden.

Frederick William Lumsden VC (1872 – 1918). Lumsden is frequently mentioned by Ryan. He was a Royal Marine Artillery Officer who, in 1915, took up a temporary appointment as Staff Officer (Intelligence), First Army Headquarters. Charteris [5, page 108] notes: 'My chief assistant, Lumsden, is a Marine major, many years older than I am.' Between 3 and 4 April 1917 at Francilly-Selency, west of St Quentin, Major Lumsden undertook to bring in six captured enemy field-guns which had been left in dug-in positions 300 yards in front of the British troops. For this action, he was awarded the Victoria Cross on 8 June 1917. The citation reads: 'For most conspicuous bravery, determination and devotion to duty. Six enemy field guns having been captured, it was necessary to leave them in dug-in positions, 300 yards in advance of the position held by our troops. The enemy kept the captured guns under heavy fire. Major Lumsden undertook the duty of bringing the guns into our lines. In order to effect this, he personally led four artillery teams and a party of infantry through the hostile barrage. As one of these teams sustained casualties, he left the remaining teams in a covered position, and, through very heavy rifle, machine gun and shrapnel fire, led the infantry to the guns. By force of example and inspiring energy he succeeded in sending back two teams with guns, going through the barrage with the teams of the third gun. He then returned to the guns to await further teams, and these he succeeded in attaching to two of the three remaining guns, despite rifle fire, which had become intense at short range, and removed the guns to safety. By this time the enemy, in considerable strength, had driven through the infantry covering points, and blown up the breach of the remaining gun. Major Lumsden then returned, drove off the enemy, attached the gun to a team and got it away.'

©Author's collection   © Copyright expired

Portrait from *The V.C. and D.S.O Vol I: The Victoria Cross*, compiled by Sir O'Moore Creagh & E M Humphris, p 233, The Standard Art Book Co Ltd, London, 1923.

As Brigadier General commanding 14 Infantry Brigade, Lumsden was killed in action at Blairville, near Arras, France, on 4 June 1918. He is buried in Berles New Military Cemetery, Berles-au-Bois.

Wednesday 21 April 1915. 2nd Army casualties reported to be about 2500.

©Author's collection

21-4-15

My own darling

Here is the usual bit of script to you and ours. As Mrs B [Bostock] is full of her little self and her John, it is really nice to find she is so proud of her hubby. I am sorry about her brother-in-law, but you will probably find there is nothing in it. I am writing this in Yates's office after dinner having just got yours. He is full of himself as he has been promised his two day's leave. How I too should love to go but I would not condescend to ask for it as I know the difficulty and red tape about getting a chap to do my duty, and it is much better to wait for a decent week. I felt after the last spell that I wanted to go back again at once and I don't think it is worth going for two days though a lot might be done in that time so I regret there is not a slightest chance of converting your dream into a reality. There is still a stiff fight going on about Ypres. They shelled hell out of the poor little town again today with some very big guns. The postman is just collecting so I must close with billions of kisses to you, Florrie and kiddies.　　　　Your loving & lonely poor old thing　Jane

Second Ypres: April – May 1915

On 22 April 1915, the German IV Army launched an offensive on the French positions around the Ypres salient when 'for the first time the Germans made use of poison gas with far greater effect than they had themselves anticipated or were prepared to follow up. The First Army, however, took no part in this battle beyond sending reinforcements and endeavouring to learn from it such lessons as might prove of assistance in the future' [9, page 241]. After an intense bombardment, the German infantry attacked behind clouds of chlorine gas released from cylinders. Without protection against the gas, the French were forced to retreat, leaving a gap in the line to the left of the Canadian I Division. However, the Germans had insufficient reserves to exploit the situation. By 24 April, the British and Canadians had reconstituted the defence and a series of unsuccessful counterattacks ensued.

HD Friday 23 April 1915. It seems the whole of the XXVI-th German Corps carried out the attack last night on the line Langemarck – Bixchoote. The enemy used asphyxiating gases and forced (it is said) the French to retire. The latter are only Territorial Infantry. A prisoner stated that the asphyxiating gas is contained in metal cylinders, 4ft. long, which are sunk in the earth at bottom of trench. Pipes are attached to cylinders and the nozzles project over the parapet. The gas is a yellowish colour, probably chlorine, and drifts down wind over the opposite trenches.

Friday 23 April 1915. Report of French reverse NE of Ypres. We still hold Hill 60. The Germans reported firing asphyxiating shells. Day very cold.

On 24 April, Charteris [5, page 88] recorded: 'We have not yet got full news of the fighting around Ypres. I am going up there tomorrow to see the Intelligence people. Apparently the Germans used heavy asphyxiating gas, which they released from their trenches. The wind drifted it on to the French line ... which gave way very badly. We have had to send up some troops ... from the First Army to help restore the situation.' On 28 April, he [5, pages 88-89] comments further: 'Ypres has been a very sad affair. All this week there has been very fierce fighting with very varying results. We were hopelessly let in by some French Territorials, and have had very heavy losses. ... We shall of course now have to use gas ourselves, as soon as we can get it going. The horrible part of it is the slow lingering death of those who are gassed. I saw some hundred poor fellows laid out in the open, in the fore-court of a church, to give them all the air they could get, slowly *drowning* with water in their lungs – a most horrible sight, and the doctors quite powerless.'

Saturday 24 April 1915. Hellish battle north of Ypres. The French retire several kilometres (6) exposing our left flank held by Canadians - where casualties are very heavy. They did excellent work but owing to being outflanked had to retire, losing some guns. It is reported that the horses even refused to go near the guns.

Sunday 25 April 1915. Day cold. Still severe fighting going on at Ypres. 2nd Army reinforced by Cavalry. The French also sending reinforcements.

Monday 26 April 1915. Battle still raging. Things are a bit mixed but Germans are being hard held. Casualties reported heavy on both sides. Mac [Macpherson] sent from 1st Army to help 2nd Army.

Tuesday 27 April 1915. The Germans are being driven slowly back. Very severe cannonading can be heard at Aire. Heavy casualties among Lahore Division.

Wednesday 28 April 1915. Report that Germans are driven across the Yser & that we have recovered as far as St Julien NE of Ypres. 29,000 landed at Gallipoli in Dardanelles.

Friday 30 April 1915. The Germans still using gas round Ypres, & 'pipes' protruding from German trenches in several places in front of us. Precautions have been issued to all our troops.

Saturday 1 May 1915. Lovely day. The Boshes still using gas, but not making progress. My mare gone lame from sanderack [fissures in the hoof].

Sunday 2 May 1915. My mare still lame. 225 of Dorsets reported poisoned with gas near Ypres.

Friday 7 May 1915. Eve of battle - Neuve Chapelle & La Bassée. Our advanced Reporting Centre got to Merville. Rain nearly all afternoon but still very warm.

Fighting renewed around Ypres on 8 May and continued until 13 May, and then again on 24–25 May, with repeated use of gas attacks. Towards the end of May, logistical difficulties and shortages of reserves forced the Germans to call off the offensive. Losses during the Second Battle of Ypres are estimated at 59,000 British troops and 10,000 French troops, against 35,000 German, the difference in numbers partly explained by the use of chlorine gas.

The sinking of R.M.S. Lusitania

©Author's collection

Saturday 8 May 1915. Heavy fighting going on Ypres direction. Our show postponed 24 hours owing to rain. The French attack south of La Bassée is on the start. The Lusitania reported sunk off Old Head of Kinsale with loss of 1300 souls. Great indignation.

On 1 May 1915, the Cunard liner *RMS Lusitania* sailed from New York en route for Liverpool. On the previous day, the German submarine U20, under the command of Kapitänleutnant Walther Schwieger, had sailed from Borkum in the East Frisian Islands off the north German coast. Having passed north of Scotland and the Atlantic coast of Ireland, U20 was off the shores of County Cork by 5 May. On 7 May, U20 sighted the *Lusitania* 8 miles from the Old Head of Kinsale and, at 2.10pm, fired a single torpedo at a range of 700 yards. Kapitänleutnant Schwieger's log records: 'Torpedo hits starboard side right behind the bridge. An unusually heavy detonation takes place ... '. The *Lusitania* sank in 18 minutes, with the loss of 1,198 of the 1,959 people aboard, many of whom were US citizens. The sinking turned public opinion in many countries against Germany: it was greeted with outrage by the US public and contributed significantly to the decision of the United States to declare war on Germany in April 1917.

Aubers Ridge, Festubert, Givenchy: May – June 1915

Aubers Ridge. On 9 May 1915, Charteris [5, page 91] wrote: 'The curtain has rung up on another act in the great drama. It is a perfectly gorgeous morning, and a great battle has begun.'

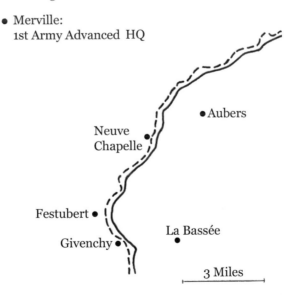

Front Lines on 9 May 1915.   ©Author's collection

Charteris was referring to a renewed assault on Aubers Ridge by British and Indian troops of First Army, coinciding with a French attack near Arras. On 11 May, he recorded the outcome [5, p.92]: 'Our attack has failed, and failed badly, and with heavy casualties. That is the bald and most unpleasant fact. ... We had not enough ammunition, and much of what we had was defective.

The bombardment had not destroyed the German wire when the infantry attacked, and they could make no progress.' The Official History identifies three causes of the failure: 'first, the strength of the German defences and the clever concealment of machine guns in them; secondly, the lack on the British side of sufficient shells of large calibre to deal with such defences; and thirdly, the inferior quality of much of the ammunition supplied ...'

In [13, page 137], Harris quotes a first-hand account by a subaltern of the Welsh regiment: 'We were told that after the bombardment there would not be many people left in the German first and second lines. We were all quite confident of the result and were very cheery ... My platoon was not to leave the trench for two minutes after the first two platoons had gone. At 5.37 am the first two platoons jumped over the parapet ready to charge but they were met by a perfect hail of bullets and many men just fell back into the trench riddled with bullets ... My company commander then turned to me before my two minutes were up and said I had better try. So I took my platoon and the other platoon in the company also came and we jumped over the parapet to charge but we met the same fate ... I was the only officer left in my company'.

First Army had suffered 11,000 casualties by the time the attack was abandoned on 10 May.

Sunday 9 May 1915. Terrific bombardment started by us this morning at 4 am. The 8th Division have got the front line trenches by 7 am, some other places held up by wire & maxims. Great slaughter near Ypres. 5 German assaults severely repulsed.

Monday 10 May 1915. Several very severe bombardments yesterday. Losses on both sides heavy. We took several prisoners who got nasty. The French south of Arras doing very well. Went all round C.C.S. *[Casualty Clearing Stations]* with Dwyer. Chocques choked with blessés.

Tuesday 11 May 1915. The French took over 2000 prisoners, 32 maxims, 6 field guns near Arras. We are keeping the enemy on our front hotly engaged.

Wednesday 12 May 1915. The French near Arras making very good progress. Advanced over 4 kilometres over a 7 mile front. ...

Thursday 13 May 1915. ... The French doing splendidly, capturing Notre Dame de Lorette, Cruency & two other villages. Prisoners 4129 & guns of various kinds including 6 heavy field guns. Raining all day today.

Saturday 15 May 1915. ... We are about to attack tomorrow *[Battle of Festubert which, in fact, opened at 23:30 on 15 May]*. Béthune shelled during night.

Festubert. Under pressure from GHQ to resume the offensive as soon as possible after the failure of Aubers Ridge, an attack further to the south at Festubert was planned, preceded by a lengthy bombardment on 13–15 May. The infantry attack began at 23:30 on 15 May. On 16 May, Charteris [5, page 92] records: 'Another attack yesterday and good news. We made some progress. To-day we have advanced still farther, about 1 mile on a front of 2 miles; we may be able to enlarge the gap to-morrow.' On 18 May he states: 'We made progress yesterday; it is terribly slow and expensive in life. We are really only pushing on to assist the French attack on our left, and not in the hope of accomplishing anything very big ourselves ... The weather has gone against us. It has rained pretty continuously the last two days, and the ground is a quagmire again. ... In the last three weeks we have lost 50,000.' On 25 May, Charteris [5, page 93] observes: 'The battle is over as far as we are concerned, and we can take stock. It is not a satisfactory stock-taking for us in the First Army. We have not done nearly as well as we had hoped to do, and our casualties are heavier than we had anticipated ... We did our part by holding the Germans down to the ground in front of us, while the French, who had larger forces engaged than we had, fought their way forward on our right ... Our artillery was ineffective, due to lack of ammunition and faulty ammunition.'

Over the 11 days of the Battle of Festubert, First Army suffered approximately 17,000 casualties.

Sunday 16 May 1915. A number of officers including Generals Macpherson, Hobbs, Rice etc went to church to celebrate Joan of Arc. A great fight progressing well for us, capturing 222 prisoners & gaining about 1200 yards.

Monday 17 May 1915. We continue to progress, the Germans surrendering in numbers. Took about 400 prisoners, others surrendering fired on by their own guns & ours.

Tuesday 18 May 1915. Raining, cold & cloudy rendering observation impossible. Battle easing off in consequence.

Wednesday 19 May 1915. Weather still bad. Shelling going on & occasional infantry attacks. Lunched with Sir Douglas at Merville. Fletcher indisposed.

Thursday 20 May 1915. The Canadians made a night attack & progressed about 500 yards taking several prisoners. I went to Merville to see Fletcher who is slightly improved. Weather improving.

Friday 21 May 1915. Fletcher much better. Day fine. Great shelling. Béthune again shelled. 1st Corps shifted to Chocques. The Canadians gained some ground again last night. Indians repulsed.

Saturday 22 May 1915. Day fine. Shelling intense 2-5 ... Made some progress again last night.

Sunday 23 May 1915. Went to Merville before lunch, rode after. Intense shelling going on. We were heavily counterattacked killing a large number of the enemy. Béthune heavily shelled. All Field Ambulances cleared out.

©Author's collection

Monday 24 May 1915. Day very hot. Enemy tried on gas again last night & this morning near Ypres. Some were suffocated. Progressed in attack again yesterday & last night.

Givenchy. On 11 June 1915, Charteris [5, page 98] commented: 'We are planning another small operation to help the French, who are still pegging away at their big attack to the south of us. It will be quite a small affair, for we have not enough ammunition for serious attack.' He was referring to the Battle of Givenchy, the preliminary bombardment for which took place during 13–15 June. The infantry assault commenced at 6pm on 15 June: over much of the front, the wire was intact and the attack failed to reach the German lines. In those few places where the wire had been cut, there were some gains – but by 16 June the Germans had countered and driven the British troops back. The First Army suffered 3,500 casualties. Charteris [5, page 98] summarized the outcome on 18 June: 'We have had our little attack, and it has failed. We had departed from the Neuve Chapelle plan of infantry attack after a short bombardment, and adopted the French system of a long bombardment. The Germans were well prepared, and though we got into their line at several places, we could not make progress or even hold what we had gained, and are back in our own front-line trenches. There are three reasons for this failure - not enough artillery, the Germans had excellent deep dug-outs that our fire could not reach, and in the middle the French on our left asked for assistance to meet a German counter-attack. Of these, the vital one was the second, the deep German dug-out. The Germans are admirable military engineers. We must expect better and better defences as time goes on, unless we attack constantly and keep them occupied.'

Sunday 13 June 1915. Went to Boulogne got stores, returned to Aire for lunch. Rode with Morgan to see Grand Gymkhana given by Indians at which the King & Queen of Belgians were present ... During the performance shelling was loud & intense by 1st Army and French near Souchez.

Grand Gymkhana. A similar incongruous event on Thursday 24 June was noted by Charteris [5, pages 99-100]: 'The kaleidoscope of war gave another quite paradoxical view to-day. The Indian Cavalry ... staged a Horse Show at a little place with a natural amphitheatre (Estreblanche). It was so utterly out of place - some 20 miles from the front-line trenches, where the infantry are cheek by jowl with the Germans, and the French just finishing off an enormous battle next door to us! And then a Simla horse show with French military bands playing music to us! Every one of the competitors, and most of the spectators, beautifully turned out; all the horses' harness polished till it shone in the bright sun, motor cars grouped round the ring, subalterns - and even generals - flirting with young women in neat uniforms, a tent with drinks, and Indian mess servants.'

Haig also witnessed the event on 24 June: in his journal entry for that day he wrote 'Major General [*Hubert*] Gough came to see me and stayed to lunch.

He and [*Major General Harvey Frederick*] Mercer accompanied me to Estrée Blanche where the Indian Cavalry Corps held a Horse Show. ... It was strange to see such an animated and peaceful scene so close to the Battle front'.

Tuesday 15 June 1915. We attacked and found 1st line trenches all along the line but nearly driven out of all by the intense counter attack in which the Germans used evil smelling bombs.

©Author's collection

Liquid fire: July 1915

Thursday 8 July 1915. KoK [*Kitchener of Khartoum, Secretary of State for War*] inspecting here today. Asquith lunched with Sir D. Raining at intervals.

Sunday 25 July 1915. Motored to Armentières with Lumsden. Town knocked about by shells. Went to see Royal Scots 900 yds from trenches.

Thursday 29 July 1915. Enemy attacked near Hooge using liquid fire, 'petrol & tar', occupying our front trenches. 1100 casualties.

Liquid fire: the first use of flamethrowers by the Germans. Charteris [5, page 102] records: '... on to the Ypres area to investigate the new devilry that the Germans have introduced - liquid fire. It was apparently very terrifying but did little harm. The attack was on our old Head-quarters in October, Hooge Château. The fire came like a stream of water out of a kind of hosepipe, with a bright flame followed by a thick black smoke-cloud. The first use of this ... lost us some trenches - but afterwards when the Germans tried them again, the men carrying them were shot down quite easily before they could be used.'

No 18 CCS, Lapugnoy: August 1915

A Casualty Clearing Station (CCS) was part of the casualty evacuation chain, further back from the front line than the Aid Posts and Field Ambulances. It was manned by the Royal Army Medical Corps, with attached Royal Engineers and men of the Army Service Corps. The role of the CCS was to treat a casualty sufficiently for his return to duty or, in most cases, to enable him to be taken to a Base Hospital. It was not a place for a long-term stay. CCSs were generally located on or near railway lines, to facilitate movement of casualties on to the Base Hospitals. In August 1914, only six CCSs (then known as 'Clearing Hospitals') accompanied the BEF: by 1916, there were approximately fifty CCSs in France and Belgium, each typically accommodating between 500 and 1000 casualties.

In a letter to his wife on 8 June 1915, Haig had written: '... Also Ryan – I am anxious to get him command of a "clearing station" should any vacancy occur.' One such vacancy occurred in August 1915.

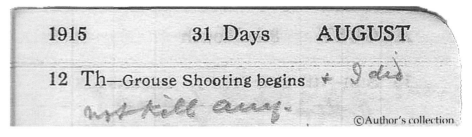

©Author's collection

Thursday 12 August 1915. Grouse Shooting begins & I did not kill any. Nothing doing. GHQ wired & asked me for an interview. Offered No 18 CC Station.

HD Sunday 15 August 1915. Surgeon General Macpherson came to report today. A vacancy for the command of a 'Casualty Clearing Station' has occurred. I approved of Major Ryan (Medical Officer with my Head Quarters) being given it.

On 15 August, Ryan received orders to take over, from Lieutenant Colonel John David Ferguson RAMC, as Commanding Officer, No 18 Casualty Clearing Station located at Lapugnoy, to the west of Béthune. He held this command for just over a year. On 23 August 1916, Ryan received orders to take over command of No 4 Casualty Clearing Station at Beauval (south of Doullens); this command was short lived as three days later, on 26 August 1916, he was requested by Haig (who was by then Commander-in-Chief of the BEF) to rejoin his personal staff.

Sunday 15 August 1915. Orders came for me to take over No 18 Casualty Clearing Station from Lt Col Ferguson but was unable to do so as Winder who is to relieve me is on leave.

Monday 16 August 1915. Had a look at 18 C.C.Stn. 2 sections at Aire, one at Lapugnoy.

On the same day, he wrote to Sadie.

Monday 16th '15

My dear little one,

I have just got my orders to take over command of No. 18 Clearing Station from Col Ferguson [*John David Ferguson*]. Winder is to take my job but he is on leave till 18th so I will probably wait till Thursday. It is a new clearing station. It has just come out from England. Ferguson is that one that was at the Depot when we arrived in Aldershot. The other one [Nicholas Charles Ferguson] is still with a division out here. He is not getting the depot. I am glad I am going as I will have much more interesting work. I hope ye are all splendid. I am in a great hurry as I have been out all day with the Surgeon General and find several things to be done. Love hugs & kisses to you & ours & kindest regards to all at Ocean Wave Lodge. ...   Your loving Jane

Tuesday 17th '15

My darling Sall,

I have been up to my eyes in work taking over from Ferguson today. I returned to my old digs at 7.15pm and have got to do the two jobs for another day or two as Betsy *[Winder]* is on leave and does not return till tomorrow night. He … then comes here so I will probably shift on Friday or Saturday. It is quite a new unit just out from England, knows nothing of the country or local conditions with only one regular RAMC officer and he has only two year's service and two amongst the rank and file. However it will be a more active life as far as work is concerned and I hope to do some surgery again. It rained here most of the day today. There are some possibilities of making this a rather good affair and I am going to have a good try. I am very fit. …

Your loving Jane.

Wednesday 18 August 1915. Took over command of 18 C.C.S & motored to Lapugnoy in afternoon & returned to Aire at 9.15.

18.8.15

My darling little scamp,

Not a scrawl today. However I know it is the postal arrangements are wrong from your wild and beautiful Kerry. I took over today from Ferguson. … I returned here at 7.30 as Betsy *[Winder]* has not yet put in an appearance and I cannot go definitely until I have handed over to him. He returns from leave tonight so he will probably blow in here tomorrow or after. I spent all day in my camp, no house or suitable buildings being available and I mean to make a very fine show of it though the locality is a very poor and rotten one. I will be within five miles of Sir Douglas and he expects me to go and see him occasionally. Things are very quiet, but we are getting in some 'eggs' *[artillery shells]* and hope to have a good supply pretty soon. Give my very best love to all your numerous visitors. … Your own loving Jane.

Thursday 19 August 1915. Motored to Lapugnoy again today where I spent some hours seeing to get camp ready. Betsy arrived at Aire at 6pm.
Friday 20 August 1915. Handed over to Betsy. Went to Hinges to see Sir D. Reached camp at 12 noon & busy all the afternoon bridge building etc.
Saturday 21 August 1915. Busy in camp. Saw paymaster – opened imprest a/c, 500 frs. Spent all day after in camp. Sent wire to DMS *[Director of Medical Services]* 'ready for patients'. Still improving & getting camp ready.

No 18 Casualty Clearing Stn.
1st Army   21.8.15

My darling Sall,

I was relieved by Betsy yesterday morning and came along here to my new command. As far as I can see I have a nice lot of chaps here, none of which with the exception of the Sgt. Major has more than 6 months service. However I think they are capable of being licked into shape. I am camped in a small valley beside a small river and railway line. I think it will be O.K. until we are washed out. The weather is cool, quite different to what it was at this time last year. ... I am writing this at 7am. We are early birds here, our post leaves before breakfast. ...   Your loving Jane

The site of No 18 CCS, Lapugnoy.
©Author's collection

No 18 Casualty Clearing Station was situated in what is today the Parc de Loisirs at Lapugnoy. The small river (La Clarence) and the railway line, referred to by Ryan in his letter of 21 August, remain.

Sunday 22 August 1915. Visit from Sir Arthur Sloggett, Sir Wm Leishman, S.G *[Surgeon General]* Mac *[Macpherson]* & Burtchaell who expressed themselves as pleased with camp. Shelling prevalent.

Monday morning *[23.8.15]*

My darling Sall,
    ... I am located about $3\frac{1}{2}$ miles from Sir D, who by the way is very well *[Haig's HQ was at Hinges, a few miles north east of Lapugnoy]*. Yesterday was a beautiful day. I had a visit from Sir Arthur Sloggett, Sir William Leishman, Surg Genl Macpherson and Col Burtchaell about 3 to 4 yesterday. They were pleased with my camp and naughty Arthur was full of buck. After tea I went for a ride up to the top of an adjacent hill and saw five captive ballons up and about 15 aeroplanes all more or less being fired at. It was a very beautiful sight. I am getting my first patients in today. We are all working like troopers getting the place ready and trying to make it as nice as we can. I have 8 officers, all with one exception being temporarily commissioned, but very nice chaps. No more news. ...   Your loving Jane

Monday 23 August 1915. Visit from Sir Douglas etc. Camp now in good order. ... Padre whom I was called to attend died today. Haemorrhage of brain. Col Wallace visited camp. *[Colonel Sir Cuthbert Sidney Wallace, consulting surgeon, 1st Army.]*

HD Monday 23 August 1915. In the afternoon I rode to Lapugnoy and inspected ... Clearing Hospital which Major Ryan has just taken over. It arrived from England about 6 weeks ago and is most complete in every way. Some 20 or 30 large Indian Tents are arranged with stretchers for the accommodation of 4 or 500 wounded. There is room in an adjoining meadow for more tents so that 800 wounded could be taken in. The Ambulance Trains are 'stabled' at Lapugnoy Station so that stretchers can be carried straight from the tents & put into the Train. Ryan is very pleased with his command and showed me round, with much pride, the operating tent, store, receiving tents etc. etc.

Tuesday 24 August 1915. Received 120 patients to-day. Everything working well. The S.G. visited the camp.

Tuesday morning 31st *[31.8.15]*

My darling Sall,

I had not time yesterday morning to drop you a line; things are getting very nice here. It rained a bit yesterday and it is beautifully cool and fresh this morning. Kelly is with a clearing station about a mile from me, and he may possibly come on to me as I hear I am getting an extra section from the clearing station that he is with. I had a visit from Claude *[Major Morgan RAMC]* yesterday, also Col Wallace who is consulting surgeon 1st Army. Seven nursing sisters arrived for duty on Sunday. They are a pack of beauties too. The one in charge is a copper coloured sister from India, the other six are all frae Glaskey, and auld Reekie. I hope ye are all enjoying life and that you are getting much stronger also the kiddies. Give my chin chin to all at Ocean Wave and with lots of love to you and kiddies.

Your loving Jane

Sept 1st 15

My darling Sall,

A blustery and windy morning. I have now about 140 patients in and have got rid of about another 100. I had a visit yesterday from Col Pike[4], Col Murray Irwin[5] (that nice man I met at the war office when I returned from Malta) and Morgan. I showed them all round my camp and all seemed very pleased. There are two of my officers who are inclined to be slack and if they don't buck up I will give them a warm time and send them up to the trenches. I hope ye are all splendid. No more news. ...   Your loving Jane.

Wednesday morning *[8.9.15]*

My darling Sall.

Weather fine again DV, things are looking well. Fighting is not very heavy at times but we are getting a run of about 80 per day into this place so it just keeps us nicely busy. I have no news. My staff is gradually increasing and yesterday I got rid of one of the 'marked ones' and got an excellent chap in

---

[4]Colonel William Pike RAMC.
[5]Colonel James Murray Irwin RAMC.

exchange for him. I hope ye are all very fit and that you enjoyed that motor trip. Give my kindest regards to all at Ocean Wave and with tons of love and kisses to you and ours.   Your loving Jane

17 September 1915. Ryan was appointed temporary Lieutenant Colonel.

> ARMY MEDICAL SERVICE.
>
> *Royal Army Medical Corps.*
>
>   Major Eugene Ryan to be temporary Lieutenant-Colonel whilst in command of a Casualty Clearing Station. Dated 17th September, 1915.

Supplement to the London Gazette, p.3259, 25 March 1916. ©Crown Copyright

18 September 1915. In her diary[6] entry for that day, Emma Maud McCarthy, Matron-in-Chief, BEF, 1914–1919, records a visit to No 18 CCS.
'. From there to Lapugnoy, 18 Casualty Clearing Station just establishing. Under canvas, accommodation 400 men, 22 officers. A large number of men just admitted, some very seriously. Major Ryan in charge, Miss White QAMNS for India Sister in Charge. There seems every prospect of this being a very excellent unit, every detail for the comfort and convenience of the patients very well thought out, and the Staff very keen and capable looking.'

Loos: September – October 1915

The Battle of Loos formed part of a wider offensive conducted by the French and British in September 1915: the British assault took place at Loos, and that of the French in the Champagne region. Harris [13, page 176] comments as follows. 'The Battle of Loos was launched because the British needed to prove to their allies ... that they were prepared to make serious offensive efforts on the Western Front. ... Haig was pushed into mounting an offensive ... against his better judgement.'
    Among Haig's concerns were a shortage of shells, the fatigued state of his troops, and the unfavourable nature of the terrain – a flat open plateau dominated by the Hohenzollern Redoubt, from the elevated position of which the Germans could direct artillery fire. The attack on Loos began early on the morning of 25 September: it was the first occasion in which the British used poison gas which, at that time, was released from cylinders and was heavily dependent on a favourable wind. On the eve of the battle (24 September), Charteris [5, page 113] observed that ' ... the weather reports were bad. The wind had changed and was blowing from the enemy's trenches.' On 25 September, Charteris [5, pages 113-114] records the opening of the battle in the following terms. 'At 5 he [Haig] came to our office with Fletcher. There

---

[6]Crown Copyright: The National Archives, WO 95/3988.

was quite a faint breath of wind then, and Fletcher's cigarette smoke moved quite perceptibly towards the Germans. But it died away again in a few minutes, and a little later D.H. sent down a message to inquire whether the attack could still be held up. Gough [*Lieutenant General Hubert Gough, Commander I Corps*] replied that it was too late to change.'

Following a preliminary artillery bombardment, 5,100 cylinders of chlorine gas were released from the British front line with mixed results. In places the wind blew the gas back into the British trenches, resulting in many casualties (but few fatalities).

Haig's strategy involved the deployment of I and IV Corps in the gap between Loos and La Bassée Canal. The southern section of the attack, conducted by IV Corps, made significant progress on the first day of the battle, capturing Loos and advancing towards Lens.

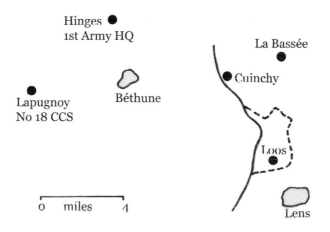

---- Front line at nightfall 25 September 1915
(the solid line is the Front at the opening of the Battle of Loos).
©Author's collection

However, a shortage of reserves brought the advance to a halt by nightfall. Haig had asked the Commander-in-Chief, Sir John French, to make XI Corps available for reserve use the same day, but French had argued that they would not be required until the following morning. The troops were eventually released during the afternoon, arriving at night.

The delay in making available the reserves was crucial: it allowed the Germans to bring up their reserves and to reconstitute their defences. In advancing towards the German line on 26 September, without the benefit of a preliminary artillery bombardment, the British came under intense machine gun fire and suffered heavy casualties. Charteris [5, page 115] summarized the situation. 'It was the old story, "too late". During the night the Germans had reorganized their line. The new divisions were worn out with their long march up during the 25th, and they had never been in action before. They went forward with great gallantry ... But they came under unexpectedly heavy fire ... They broke and came back.' After some further days of sporadic fighting the British were eventually forced to order a retreat. The Loos attack was renewed on 13 October, when further heavy losses combined with poor weather caused the offensive to be called off.

Loos: Ryan's diary

Sunday 19 September 1915. 20 French aeroplanes, large type, passed over our camp. A beautiful sight. Day fine.

Monday 20 September 1915. A violent bombardment along our line, more especially from Givenchy to Loos. The enemy also bombarding & we are getting a fair number of wounded.

Tuesday 21 September 1915. Bombardment still continues night & day.

Wednesday 22 September 1915. Nothing but booming of guns heard - continuous.

Thursday 23 September 1915. Still gunning & more intense.

Friday 24 September 1915. The cannonade was so intense that all the windows in village of Lupugnoy were shaking. Noise is really deafening.

©Author's collection

Saturday 25 September 1915. The battle of Loos started this morning. Wounded arriving all the evening. Everybody very busy & worked right through the night. Loaded an ambulance train about 2 a.m. The Surgeon General was in the camp at 2.30 a.m. The severely wounded cases are being brought to my hospital. The more lightly wounded cases going to No 23 Casualty Clearing Station & Lillers.

[No 23 CCS was located a few miles north-west of Lapugnoy at Lozinghem, wryly known by the Tommies as Losing 'em.*]*

Sunday 26 September 1915. Battle still raging. News good. We have taken Loos & Hill 70. Wounded many & wounds very severe. Everybody in camp hard at it. Taking in about 1000 wounded today.

Monday 27 September 1915. Have received 2600 wounded today. Got rid of 1440 by four ambulance trains & had 1160 left in camp at 9 p.m., none without food shelter & attendance. Raining hard.

[Arithmetic consistency would indicate that the figure of 2600 wounded is the cumulative figure for admissions over the period 25–27 September.]

Tuesday 28 September 1915. Took in another 1100 today, all up to the present being mostly seriously wounded cases, the lightly wounded going to 23 CCS *[Lozinghem]* & Lillers. All officers & sisters hard at it. Raining away.

Wednesday 29 September 1915. Things are slightly quieter. About 900 admitted today. Visit from Commander-in-Chief *[Sir John French]* who expressed himself as being highly pleased with all he saw.

Thursday 30 September 1915. Got five extra Medical Officers & some personnel to help me. Some arrived on Tuesday night. Battle practically over but wounded still coming in. Got a lot of help from 1st Cavalry Division & Gunners on loading trains etc.

The above diary entries indicate a total of 4600 admissions during the period 25–30 September. This is an overestimate: in the War Diary for No 18 CCS *[The National Archives, Kew, Ref WO 95/344]*, Ryan gave more accurate figures.

War Diary No 18 CCS, Thursday 30 September 1915. From the 25th to 30th of Sept. there were 3711 admissions to this Clearing Station nearly all wounded. The wounded cases were very severe indeed, as we were only taking in the lying down cases, the lightly wounded cases going on to No 23 C.C. Stn at Lozinghem and the C.C. Stations at Lillers. The number of officers admitted during this period was 233, nearly all of which were wounded. A few suffered from the effects of gas, shell concussion & nerves etc. Of the 233 admissions a large percentage were very seriously wounded through the chest & abdomen and 8 officers of this class died. Three officers were returned to duty, three remain in station at present and the rest were evacuated to the base. In addition to those, 28 officers were evacuated from 23 C.C.Stn through this Clearing Stn. Of the other ranks admissions total 3468 also nearly all seriously wounded lying down cases and of these 42 died, 87 remain at present and the rest were evacuated to the base.

Surgical notes. About 300 operations were performed during the six days, the large majority consisting of drainage of dirty wounds, extraction of shell fragments and bullets, adjusting fractures of the bones of the leg, arm & jaw in splints etc. Abdominal operations have been contraindicated in a large number of cases as patients had been lying out for some days in some instances,

and were either moribund on admission or so localized that immediate interference was not indicated. The general condition of the patients after such
exposure was grave in most cases but of those operated upon, 12 in number,
6 are progressing well, 3 having already gone to the Base in excellent condition. A small number of abdominals which are doing well without interference
are still in Hospital. Head cases have been mainly sent to the base after having the head shaved and dressed. Of eight head cases [which] were operated
upon, two have died, the others which were kept in hospital for a few days
and evacuated owing to a large number of patients coming in, had shown a
marked improvement, consciousness having returned and general condition
quite compatible with transport.

Friday 1 October 1915. ... We filled thirteen ambulance trains from 26-30
September ... Things much quieter.
Sunday 3 October 1915. 4519 cases evacuated since start of battle. This in-
cludes 268 officers. Of this number, 23 officers & 839 other ranks came from
No 23 Casualty Clearing Station.
Monday 4 October 1915. Things are quiet now & weather much better. It was
very bad during the battle.

War Diary No 18 CCS, Wednesday 6 October 1915. 4pm. The G.O.C. 1st Army
[*Haig*] & staff visited the camp and asked me to thank all officers, NCOs and
men for the good work done during the fight of last week.

HD Wednesday 6 October 1915. In the afternoon I rode to Lapugnoy Clearing
Hospital and saw Major Ryan commanding it. I had already issued an order
to the Medical Services thanking them for the splendid way in which they
had looked after the wounded. I wanted personally to tell Ryan how fully I
realised the continuous hard work which he and the personnel of his hospital
had had.

   This was but one of several visits that Haig made to Ryan's hospital. No
18 CCS was only one of many on the Western Front (in September 1915 there
were in excess of 40 CCSs in France & Flanders) to which Haig made similar
visits. Harrison [14, pages 34-35] comments that 'Sir Douglas Haig ... regularly made a point of visiting his CCSs ... Haig's familiarity with the work of
the CCSs may well have convinced him of their importance ... .' This does not
accord with the frequently-promulgated image of Haig as a distant commander immune to the casualties sustained and their effect on morale.

Wednesday 6 October 1915. Taking in about 100 daily & fair percentage of
sick.

Loos: casualty count

No 18 CCS War Diary records 3711 admissions during the period 25–30
September. Haig's diary entry for 4 October notes the total number wounded
at Loos during the period 25 September to 1 October as follows.

HD Monday 4 October. Surgeon Genl Macpherson came to report. All our medical arrangements have worked well. The total number of wounded between 25th Sept. and 1 Oct amounts to 28,196.

Ryan's personal diary records that, by 3 October, 4519 cases were evacuated from his clearing station. Casualties sustained in the overall period, 25 September to 14 October 1915, of the Loos offensive are estimated at 50,000, of which approximately 8,000 were fatalities. These figures indicate that approximately 10% of those wounded at Loos passed through No 18 CCS.

In [5, pages 116-117], Charteris records this sterling effort in his diary entry for 1 October 1915. 'On my way to examine a captured German aeroplane, I happened to find myself near Ryan's hospital, and looked in to see him. I meant to spend half an hour and ended by being there 2 hours. He insisted on showing me over the whole show. His record of work during the battle is something to be proud of. The nurses worked without a break for 72 hours - just eating biscuit in the wards as they carried on. One surgeon operated continuously for 19 hours, then had to rest. The theatre sister carried on with the new surgeon for another 10 hours - she looks about 25 years of age. The matron wrote a note to the relatives of every one of the 369 officers who passed through the hospital, and made the sisters write to the relatives of every case that was reported "Serious" or "Dangerous". Amidst all the grouses and grumbles that one hears, there is never a word against our medical service. They are really magnificent - and there is no other word - in their efficiency.' In [5, page 148], Charteris also comments that 'Ryan at Loos used one of the padres to give coffee to the wounded as they arrived and another to write letters home, and two more to help dig the graves!'

Loos: the aftermath

The failure of the Loos offensive discredited Sir John French and contributed to his being replaced as Commander in-Chief by Haig in December 1915. On 27 September, Charteris [5, page 116] writes that 'Sir J. French is played out. The show is too big for him and he is despondent. ... I do not think that after Loos, D.H. and French can work satisfactorily together. One or other will have to go elsewhere.'

In his diary, Haig is unequivocal in his criticism of French's performance.

HD Saturday 9 October 1915. ... The main criticism to my mind is the fact that the Reserves were not at hand when wanted. The causes for this seem to me to be
1. Neither the C in C nor his Staff fully realised at the beginning (in spite of my letters & remarks) the necessity for Reserves being close up before the action began.
2. The two divisions were billetted in depth a long distance from where they w[oul]d be wanted, and no attempt was made to concentrate them before the battle began.

3. When the course of the fight showed that reserves were wanted at once to exploit the Victory, the two divisions were hurried forward without full consideration for their food etc. with the result that the troops arrived worn out at the point of attack and unfit for battle.

4. But the 21st & 24th Divisions, only recently arrived in France, with Staff and Com[mande]rs inexperienced in war, should not have been detailed for this work. It was courting disaster to employ them at once in fighting of this nature.

There were other divisions available as shewn by the fact that these arrived 1 to 3 days later upon the battlefield, namely the 28th Div. the 12th Div. and the Guards Div[isio]n.

... the arrangements for the supreme command during the battle were not satisfactory. Sir J. French was at Philomel (near Lillers) 25 miles nearly from his C.G.S. who was at St. Omer. ... Many of us felt that if these conditions continued, it would be difficult ever to win!

HD Sunday 24 October 1915. ... After dinner the King asked me to come to his room, and asked me about Sir J. French's leadership. I told him that I thought the time to have removed French was after the Retreat [from Mons], because he had so mis–managed matters, and shewn in the handling of the small Exped[itionar]y Force in the Field, a great ignorance of the essential principles of war. Since then, during the trench warfare, the Army had grown larger and I thought at first that there was no great scope for French to go wrong. I have therefore done my utmost to stop criticism and make matters run smoothly. But French's handling of the Reserves in the last Battle, his obstinacy, & conceit, shewed his incapacity and that it was impossible to prevent him doing the same thing again. I therefore thought strongly that for the sake of the Empire French ought to be removed. I personally was ready to do my duty in any capacity, and of course w[oul]d serve under anyone who was chosen for his military skill to be C in C. The King said that he had seen Generals Gough and Haking[7] that afternoon, and they had told him some startling truths of French's unfitness for the Command. Gen. Robertson[8] also told him that it was impossible to deal with French: his mind was never the same for two consecutive minutes!

Having lost the confidence of the King, the Prime Minister (Asquith), the Secretary of State for War (Kitchener) and Haig, the writing was on the wall for John French. In his papers Asquith recorded that, in November 1915, he 'entrusted to Lord Esher as an old and most attached friend of Sir John French the duty of conveying to him ... that owing to the strain of the previous months he was no longer able to conduct that campaign' (vide [15, page 277]). Thus, in December 1915, French was forced to resign his command of the BEF. He returned to England and took command of the Home Forces. Haig succeeded

---

[7]Lieutenant General Richard Cyril Haking.
[8]General Sir William Robert Robertson, French's Chief of Staff.

him as Commander–in–Chief of the Army in France and Flanders.

Lord Esher: Reginald Baliol Brett, 2nd Viscount Esher, was a highly influential figure in British politics and in royal circles: he declined high office, preferring instead to manipulate from behind the scenes. During much of the war, Esher (whose mother was French) was – in all but name – a pivotal figure in British Intelligence in France, reporting on the French domestic and political situation. Charteris [5, page 85] observes that Esher 'has some kind of unofficial mission in France ... his chief characteristic is that he is always close friends with those that matter.'

Légion d'Honneur: November 1915

War Diary No 18 CCS Friday 5 November 1915. ... 5pm. The GOC 1st Army [*Haig*] visited the camp at 4 pm & discussed the prevalence of chilled feet etc and any precautions taken to counteract it. He also spoke about getting schools as a site for winter.

HD Friday 5 November 1915. ... In the afternoon I rode to Casualty Clearing Station at Lapugnoy. It consists of tents in low lying fields. I was anxious to see how the recent wet weather had affected it. I saw Major Ryan. He has made roads and drained the ground so that at present matters are satisfactory. He is arranging to move, and will either occupy the Schools in the village, or go to La Beuvrière. He can take in 800 wounded now: in the winter so large an amount of accommodation will not be necessary.

Friday 5 November 1915. Rung up on phone by Morgan who informed me that I was to be presented with Légion d'Honneur.

Saturday 6 November 1915. Got presented with the Légion d'Honneur [*Chevalier de l'Ordre National de la Légion d'Honneur*] today at Vaudricourt. About 15 officers including Potter[9] of the Liverpools and Colonel [*Herbert*] Holman. Met Colonel [*William*] Gray, ADMS 2nd Division, who came to lunch with me at Lapugnoy. Colonel Gray relieved Colonel Holt as ADMS 2nd Div, Holt going as ADMS 28 Division which has left for Salonika. My health was cheerily drunk at dinner by the mess when Padre made a great speech.

©Author's collection

HD Saturday 6 November 1915. ... 9.30 I motored to Vaudricourt (H.Q. XI-th Corps) and presented French decorations (Legion of Honour, ...).

---

[9]Major Herbert Cecil Potter who, in a letter to his mother, ruminated on the reason for the award: 'for trying to do my job, I suppose'.

No 18 CCS, Lapugnoy: November – December 1915

War Diary No 18 CCS, Tuesday 9 November 1915. ... Colonel Wallace, Consulting Surgeon 1st Army, was here today. We discussed the prevention of chilled feet etc. Apparently neither the Regimental M.O.s [n]or Platoon Officers are taking sufficient care of the men's feet as antifrostbite grease has not yet been applied except in very few cases. I am making a full report each evening of the cases admitted here relating to number of days spent by each in the trenches, what they were wearing, whether antifrostbite grease was applied or gum boots issued.

Thursday 11 November 1915. There was a cyclonic storm yesterday. ... Raining all day. River nearly overflowing.

War Diary No 18 CCS, Saturday 13 November 1915. ... The Commanders of 1st Army [Haig] & 4th Corps [Rawlinson] visited the camp at 4pm. General Sir Douglas Haig stated we should have to move as the camp was unsuitable for treatment of sick & wounded.

Saturday 13 November 1915. Blew a hurricane this morning & afternoon. ... Took in 206 cases today including 60 chilled feet.

13 Sat—☽ Moon's first quarter 11.3 p.m.

©Author's collection

Severe weather conditions and the high water level in the adjoining river, La Clarence, necessitated the moving of the CCS.

War Diary No 18 CCS, Sunday 14 November 1915. ... The DMS [Director of Medical Services, 1st Army] visited the camp at 11am. Made enquiries about patients' feet etc and stated pressure was being brought on French Authorities to get the Schools as accommodation for this Clearing Station. In the meantime we are shifting tents in lower field into the higher one adjoining where the Officers' tents are. Three EPIP tents are pitched together making one ward of 30 beds. Weather fine.

[The EP (English/European Privates) tent was the standard issue tent in use in India in the late 19th century. When used outside India it became the EPIP to distinguish the Indian pattern (IP) tent from its British equivalent.]

War Diary No 18 CCS, Monday 15 November 1915. ... 5pm. 18 EPIP tents have been taken from lower field and repitched in higher field in bunches of 3 tents each ward.

War Diary No 18 CCS, Tuesday 16 November 1915. ... 9am. An order has

come from DMS closing our camp from 15th to 18th for reception of patients while tents are being transferred.
... 5pm. The Commander [*Rawlinson*] of the IV Corps & staff visited the camp this afternoon and went through the new lines questioning the patients etc about chilled feet etc.
Friday 19 November 1915. Took in 102 cases today, 27 chilled feet amongst them. Weather cold & blustery. A heavy cannonade nearly all day being especially severe between 9 & 10 pm.
War Diary No 18 CCS, Saturday 20 November 1915. ... 5pm. ... Surg-Genl O'Donnell & Lt-Col Webb (Sanitary Officer) visited the camp at 3.30 and agreed that the new camp looked very serviceable & thought the drying tent and heating arrangements good.
War Diary No 18 CCS, Sunday 21 November 1915. ... 5pm. Sir H Rawlinson & the new DADMS [*Deputy Assistant Director of Medical Services*] 1st Army (Brevet-Col Ensor DSO) visited the camp.

HD Tuesday 14 December 1915. ... I rode back by Lapugnoy Casualty Clearing Station and went round the Hospital and saw the arrangements for winter. Tents have been pitched on rising ground: they have been boarded and big trenches dug all round: good oil stoves were burning, and a system of electric light is being introduced at a small cost. Everything seemed most comfortable. Today was the day for receiving cases, and when I was there numerous motor ambulances arrived with wounded & sick. Major Ryan told me he had about 100 cases remaining as he kept all the slight cases now. If the men are allowed to go to the Base we never see them again!

In the context of the latter comment, Sheffield [18, page 143] conjectures that '[i]t was Ryan who seems to have persuaded Haig of the value of treating as many men as close to the front as possible ...'. In a similar vein, Harrison [14, page 34] remarks that 'the principle of forward treatment would be adopted across the board and when Haig became Commander-in-Chief of the BEF in December it was further refined and enhanced.'

War Diary No 18 CCS, Wednesday 15 December 1915. ... Genl Sir Douglas Haig GOC 1st Army & Lieut-Genl Sir H Rawlinson Commanding IV Corps visited the camp yesterday. Saw the sick & wounded being taken in & went through the wards speaking to a number of the patients.
3pm. Surg-Genl Sir A Sloggett visited the camp to-day at 2.30 & went through the wards, thought the camp ground was very good & patients comfortable.

Thursday 16 December 1915. Went to Aire to see DMS about beds etc. Called to IV Corps to see General Montgomery.[10]
Friday 17 December 1915. Took in 120 sick & wounded today, 11 trench feet. Sir D appointed to command Army in France.
Saturday 18 December 1915. Weather fine but cold. Went again to IV Corps Headquarters. Went to see Sir Douglas.

---

[10]Brigadier General Archibald Montgomery, Rawlinson's principal staff officer, IV Corps.

Haig appointed Commander-in-Chief: December 1915

HD Friday 10 December 1915. ... About 7 p.m. I received a letter from the Prime Minister (Asquith) marked 'Secret' ... It was dated 10 Downing Street, Dec. 8, 1915, and ran as follows: 'Sir J. French has placed in my hands his resignation of the Office of Commander in Chief of the forces in France. Subject to the King's approval, I have the pleasure of proposing to you that you should be his successor. I am satisfied that this is the best choice that could be made in the interests of the Army and the Country.'

HD Sunday 12 December 1915. ... As regards my successor as GOC First Army, I recommended Sir Henry Rawlinson. Though not a sincere man, he has brains and experience. ...

On 12 December, in [5, page 125], Charteris notes: 'The great change has been made, and D.H. becomes C.-in-C. He told me ... that he intends to take me with him as head of the Intelligence of the army in France. ... Rawlinson takes over the First Army. ... Rawlinson is very able and has been in the thick of all the fighting, but I am never quite sure that he may not try to supplant D.H.'.

At noon on Sunday, 19 December 1915, Haig took over command of the Army in France and Flanders. His predecessor, Sir John French, returned to England to take command of the Home Forces.

©Author's collection

Sunday 19 December 1915. Sir Douglas took over today at 12 o'c. A brilliant sun shining at the time. Many German aeroplanes over today.

HD Sunday 19 December 1915. ... I took over Command of the Army in France and Flanders today at noon. I sent a telegram to War Office announcing the fact, and asking who was to take Command of 1st Army. I recommended Sir H. Rawlinson. Up to 11 p.m. no reply reached me. Then Sir Wm. Robertson arr[ive]d from England and telephoned from St. Omer that the Prime Minister & Lord K. had gone out of London for the week end, and nothing could be settled before Monday!! and this is war time!

On 20 December 1915, Dorothy Haig wrote to Ryan in connection with her husband's appointment.

'A very very happy Christmas to you.'

21, Prince's Gate, S.W.

20.12.15

Dear Colonel Ryan,

How nice of you writing me such a charming letter of congratulations on Douglas's appointment. It is delightful, is it not, one can't believe it is true.

You are so nice the way you say everybody is pleased. I think one owes a deep debt of gratitude to you for looking after Douglas so well during the "Retreat" and after. This has enabled him to stand the strain.

The letter continues with an update on the health of the Haigs' eldest child, Alexandra:

Xandra seems getting on well. She has been put under the tuberculine treatment (Fleming,[11] Almroth Wright's[12] understudy) by Mr Burghard.[13]. I do so hope it will be a success, it has not cured the present gland, but made it break down, however. Fleming now has got a culture from Xandra & one does hope that will succeed. ... Xandra goes back to Wales next Wednesday so she is on the road to recovery.

With warm informality, the letter concludes:

Again thanking you for your kind letter. How I wish I could see your hospital. Douglas tells me it is so well run. Of course it would be with you at the head.

Very sincerely yours

Dorothy Haig

©Author's collection

---

[11]Sir Alexander Fleming, discoverer of penicillin.
[12]Sir Almroth Wright, a pioneer in immunology.
[13]Frederic Francois Burghard

Monday 20 December 1915. Day fine. They have started to put down fittings for electric light in camp.

Tuesday 21 December 1915. Day showery. Took in 130 today about 30 of which were wounded. Hair pin trench fighting near Loos.

©Author's collection

Wednesday 22 December 1915. Still attending General Montgomery, IV Corps. He is better. Day showery. Saw Charteris who has just been made Brigadier-General.

As in 1914, 'Micky' Ryan's 1915 diary finishes on a workmanlike note.

Friday 31 December 1915. Took in 6 wounded this morning at 3 a.m.

4
First World War: 1916

At a conference in Chantilly in early December 1915, shortly before his being replaced as Commander-in-Chief by Haig, Sir John French agreed to British participation in coordinated offensives across all fronts by the allies: France, Russia, Italy, Belgium and Great Britain. Haig inherited this agreement and, consequently, the early months of his command were largely taken up in the planning of and preparation for the Anglo-French offensive on the Western Front, leading inexorably to the Battle of the Somme – which comprised, in fact, a sequence of battles fought over the period July to November, incurring casualties at levels hitherto unheard of.

January – March 1916

Diary Tuesday 4 January 1916. My name was mentioned in dispatches in to-day's list.
[Second Mention: Field Marshal Sir John French's Dispatch of 30 November 1915.]
Thursday 27 January. ... Some heavy cannonade on both sides.
Friday 28 January. Heavy shelling continues. Weather fair & cloudy.
Saturday 29 January. Shelling still continues.
Sunday 30 January. Cannonade intense last night. Very cold & foggy. Report of Zeppelin raid on Paris.
Monday 31 January. An intense cannonade last night & this afternoon.
Tuesday 29 February 1916. Visit from H.R.H. Prince Arthur[1] with Staff. Went round & talked to a number of wounded officers & men.
Friday 3 March. Very busy night taking in 280 wounded.

---

[1]Prince Arthur of Connaught, grandson of Queen Victoria and aide-de-camp to Haig.

HD Wednesday 15 March 1916. ... I called at Major Ryan's Collecting Station at Lapugnoy. His hospital is very well arranged and consists of large E.P. Tents. There were two sad cases of men who had to have their legs amputated through the air microbe. Owing to the highly cultivated nature of the soil many wounds get poisoned and this "air bug" develops: the limb swells up and amputation becomes necessary to save life.

Harrison [14, page 27] notes that 'the richly-manured fields of France and Flanders nurtured lethal microbes like those causing tetanus, gas-gangrene, and septicaemia'. The two amputations referred to by Haig appear to have been the result of gas gangrene.

The above diary entry serves to provide further evidence of Haig's interest in, and familiarity with, the work carried out in his Casualty Clearing Stations.

March – April 1916

Distinguished Service Order

From Tuesday 21 March to Sunday 2 April 1916, Ryan was on leave in London and Ireland. On Wednesday 29 March, whilst at his wife's family home in Kanturk (Co Cork, Ireland), Ryan received a summons to Buckingham Palace for appointment to the Distinguished Service Order (DSO).

©Author's collection

To: Major Eugene Ryan, Kanturk, Co. Cork.
Your attendance is required at Buckingham Palace on Saturday morning next the 1st April at 10:15. Service Dress. Kindly telegraph acknowledgement.
Lord Chamberlain London

Saturday 1 April 1916. ... Arrived Buckingham Palace at 10 a.m. Got presented by H.M. with D.S.O.

©Author's collection

Charteris's health: bronchitis

Charteris's Diary Entry [5, page 42].

April 2. Rather a sharp go of bronchitis; the doctor says it means a few days in bed. D.H. has telegraphed for Ryan!! I am in the Duchess of Westminster's Red Cross Hospital, Casino, Le Touquet, and very comfortable, but I get little sleep and am tired out.

Haig's letter to his wife, 3 April 1916. I sent for Major Ryan to see Charteris who is in Hospital with bronchitis (really over cigarette smoking) in order to insist on the Doctors at the Hospital being strict with him and keeping him under control until he is quite better. Ryan asked most kindly for you & the children, and asked me particularly to send you his kindest regards. He will be back here on Wednesday to see Charteris & will I hope stay the night.

Monday 3 April 1916. Went to Le Touquet to see General Charteris, also to see C. in C. Charteris very bad with bronchitis. Dined with C. in C.
Wednesday 5 April 1916. Again went to Le Touquet to see Charteris. Also reported to C. in C. that his condition was serious. ...
Friday 7 April 1916. Again went to Le Touquet ... Charteris much improved.
Sunday 9 April 1916. Saw Charteris. Better.

The Somme: July – November 1916

Prelude. The Allied strategy for 1916 had been formulated in the conference at Chantilly in December 1915: it was decided that simultaneous offensives would be mounted by the Russians on the Eastern Front and the Anglo-French on the Western Front. Haig favoured a British offensive in Flanders, close to BEF supply routes via the Channel ports. However, the numerically inferior British had to comply with French policy: the decision was made to mount a combined offensive – in summer 1916 – where the French and British armies met, north and south of the river Somme in Picardy. In February 1916, plans for the joint offensive were compromised by the launch of a German attack against the French at Verdun. As the French had to commit troops and re-sources to defending Verdun, their capacity to carry out their intended role on the Somme diminished, and it became clear that the British would assume the main role in the Somme offensive. Sheffield [18, page 164] summarizes the situation thus: 'Ultimately, the BEF fought on the Somme because of the de-mands of coalition warfare. The French, the senior partners, set the agenda, and the British had to fall in with it.'

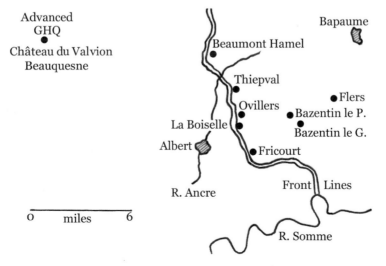

Front Lines at the opening of the Somme offensive on 1 July 1916. ©Author's collection

First day of the Battle of the Somme. The Battle of the Somme was preceded by an eight-day artillery bombardment, during which 1.7 million shells were fired. The infantry assault was originally scheduled for 29 June, but bad weather forced a postponement to 7.30am on 1 July. The axis of the advance was to be the Roman road from Albert to Bapaume 12 miles to the northeast. The advance artillery bombardment failed to destroy either the German front line barbed wire or the heavily-built bunkers or dug-outs: in addition, many of the munitions used by the British were defective. The cessation of the bombardment signalled the start of the infantry attack: the Germans emerged from their bunkers and manned their machine guns to great effect. North of the Albert-Bapaume road, the British advance was a failure from the outset. Whilst a few units managed to reach the German trenches, they could not exploit their gains and had to fall back. South of the road, in the Fricourt area, the British made some progress – but overall the first day was a catastrophe. The fate of the Newfoundland Regiment (with the 29th Division) at Beaumont Hamel encapsulates the disaster. Ordered forward at 8.45am, 22 officers and 758 other ranks began their advance. Within 20 minutes, all officers and some 650 other ranks had become casualties. By the end of the day, the British had suffered 60,000 casualties, with approximately 20,000 fatalities. The first day of July 1916 marks the nadir of Haig's command. In [21, page 207], Terraine comments as follows. 'What is difficult to grasp, from the vantage point of today, is how a disaster of such proportions could fail to be instantly apparent. Yet such was the case. It is perfectly clear from Haig's Diary that he had no sense whatever, on July 1st, of the catastrophe that had befallen his army.'

HD Saturday 1 July 1916. Glass rose slightly during night. A fine sunny morning with gentle breeze from the west and southwest. At first some mist in the hollows. This very favourable because it concealed the concentration of our troops. The bombardment was carried out as usual, and there was no increase of artillery fire but at 7.30 am (the hour fixed for the infantry to advance) the artillery increased their range and the infantry followed the Barrage. Reports up to 8 am most satisfactory. Our troops had everywhere crossed the Enemy's front trenches. By 9 am I heard that our troops had in many places reached the 1.20 line (i.e. the line fixed to be reached 1 hour and 20 minutes after the start).

Ryan's diary entry on 1 July is optimistic. 'Battle of Somme started. Everything so far going on well. Fricourt, La Boiselle & Ovillers taken.'

©Author's collection

In [5, page 152], Charteris's diary entry for 1 July is also optimistic: 'On the whole, our interpretation of the information received has been fairly good.'

Continuation of the offensive. Despite the heavy losses of the first day, Haig persisted with the offensive in the following days. Advances were made, but these were limited and often ultimately repulsed. On 11 July, German troops were transferred from Verdun to the Somme. In a surprise dawn attack on 14 July, the British broke through the German lines on a 3 mile sector along the Longueval ridge: Bazentin-le-Petit was taken.

©Author's collection

Friday 14 July 1916. Battle of Bazentin Le Petit et Bazentin Le Grand & Longueval. Good progress & many guns & prisoners.

Thursday 27 July 1916. Ryan received an aerial photograph of his CCS. *[Taken from an aircraft of No 25 Squadron based at Auchel Aerodrome, near Lozinghem.]*

Signed by Captain Richard Raymond de Cruce Grubb.   ©Author's collection

No 18 Casualty Clearing Station, Lapugnoy, July 1916. ©Author's collection

Ryan's diary continues:
Wednesday 23 August 1916. Got orders this afternoon to proceed to No 4 Casualty Clearing Station *[Beauval]* ...
Sunday 27 August 1916. A great battle round about Guillemont.
Monday 28 August 1916. We took in *[to No 4 CCS, Beauval]* about 400 wounded.
The good old XVI Irish Division takes Guillemont.

The German-held village of Guillemont lay at the junction of the British and French sectors, hampering Allied operations. On Sunday 3 September, it was attacked by the 20th Division and the 16th Irish Division, and taken on Monday 4 September. Curiously, Ryan records this action as having occurred precisely 1 week earlier: this probably has a prosaic explanation – Ryan simply wrote his entries on the wrong page of his diary. On 9 September, the 16th Irish Division took the village of Ginchy, thereby depriving the Germans of a strategic observation point. In his diary entry for 10 September, Ryan correctly dates this action and his Irish pride again surfaces in recording that 'XVI Division again did famously yesterday taking Ginchy'.

The next major British offensive was mounted on 15 September in an action now known as the Battle of Flers-Courcelette in which tanks were used for the first time. In 1914, Ernest Swinton had proposed the construction of an 'armed engine capable of destroying machine guns, breaking through entanglements and climbing earthworks'. This idea was promoted by Winston Churchill who, in February 1915, established a War Cabinet committee – the Landships Committee to oversee the development of 'an armoured trench-crossing vehicle'. The result was the first British experimental tank, attributed jointly to Major Walter G Wilson and Sir William A Tritton. Following development of this prototype, the Mark I tank entered service in August 1916 and was first used in action at Flers-Courcelette. Haig's decision to use the small number of tanks (then a secret weapon) that were available at the time was criticized by some. Winston Churchill commented: 'This priceless conception, containing if used in its integrity and on a sufficient scale, the certainty of a great and brilliant victory, was revealed to the Germans for the mere petty purpose of taking a few ruined villages'. Such criticism was unequivocally rebutted by General John Frederick Charles Fuller, principal staff officer, Tank Corps' HQ (who, on other occasions, was not averse to criticizing Haig): 'The use of tanks on 15 September, 1916, was not a mistake. Serious mechanical defects manifested. No peace test can equal a war test.'[2] In his book *A Short History of World War I* (Oxford University Press, 1951, page 189), J E Edmonds comments on the use of tanks at Flers-Courcelette as follows. 'The comparative failure of the tanks seems to have misled the enemy as to their potentialities; the Allies had copied his gas with great effect, but he did not attempt to follow suit in tanks and only produced in 1918 a few vehicles as cumbrous as their German name *Panzerwagenmitraupengetriebe*; but Haig sent to the War Office on 19 September a request for a thousand tanks'. The latter remark attests to Haig's prescience: clearly, he recognized the tank's potential and acted accordingly – this runs counter to the frequently-aired thesis that Haig was a cavalry-obsessed technophobe.

Further British attacks in the Flers area occurred between 25 and 27 September, in the Battle of Morval and the Battle of Thiepval Ridge. Advances were small but were consolidated. Other attacks launched by the British included

[2]Ref LH 1/302/100, Liddell Hart Centre for Military Archives, King's College, London.

the Battle of the Transloy Ridges (1–20 October) and the Battle of the Ancre Heights (1–11 October). Torrential rains in October turned the battlegrounds into quagmires. On 13 November the British made a final assault, the Battle of the Ancre, in which they captured Beaumont Hamel. Notwithstanding the slow but progressive British advance, adverse winter weather conditions brought the Somme offensive to a halt on 18 November. During the 5-month offensive, the British and French had advanced only some 10 kilometres – at the cost of approximately 420,000 British and 500,000 German casualties.

George V at No 18 CCS, Lapugnoy: August 1916

On Friday 11 August 1916, King George V, accompanied by his Private Secretary, Lord Stamfordham (Arthur Bigge), and his son Edward, Prince of Wales, visited No 18 Casualty Clearing Station.

©Author's collection

Friday 11 August 1916. His majesty, King G, with Lord Stamfordham, Prince of Wales, etc. visited my camp this afternoon. Inspected the sick & wounded officers and also the other ranks sick & wounded. He expressed himself very pleased with the camp, and the general arrangements made for the comfort of the patients. I introduced His Majesty to my Officers & Sisters, also Sgt Major.

Ryan escorting George V. The tall figure on the right of the centre pair is Lieutenant Colonel Sir Derek Keppel, Master of the Household. On the left in the rear pair is Edward, Prince of Wales.   ©Author's collection

In the **War Diary for No 18 CCS, 11 August 1916**, Ryan elaborates further: His Majesty visited the camp this afternoon and inspected the Hospl between 4 and 4.45 going through all the wards and speaking to nearly all the patients who numbered 138. ... Weather hazy & warm, wind from N.W.

Ryan in conversation with an officer (possibly Stamfordham) while George V is greeted by a nurse. The figure third from left is Surgeon General Robert Porter, Director of Medical Services, 2nd Army. ©Author's collection

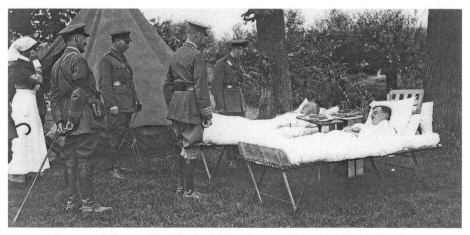

Ryan and George V at the bedside of a casualty. ©Author's collection

The visit was filmed by Geoffrey H Malins (one of two official British photographers assigned to the Western Front during the War) and forms a Chapter, under the heading *A Visit to the Wounded at a Casualty Clearing Station*, of a newsreel entitled *The King Visits His Armies in the Great Advance* (Imperial War Museum Archive No IWM 192). In Chapter 19 of his memoirs *How I Filmed the*

War (edited by Low Warren and published by Herbert Jenkins Ltd, London, 1920), Malins gives an account of the filming of the visit.

'His Majesty was now going to view some ruins near the front, but unfortunately, owing to burst tyres, I could not keep up with the party, and by the time I got on the move again it would have been impossible for me to reach the place in time to film this scene. Therefore, knowing that he was due at No. 18 C.C.S. or "Casualty Clearing Station", I made hurried tracks for it. A most interesting picture promised to result. I arrived at the C.C.S. and was met by the C.O. *[Ryan]* in charge. ... Half an hour later the royal car drew up. The King and the Prince of Wales alighted, and were conducted around the hospital by the C.O.. I did not miss a single opportunity of filming, from His Majesty's talk to some wounded officers, to his strolling through the long lines of hospital tents and entering them each in turn. At one point my camera was so close to the path along which the King passed, that the Prince of Wales, evidently determined not to run into my range again, quickly slipped away and crossed higher up between the other tents. An officer standing by me remarked with a laugh, "The Prince doesn't seem to like you". A touching incident took place when the King was on the point of leaving. He stooped down and tenderly picked up a small puppy, and gently caressed and kissed it ...

George V with Surgeon General Robert Porter and Ryan in background.
©Author's collection

I had just finished turning, when an officer came up to me and said in a low tone: "That's funny." "What's funny?" I asked. "Why that incident. Do you know that dog only came in here yesterday, and he has done so much mischief through playing about, that at last the C.O. determined to get rid of him. But we won't now. I shall put a red, white, and blue ribbon round his neck and call him George. He shall be the hospital's mascot." '

No 4 CCS, Beauval: August – September 1916

On 23 August 1916, Ryan received orders to take over command of No 4 Casualty Clearing Station at Beauval (south of Doullens): this command was short lived as three days later, on 26 August, he was requested by Haig to rejoin his personal staff as Medical Officer. This Ryan did on 8 September 1916, when he moved to Haig's Headquarters at Beauquesne.

Wednesday 23 August 1916. Got orders this afternoon to proceed to No 4 Casualty Clearing Station & take over from Major Rahilly.[3]

Thursday 24 August 1916. Surgeon-General Pike, [*Director of Medical Services, 1st Army*] made a hell of a speech about my leaving the unit etc.

Friday 25 August 1916. Arrived at Beauval at noon & took over in the afternoon. Was not impressed with what I saw.

©Author's collection

Saturday 26 August 1916. Was called to see General Kiggell C.G.S.[4] at Château [*Valvion*]. Met the C. in C. also General Butler[5] who asked me to give up the Casualty Clearing Station. I consented.

©Author's collection

Wednesday 30 August 1916. Called to see Sir D. who has some fever, temp 101.2, with diarrhoea. Saw him again in evening, temp 100.

---

[3]Major John Maurice Rahilly RAMC.
[4]Lieutenant General Sir Launcelot Kiggell, Chief of the General Staff.
[5]Major General Richard Harte Butler, Deputy Chief of the General Staff.

Thursday 31 August 1916. The C. in C. improved, temp 99.6.

Friday 1 September 1916. The C. in C. better but kept him in bed.

Advanced HQ Beauquesne: September 1916

On 8 September 1916, Ryan joined Haig's Personal Staff at Advanced HQ, located at the Château du Valvion, Beauquesne.

Letter to Haig from the War Office, London, dated 9 October 1916.

Sir,

With reference to your letter of the 5th ultimo, No. 17915, I am directed to acquaint you that the appointment of Major (Temporary Lieut.-Colonel) E. Ryan, D.S.O., Royal Army Medical Corps, as medical officer on your Personal Staff is approved.

He may retain his temporary rank of Lieutenant-Colonel and receive additional pay at the rate of 10s. a day from the 25th September, 1914, and while he continues to be employed in this capacity.

Sheffield [18, page 134] explains that 'Haig liked to have familiar faces about him. Colonel Ryan … returned to GHQ in September 1916. Alongside his formal job of medical officer, Ryan had a clearly understood role of simply being there for Haig.'

In [11, page 33], Reverend George S Duncan (Haig's chaplain) records that 'Ryan came with Haig to GHQ and remained with him to the end. I do not know how his duties were defined. But he was an invaluable member of our GHQ fraternity, welcome in every company, and always ready to undertake some special commission. His greatest service of course lay in the influence he exercised over the Chief. Haig was no valetudinarian - the fact that he carried on during the whole period of the war with scarcely a day's illness is sufficient evidence on that score. But it meant much to him to have close at hand a man like Ryan who could keep a watchful eye on him, and whom he had come to trust implicitly, not merely for his professional gifts, but above all for his robust and cheerful attitude to life and his unfailing commonsense. In his genial way Ryan continued to "bully" Haig as no one else would have dared to do, laying down the law when occasion arose with regard to food, hours of sleep etc.; and the Chief would meekly reply: "All right; I'll do as you tell me".'

A somewhat different view on Haig's attitude to health is put forward by John Bourne in *Who's Who in World War One* [2]. 'Colonel Ryan was Chief Medical Officer at GHQ under Field Marshal Haig. Haig was an asthmatic. He is regarded by some of his detractors as a valetudinarian if not a hypochondriac. ... He had great faith in Ryan's medical judgement and would submit meekly to him when ordered to rest or take medication. Ryan's ability to do this was regarded with amazement by the rest of Haig's staff.'

Charteris [4, page 205] comments that 'each day his own doctor found an opportunity of visiting him. ... If he was late in going to bed, if he omitted his physical exercises, if his rest was disturbed and his appetite failed, Secrett *[Haig's personal servant]* reported it to Col. Ryan, and Ryan exercised all the authority of a house physician in a great hospital on a recalcitrant patient. Senior Officers, whose whole day was coloured by a word of praise or blame from the Chief, would listen with amazement to Ryan "telling off" the Chief. "If you don't sleep you won't last," Ryan would say sternly. "I told you to go to bed at eleven." And the Chief would reply mildly – though with the suspicion of a twinkle in his eye: "All right, I'll be good".'

Ryan's 'genial bullying' of Haig continued up to their final departure from France in April 1919. In his diary entry on 13 January 1919, Haig remarks: 'Ryan allows me to get up & sit in an arm chair in my bed room'.

Friday 8 September 1916. Handed over to Rahilly & came to Beauquesne ... Reported my arrival to GHQ. Asquith here with C. in C.

Haig's letter to his wife, 8 September 1916. You would have been amused at the Prime Minister last night. He did himself fairly well – not more than most gentlemen used to drink when I was a boy, but in this abstemious age it is noticeable if an extra glass or two is taken by anybody! The PM seemed to like our old brandy. He had a couple of glasses (big sherry glass size!) before I left the table at 9.30, and apparently he had several more before I saw him again. By that time his legs were unsteady, but his head was quite clear, and

GHQ Montreuil: November – December 1916

At the opening of the Somme offensive, Haig had set up his Advanced Head Quarters near to the front line at the Château du Valvion, Beauquesne. At the close of the offensive in November 1916, Head Quarters moved back to Montreuil-sur-Mer. GHQ at Montreuil was a vast administrative organization. An interesting account, by a staff officer attached to the Quartermaster General's section, of the work carried out at General Head Quarters, is contained in *G.H.Q. (Montreuil-sur-Mer)* by Sir Frank Fox (writing under the pseudonym 'G.S.O.'), first published by Philip Allan & Co (London) in 1920 and reprinted in 2009 by the Naval & Military Press.

Haig and his immediate entourage resided not at Montreuil but at the nearby Château de Beaurepaire, in the hamlet of St. Nicolas, between Montreuil and Brimeux. In [13, page 193], Harris comments: ' ... pre-war Montreuil had been the base of the great École Militaire, the buildings of which afforded very suitable accommodation for GHQ. Haig and his personal staff did not live at Montreuil itself, but had a small château, the Château de Beaurepaire, about two miles outside the town. ... Haig's personal staff consisted of an Assistant Military Secretary ..., a private secretary (Captain Sir Philip Sassoon), a Medical Officer (Colonel Eugene "Micky" Ryan: by training a surgeon but serving, in effect, as Haig's personal physician), an officer in charge of escorts *[Captain George Balfour Black, killed in action 23 August 1918]* and five ADCs.' Reid [16, page 281] elaborates further. 'Far from conforming to the image of palatial surroundings for the generals, the Château Beaurepaire is a modest building, ... and it must have struggled to accommodate Haig's staff.'

Château de Beaurepaire   ©Wikipasdecalais - Creative Commons licence.

What is remarkable is the disparate makeup of Haig's personal staff, each of whom was unswervingly loyal to him. At one extreme was his private secretary, Sir Philip Sassoon MP, a flamboyant and immensely rich aesthete of Baghdadi Jewish descent, and a second cousin of the poet Siegfried Sassoon. Philip described his kinship with Siegfried thus: 'My Wagnerian antonym is a distant relation, the grandson of an old aunt of my father's' (vide [20, page

81]). These cousins first met in 1925, after which meeting Siegfried noted in his diary 'introduced to Sir Philip Sassoon. He looks a bit of a bounder ...' (vide [20, page 155]). Philip Sassoon's flamboyance is encapsulated in his own description, in a letter to the 2nd Viscount Esher in 1917, of his houses at Park Lane in London, Port Lympne in Kent, and Trent Park in Hertfordshire: 'I find myself the reluctant possessor of Park Lane with its *leitmotif* of sham Louis XVI, Lympne which is Martini *tout craché*, and Trent which isn't even Lincrusta when my own period is Merovingian or Boiling Oil. *Le monde est toujours mal arrangé*' (vide [20, page 75]).

At the other extreme, what Ryan, a down-to-earth career officer with a Catholic Irish nationalist family background, would have made of such extravagance is moot, yet the unusual amalgam of personal staff seemed to gel – presumably united by a shared affection for the taciturn 'Chief'.

In the commemorative issue of the *British Legion Journal* (vol.7, no.9, page 252, March 1928), Philip Sassoon wrote that Haig 'enjoyed in a supreme degree the rare gift of being able to inspire those who worked for him, not only with the certain knowledge that nothing short of their best and most efficient work would pass his critical and sure judgement, but with a personal affection for himself which ensured that, in great things or in small, they did in fact give him of their very best. ... Sir Douglas Haig did not choose his friends lightly; but once made he remembered them.'

Ryan celebrated Christmas 1916 with the Commander-in-Chief.

Haig's letter to his wife, 25 December 1916.
I have all the ADC men coming to dine tonight. Ryan is one of that mess.
Haig's letter to his wife, 26 December 1916.
We had great fun with your crackers last night. ... As regards the mottos, you would have laughed when from the first cracker I pulled with Ryan R.A.M.C. (who was on my right) came the motto 'What is it which you often feel but never see?' I read it out of course & delayed to give the answer.

5
First World War: 1917

Despite the heavy casualties for little gain in 1916, at a conference in Chantilly in November the Allies agreed on a programme for 1917 which closely resembled that of 1916. A spring offensive was planned: the French assault would be concentrated in the Aisne area (the principal attack would focus on the Chemin des Dames), with supporting British operations in the Arras region. Plans were somewhat compromised by an unexpected German decision to make a substantial strategic withdrawal from the Bapaume region to a heavily fortified position known as the Hindenburg Line. This withdrawal took place during February and March 1917.

HD Sunday 18 March 1917. ... *Information from prisoners.* German officers have told their men that reasons for withdrawal are:
1. to obtain a better position
2. to shorten the line
3. to give battle on ground favourable to Germans.
The opinion of prisoners themselves is that withdrawal was because the line was untenable.

Ryan's 1917 diary is lost and no letters to his wife in that year survive. However, notes at the end of his 1916 diary include a summary of 1917, which interweave the narrative in this chapter.

1 January 1917. In today's list of awards I was appointed Brevet Lieut. Colonel. [Third] Mention [in Dispatches].
8 - 19 January 1917. Leave followed by 5 weeks of continuous frost.
18 March 1917. Germans retreat from Bapaume-Peronne to Hindenburg line, destroying everything.

©Author's collection

Haig's letter to his wife, 3 February 1917. Ryan was here today and asked so kindly for you & the children. He always says I am the fittest of them all. He himself had a bit of a cold due to getting up in the night & going out with scanty garments to attend to an old Frenchman who had been knocked over by a motor lorry.

In early 1917, Haig's strategic focus was Flanders, with a view to an offensive to secure the Belgian coast, thereby countering the threat, posed by German U–boats, to Britain's 'Atlantic lifeline'. However, his plans were thwarted 'as the BEF had to fight an unwanted battle at Arras at the behest of a new French Commander-in-Chief, after Haig had fought a fierce and unexpected battle with his own government' [18, page 199]. The new French C-in-C was General Robert Nivelle, who had replaced Marshal Joseph Joffre in December 1916. In the same month, David Lloyd George had succeeded Herbert Asquith as British Prime Minister. The views of Lloyd George and Haig on strategy and the conduct of the war were at variance. Their mutual dislike and mistrust was long standing. In his diary entry for 30 January 1916, Haig commented that Lloyd George (who was then Minister of Munitions in Asquith's Government) 'seems to be astute and cunning – with much energy and push but I should think shifty and unreliable'. In February 1917, Lloyd George sought – or indeed intrigued – to place the BEF under the command of the French: this was averted by Haig and his supporters (amongst whom the Chief of the Imperial General Staff, General Sir William Robert Robertson, was a major player), but the affair left Haig in the position of the junior party in the coalition. In [15, page 299], Lees-Milne comments on the intrigue. 'The rock-like quality of Douglas Haig was emphasized during this crucial time by its contrast with the irrational and often hysterical behaviour of most of the leading politicians and soldiers, whether British or French. Throughout their tantrums, irresponsible conduct, disloyalties and sheer pettiness Haig remained unmoved, calm, determined, resolute – on a plane above them all.' In his diary entry for 28 February 1917, Haig comments: 'It is too sad at this critical time to have to fight with one's Allies and the Home Government, in addition to the Enemy in the field!'

Arras: April – May 1917

The first of the 1917 Anglo-French offensives took place at Arras in early April. In his diary entry for 8 April, Charteris [5, page 210] sets the scene. 'We are again on the eve of battle; although it is only to help the French it is a big thing. Three corps, each with four divisions, are making the main attack, and the Canadians are attacking on their left. The big French attack is being held back on account of the weather, but will not make very much difference to us, as far as the immediate fighting is concerned, always provided that the French Government does not at the last moment ... stop the attack altogether; if they do that we shall have the whole German Army on our heads here in a month.'

After a 5-day preliminary bombardment, the infantry attack began – in snow, sleet and rain – on Easter Monday, 9 April. The first day of the battle saw the greatest advance since November 1914: the British pushed forward over a distance of 3 miles; the Canadians took Vimy Ridge.

On April 10, Charteris [5, page 212] records: 'The attack has been a complete success. Yesterday we took more than 10,000 prisoners and 38 guns. Our first assault went straight through the German front-line trenches, and captured the whole of them within an hour. ... The one unfortunate thing is the accursed weather. It has broken again, and we are having snow and rain.'

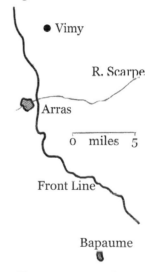

Front Line, 9 April 1917.
©Author's collection

Following the success of the first day, momentum was quickly lost: by 11 April, the Germans had brought up reserves and had consolidated their defences. In addition, the weather continued to deteriorate: blizzards and intense cold caused fatigue. The offensive was maintained only to draw attention from preparations for the French assault on the Chemin des Dames in the Aisne region: it was temporarily called off on 15 April.

The French assault was launched on 16 April. To support the French operations on the Chemin des Dames, Haig renewed the British offensive at Arras on 23 April, with heavy casualties for little gain. The offensive was halted at the end of May.

8 April 1917. Left Brimeux for Heuchin.
9 April 1917. Battle of Arras & Vimy started today. 12000 prisoners & 150 guns. Weather bad. Snow.
18 April 1917. Return to Brimeux. Weather very bad.
23 April 1917. Second Battle of Arras started.
30 April 1917. From April 9th to date, prisoners 19426 & 290 guns.
1 May 1917. Saw Peronne, Bapaume destroyed.
31 May 1917. Arras battle finished.

April 8th 1917 *left* BRIMEUX. *for* HEUCHIN
" 9th. Battle of Arras & Vimy starts to-day
12000 *prisoners*. 180 *Guns*. Weather bad. Snow
" 18. Returns to BRIMEUX. Weather very bad
23rd. 2nd battle of Arras started.
30th. From April 9th to date *prisoners*: 19436.
298 *Guns*.
May 1st Said PERONNE. BAPUME. destroyed.
31st. Arras battle finished .

©Author's collection

In the midst of military actions, with their attendant successes and failures, Haig had to entertain many visitors to GHQ, ranging from foreign dignitaries and politicians to, occasionally, artists. Although somewhat inarticulate and not a natural conversationalist, he appears to have borne this duty without complaint. The following encounter with William Orpen (portrait painter and official war artist 1917) is typical.

HD Friday 11 May 1917. Major Orpen, the artist, came to lunch. I told him that every facility would be given to him to study the life and surroundings of our troops in the field, so that he can really paint pictures of lasting value.

William Orpen's portrait of Haig, dated 30 May 1917.
From *An Onlooker in France 1917-1919* by William Orpen, 2nd Edition, Williams & Norgate, London, 1924. ©Copyright expired

In his book *An Onlooker in France 1917–1919* (Williams & Norgate, London, 1921), Orpen comments: 'Sir Douglas was a strong man, a true Northerner, well inside himself – no pose. It seemed it would be impossible to upset him, impossible to make him show any strong feeling, and yet one felt he understood, knew all, and felt for all his men ... Never once, all the time I was in France, did I hear a "Tommy" say one word against "Aig". Whenever it became my honour to be allowed to visit him, I always left feeling happier ...'.

Flanders: May – November 1917

After Arras, British attention turned again to Flanders.

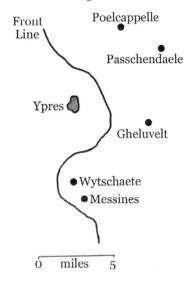

British Front Line near Ypres, May 1917.   ©Author's collection

The rationale is described by Sheffield [18, page 223]. 'The capture of the Belgian coast would help combat the menace of German submarines which was threatening Britain's very ability to go on fighting. A relatively modest advance of about seven miles in front of Ypres would drive the Germans from the half moon of high ground that faced the city. The vital communication junction at Roulers was only twelve miles from Ypres, and its seizure would put the coast within striking distance and place German logistics in Flanders in jeopardy, and might even force German withdrawal from the area. A Flanders offensive offered a big prize.'

Implicit in this rationale was the political unacceptability of abandoning Ypres, the only Belgian city not in German hands. First and Second Ypres had left the city in a highly vulnerable salient beneath the German-occupied 'half moon of high ground' from which the city was subject to remorseless shelling. Capture of the higher ground was a clear priority: of particular importance was the Messines-Wytschaete Ridge to the south of Ypres.

Messines-Wytschaete Ridge: May – June 1917

The Messines-Wytschaete offensive was meticulously planned by General Sir Herbert Plumer. The preliminary bombardment began on 21 May and continued until 6 June, the eve of the infantry attack, when Plumer is said to have remarked to his staff: 'Gentlemen, we may not make history tomorrow, but we shall certainly change the geography'. The attack was scheduled for 3.10am on the morning of Thursday 7 June. At that time 19 mines, placed in tunnels below the German lines, were detonated (it has been reported that the explosions were so large that they were heard in London). It is estimated that approximately 10,000 Germans were killed. Immediately after the explosions, a British artillery barrage further diminished the threat of German resistance. By 9am the Messines-Wytschaete Ridge had been taken. Haig did not have the necessary forces in place to exploit the initial success at Messines. Confused fighting continued until 14 June, during which the Irish Nationalist politician, Willie Redmond MP, was killed in action on 9 June, and Ryan's friend and former 1st Army HQ staff colleague, Acting Lieutenant Colonel William F B R Dugmore, was killed in action on 12 June (his death seemingly unbeknown to Ryan at the time).

©Author's collection

3 June 1917. Left Bavincourt for Blendecques.

Bavincourt, about 10 miles south-west of Arras, was the location of Haig's Advanced HQ during both the Battle of Arras and the Battle of Cambrai. During the Flanders offensive, Haig temporarily moved his GHQ to Blendecques, a few miles south of St. Omer.

7 June 1917. Battle of Ypres, Messines & Wytschaete. Willie Redmond killed. Irish troops doing good work.

[Portrait from the book *Trench Pictures from France*, by William Redmond, A Melrose, London, 1917.]

William Hoey Kearney Redmond (15 April 1861 – 7 June 1917), known as Willie Redmond, was a barrister, an Irish Nationalist, MP and member of the Irish Parliamentary Party in the House of Commons for 34 years. He was a land reform agitator – imprisoned three times – and an advocate of Irish Home Rule. At the outbreak of the war, Redmond felt that he might serve Ireland best in the firing

© Copyright expired

line - 'it Germany wins we are all endangered' In November 1914 he made a famous recruiting speech in Cork. Standing at an open window in the Imperial Hotel he spoke to the crowd below: 'I do not say to you go - but grey haired and old as I am, I say come, come with me to the war'. In 1915, he was commissioned as Captain in the Royal Irish Regiment at the age of 53: promotion to Major followed in 1916. In an attack on the Messines Ridge towards the village of Wytschaete on 9 June 1917, leading his men out of the trenches, Redmond was hit almost immediately and died in the afternoon of that day.

Willie Redmond was the younger brother of **John Redmond (1856 – 1918)**, leader of the Irish Parliamentary Party from 1900 to 1918. He was a constitutional and conciliatory politician who, in 1914, had achieved Irish Home Rule under an act which granted a form of self-governance to Ireland – the outbreak of war led to suspension of the implementation of the act. The image on the right is from *John Redmond's Last Years*, by Stephen Gwynne (Arnold, London 1919).

© Copyright expired

In [5, page 122], Charteris recounts a meeting with John Redmond on 18 November 1915. 'John Redmond came to our H.Q. yesterday. A striking-looking man and very pleasant to deal with. His view is that we need have no fear regarding Ireland if she is treated rightly ... He went right into the front–line trenches and would not hear of stopping outside the danger zone.'

Ryan was on leave for the period 16–29 June 1917, during which he visited Dorothy Haig.

Haig's letter to his wife, 1 July 1917. I saw Col. Ryan who was delighted with the children. He thought them both very hardy & fit.

At this time, Haig was involved in the preparations for an offensive at Ypres that was to become the last great attritional battle of the war and which, as 'Passchendaele', has become a potent symbol of the horrors of trench warfare.

Third Ypres (Passchendaele): July – November 1917

Monday 30 July 1917. Left Blendecques for West Cappel in Sir D's train.

July 30th. Left BLENDECQUES for WEST CAPPEL with Si Crew.

©Author's collection

Haig commanded the opening of Third Ypres from his Advanced HQ in a camouflaged train near West Cappel (approximately 16 miles north west of Ypres). On 31 July (and with limited French support on his left), he launched a major assault on the German lines.

HD Tuesday 31 July 1917. ... Fighting on our right had been most severe. ... I send Alan Fletcher and Col. Ryan round the Casualty Clearing Stations. They report many slight cases, mostly shell fire. ... Some 6000 wounded have been treated in the ten hours up to 6 pm. ... Heavy rain fell this afternoon and airoplane [sic] observation was impossible. The going also became very bad, and the ground was much cut up. This has hampered our further progress.

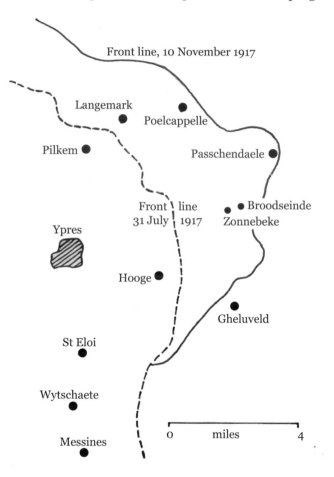

Front line, 10 November 1917

Langemark

Poelcappelle

Pilkem

Passchendaele

Front line 31 July 1917

Broodseinde
Zonnebeke

Ypres

Hooge

Gheluveld

St Eloi

Wytschaete

0   miles   4

Messines

Front line at the opening and closing of Third Ypres/Passchendaele.
©Author's collection

After a 3-day struggle, the British took the first line. By this time, the rain that was to turn the battlefield into a quagmire was unceasing. On 4 August, Charteris [5, page 241] records: 'All my fears about the weather have been realized. It has killed this attack.' The attack resumed on 10 August, directed at the German positions at Gheluvelt: the German defensive measures were effective. A renewed offensive on 16 August fared no better. On 22 August, an assault on the Menin Road secured minor gains at the expense of heavy casualties. In the realization that there would be no swift breakthrough, Haig opted for a series of attritional attacks with the intention of gradually wearing down the Germans. This successful offensive – the second phase of Third Ypres – he placed under the command of General Sir Herbert Plumer, ably assisted by his Chief of Staff, Major General Charles Harington. The Plumer/Harington partnership was formidable – characterized by meticulous planning, caution, clarity of briefings, and leaving nothing to chance. Charteris [5, page 228] observed that 'nobody knows where Plumer ends and Harington begins'.

The first of the attacks took place on 20 September on a front astride the Menin Road, followed, on 26 September, by an assault on Polygon Wood (between Zonnebeke and Gheluvelt) and, on 4 October, by the Battle of Broodseinde. These three successes, and the latter in particular, completed the second stage of Third Ypres and could be regarded as marking a turning point in the war. In the Preface to *Military Operations France and Belgium, Vol II 1917*, the British Official Historian, Brigadier General Sir James Edmonds, commented as follows. 'The successes of General Plumer in September and October are almost unknown to the British public although three times his Army broke through the much-vaunted German defence systems, causing the enemy to admit his failure to himself, and to review and change his defensive tactics again and again ... the Germans speak of it *[Broodseinde]* as "the black day of the 4th October".'

In October, the rains, which had ceased in September, returned and turned the battlefield into a morass.

22 October 1917: remnants of German wire entanglements near Zonnebeke.
©The Ohio State University, Byrd Polar Research Center Archival Program,
Sir George Hubert Wilkins Papers, wilkins52_2_2.jpg

At the opening of the final stage of Third Ypres, an attack on Poelcapelle on 9 October proved futile: the mud impeded men and guns. Third Ypres culminated in a series of actions in October & November with the aim of capturing the village of Passchendaele: these actions took place in the most appalling conditions with up to one in four of the British fatalities caused by drowning in the mud. Passchendaele was finally taken on 6 November. British casualties in Third Ypres are estimated at 245,000: the Germans suffered 260,000 casualties and the French 8,000.

25 October 1917: Château Wood near Hooge, Ypres salient.
©The Ohio State University, Byrd Polar Research Center Archival Program,
Sir George Hubert Wilkins Papers, wilkins52_1_52.jpg

The rationale underpinning Third Ypres was clear and manifold in nature: to distract the Germans from the French Armies on the Aisne – then riven by collapsed morale and mutinies following the reverses suffered in April – May 1917 in the so-called Nivelle offensive; to alleviate the unsustainable loss of merchant ships via a breakthrough to the Belgian coast and the capture of German submarine bases; and, in anticipation of Russian withdrawal from the war, to pre-empt the re-deployment of German forces from the Eastern Front to the Western Front. Nevertheless, Third Ypres/Passchendaele remains, to this day, one of the most controversial campaigns of Haig's tenure as Commander-in-Chief: the controversy largely centres on the continuation of the offensive after it became clear that a breakthrough was unlikely. In

[7, pages 58-59], Haig's Director of Operations, Major General John Davidson puts forward the following argument. 'Perhaps the weightiest reason for reaching this decision [to continue the offensive] was the need to divert German attention from the other allied fronts. ... There were also persistent and urgent pleas from Pétain [the French Commander-in-Chief who had replaced Nivelle in April 1917] to continue the Flanders operations in order to ensure that the flow of German reserves should be diverted from the French front. Moreover, the French proposed to make a limited attack in Champagne on the 23rd October ... and it was essential to prevent German reserves moving to that point. It has since been stated from several sources that Pétain had been successful in restoring, at least to some considerable degree, the spirit and morale of the French Army by this date, and it has been suggested that Haig might ... have felt justified in relying on the ability of the French to look after their own safely, and thereby release himself from the necessity of providing for their protection from attack. This would be expecting Haig to take the risk of an irreparable catastrophe, a French collapse ... Troops do not recover from the effects of a mutiny in a few weeks, especially of a mutiny of so serious a character and so widespread.'

GHQ: August – October 1917

In his diary entry of 14 August 1917, Charteris [5, page 244] marked the following anniversary.

'Three years to-day since I landed in France, and at least another year to go before we can celebrate peace. Ryan and I dined together to-night, the only two who came out with D.H. and have been with him all the time. We broached a bottle of champagne to mark the anniversary.'

Almost exactly one year later, on 16 August 1918, Charteris states [5, page 320]: 'I am afraid my own time out here is coming to an end. I was medically examined to-day by Ryan. He says no Board would pass me as fit. He wanted me to go into hospital here, but I do not want to do that. I would rather have whatever is necessary done at home. It is rather maddening not to see the last few months out in France, but I am at the end of my tether. I am getting a few weeks' leave.'

As a result of Charteris's early departure, Ryan became the only officer on Haig's personal staff who remained with him throughout the duration of the war (Ryan returned to England with Haig on 5 April 1919).

John Charteris
©Author's collection

Haig – godfather to Ryan's son Douglas

On 2 August 1917, Ryan's fifth child had been born: as evidence of their mutual respect, Ryan named his son Douglas and Haig acted as godfather.

Congratulations. Sir Douglas acting sponsor.
Ryan's telegram to his wife Sadie – 4 August 1917. ©Author's collection

Haig's letter to his wife, 1 October 1917. Some day when you have time please buy a present for the young Ryan boy. I think I told you that I had promised to be godfather! And Ryan has always been so kind in looking after you as well as me.

On 9 October 1917, Dorothy Haig wrote to Ryan:

Dear Major Ryan,

How awfully kind of you sending me the "German Surgical Case". Ever so many thanks for it. It is so interesting. Sir Eric Geddes saw it last evening. I do so appreciate you thinking of letting me have it.

It is nice to hear Douglas is very fit. I feel always he is in good hands with you there.

I was so interested to hear from Douglas that you have another son, many congratulations. I do hope the family are well.

I have been charged by D. to get his godson a present, but I don't quite know what would be the most useful thing, also, I want to get D. when he is next home to write a suitable inscription, hence the delay!!

The children thank you for your kind messages, they are very well. Again many many thanks.

Sincerely yours,   Dorothy Haig

Sir Eric Campbell Geddes (1875 – 1937) was a politician and wartime administrator. Regarded as a pioneer in what is today known as 'logistics', Geddes served as Deputy Director General of Munitions Supply (1915 – 1916), as Inspector General of Transportation in France (1916 – 1917), and as First Lord of the Admiralty (1917 – 1919).

Haig's letter to his wife, 15 October 1917. Ryan goes on leave tomorrow & will call in to see you & the children when he passes thro' London either going or returning.

Ryan's leave warrant, 16 October 1917.   ©Author's collection

Cambrai: November – December 1917

The failure of Third Ypres and the flagging morale of the troops put pressure on Haig to orchestrate a victory. The Tank Corps argued for an offensive over terrain of its choice. An assault on the German lines to the south-west of Cambrai was agreed: this was to be the first use of tanks *en masse*. At 6.20am on Tuesday 20 November, the assault on the German first line began. By the end of the day, the British had advanced some 5 miles in the area of Fontaine-Notre-Dame, taking 4,000 prisoners and 100 guns at the cost of relatively light casualties. On November 21, Charteris [5, page 270] records: 'The attack yesterday was as nearly completely successful as any attack can be. We went in without any artillery preparation and using tanks to destroy the wire. We got complete surprise.'

German countermeasures, supported by the arrival of a fresh division, signalled the start of British difficulties in consolidating their initial gains. On 22 November, the Germans regained Fontaine-Notre-Dame and repulsed a British counterattack on 27 November. The Germans went on the offensive on 30 November with a successful attack which breached the British lines near Gouzeaucourt: the intervention of tanks averted a British collapse. On the morning of 5 December, Haig ordered a withdrawal of the British back to the Flesquières Ridge: this marked the end of the Battle of Cambrai in which each side had sustained approximately 45,000 casualties with no net gain of ground.

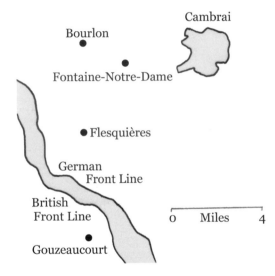

British and German Front Lines, 20 November 1917.   ©Author's collection

©Author's collection

November 19. Left Blendecques for Bavincourt [*the location of Haig's Advanced HQ during the Battle of Cambrai*].
November 20. Tank Battle of Cambrai started. 12000 prisoners & 150 guns.
November 30. Heavy counter attack by Bosch.

On 20 November 1917, at the opening of the Battle of Cambrai, Haig wrote the following note to Ryan. At first glance, it seems remarkable that, at such a crucial juncture, Haig had both the time and inclination to attend to such a minor personal matter. However, bearing in mind the relatively primitive lines of communication available in 1917 (vulnerable/unreliable field telephones, runners, etc.), once Haig had given his orders, anxious hours would have had to be endured before reports began to arrive and further decisions needed to be taken. In *The Smoke and the Fire* (Sidgwick & Jackson, London, 1980), John Terraine comments on the inevitable hiatus between the opening of an offensive and the arrival of first reports as follows: 'Generals, in fact, became quite impotent at the very moment when they would expect and be expected to display their greatest proficiency'. At such a time, a note like the following might well have helped to divert Haig's mind.

General Headquarters
British Armies in France
20 Nov: 17

My dear Ryan

I herewith a cup for my Godson & to wish him all good luck.

Yours ever

D.H.

©Author's collection

On 21 November 1917, Haig wrote to his wife:
'The gold cup for the Ryan godson has arrived. It is quite A.1. – very many thanks for choosing it. I quite agree that I can't give such presents to all children named after me ... we must only give to one or two of our intimate friends.'

On 6 December 1917, Dorothy Haig wrote to Ryan's wife Sadie.

Eastcott,
Kingston Hill,
Surrey
Dec 6th.

Dear Mrs Ryan,

I was so delighted to get a letter from you, as often have wondered how you are and the family. It was a great achievement of yours having another boy. I am also going to have another child in March, but feel certain shall go and have another girl and it will be such a disappointment! ...

EASTCOTT,
KINGSTON HILL,
SURREY.

TELEPHONE
KINGSTON 1103.

Dec 6th.

Dear Mrs Ryan,

I was so delighted to get a letter from you,
as often have wondered how you were and the family. It
was a great achievement of yours having another boy. I am
also going to have another child in March, but feel certain
shall go and have another girl and it will be such a disappoint
-ment!

Your husband always seems very cheerful
when he writes. I always feel quite happy about Douglas
when he is there. I know how well he understands him.

©Author's collection

... Your husband always seems very cheerful when he writes. I always feel quite happy about Douglas when he is there. I know how well he understands him. ...   Again thanking you for your nice letter ...

Yours very sincerely,   Dorothy Haig

Haig's correspondence with his wife, in relation to Ryan as de facto doctor to the Haig family, continues (at this time, Dorothy Haig was in the sixth month of her third pregnancy).

Haig's letter to his wife, 6 December 1917. I am glad Doria is better. Would you like me to send Ryan over to see you & the children? He might stay 2 nights so as to have a clear day with you all & return here the third day. I can manage it without any difficulty if it would please you. He knows the children's constitution & might help about the feeding etc.

Haig's letter to his wife, 10 December 1917. ... very glad to hear that Doria is much better so of course there is no need for sending Ryan to see the child. But if you would like to see him at any time I can arrange to send him over without much difficulty.

Cambrai: the aftermath

In [21, pages 379-382], Terraine comments as follows. 'The set-back at Cambrai represents the lowest ebb of Haig's career. It created difficulties for him which greatly complicated those which inevitably arrived with the return of Germany's division from the East and their offensive in the following March ... the Official History states that Haig "under-estimated the power and the tenacity of his adversary". This would seem to be entirely true, and can only be attributed to the manner in which Charteris carried out his duties.'

As Haig's Chief of Intelligence, Charteris had been the subject of criticism from many quarters for some time, mainly on the grounds of over-optimism and misleading intelligence reports. In the aftermath of Cambrai, Lord Derby (who had succeeded Lloyd George as Secretary of State for War) wrote to Haig advocating that Charteris should be replaced. Haig's loyalty to his 'band of brothers' came to the fore in a stout defence of his Chief of Intelligence. 'My dear Derby ... I cannot agree that Charteris should be made "whipping-boy" for the charge of undue optimism brought against myself ... if the charge is justified at all, I am responsible and not Charteris.' Terraine, in characteristically succinct style, cuts to the core of the situation [21, page 384]: 'This attitude on Haig's part, a mixture of habitual loyalty to subordinates, special affection for Charteris, and apprehension at what might be portended, could not survive the setback at Cambrai.'

HD Sunday 9 December 1917. ... Charteris having said to me that he was afraid the Government at home was striking at me through him. He had much rather do anything than be a source of trouble for me. I told him that I alone was responsible for the opinions which I expressed to War Cabinet, and these were based not merely on what Charteris told me but on what I learnt from Army and subordinate commanders who were in close touch with the fighting troops & so were able to form an opinion of the enemy's fighting value. Kiggell then spoke to me about Charteris. That although he did his work well at Hd.Qrs he was much disliked in Corps & Armies. I told K. to see Charteris and that if what he (K) said was based on good evidence, we ought to give Charteris another appointment but that there was no question of moving C. because of inefficiency in his work. No one could do the Intelligence work better than C. but I fully realised C's faults towards his own subordinates ...

HD Thursday 13 December 1917. General Lawrence[1] (commanding 66th Division) arrived and stayed night. I arranged for him to take over charge of the Intelligence Branch from Charteris. The latter has made himself so unpopular with authorities at War Office and War Cabinet that in order to avoid friction I am obliged to change him. I am sorry to lose him.

In a letter to his wife, Haig elaborates (with typical concern for the well being of a loyal subordinate).

Haig's letter to his wife, Friday 14 December 1917. It is over a year ago since Derby and the War Office have set their faces against poor Charteris, and although he has done his work admirably and his Intelligence Branch is in ex-

---

[1]Lieutenant General Sir Herbert Alexander Lawrence.

cellent order, I feel that it would be wrong of me to keep an officer at this time who seems really to have upset so many people and to have put those who ought to work in friendliness with him against him. ... I shall, of course, do my best to find Charteris another good job. As you know, he has lots of brains, and so in the long run it may probably turn out to have been a good thing for him to have left the Intelligence at this time, because Intelligence is rather a special kind of work which has a very small place in the Army in time of peace.

Lawrence acted as Charteris's successor only for a matter of weeks, before his promotion to Chief of the General Staff. Lawrence's place in the intelligence branch was then taken by Brigadier General Edgar William Cox. During the German spring offensives in 1918, Cox's health deteriorated under the relentless strain of the task of predicting the location and timing of successive German attacks. On 26 August 1918, Cox drowned in the sea off Berck Plage, on the coast near GHQ Montreuil.

Charteris remained with GHQ, as Deputy Inspector General of Transportation, until, as already noted, ill-health necessitated his return to England in August 1918. One of the final intelligence tasks undertaken by Charteris, before his replacement by Lawrence, was to report to Haig on the German offensive potential. In his report, he correctly predicted the German spring offensives of 1918: 'In the early spring (not later than the beginning of March) she should seek to deliver such a blow on the Western Front as would force a decisive battle which she could fight to a finish before the American forces could take an active part, i.e., before mid-summer'.

Charteris's diary, Monday 31 December 1917. I am handing over charge of Intelligence to General Lawrence. I asked to go to a brigade or a division out here, but D.H. tells me he will not let me leave G.H.Q., so I become Deputy Inspector-General of Transportation, when I come back from leave. It is a disappointment, but is softened by the verdict of the doctors that in any case they could not have passed me as fit for front-line work [5, page 277].

In the aftermath of Cambrai, Haig's Chief of the General Staff, Sir Launcelot Kiggell, also suffered criticism. It was believed that Kiggell's health was giving way under the strain.

HD Thursday 20 December 1917. Colonel Ryan and Sir W. Herringham[2] (Consulting Physician to Army) came to lunch and afterward they examined Kiggell. They then reported to me that they found Kiggell is suffering from 'nervous exhaustion due to the very exacting nature of the work he has to perform'. There is no organic disease. Personally I think Kiggell is much better now than he was two years ago when I took over from FM French. I spoke to Kiggell. He goes on leave tomorrow and returns 28 December. We agreed that if either he feels he is not up to the work, or I think he is not fit for the work then I will ask him to go home.

_____
[2]Sir Wilmot Parker Herringham, a pioneer in the treatment of poison gas casualties.

Kiggell subsequently resigned his post and, on 24 January 1918, was replaced, as Chief of the General Staff, by Lawrence. Following a period of convalescence, Kiggell was appointed Lieutenant Governor and Commander-in-Chief of the Island of Guernsey. In [2], Bourne makes the following observations on Kiggell. 'Few British officers, except perhaps Charteris, have received such a uniformly hostile press as "Kigg". He is commonly dismissed as a tidy-minded clerk ... Kiggell is also accused of being out of touch with battlefield realities and is principally remembered for breaking down in tears when finally confronted with them at Passchendaele, a story that is almost certainly apocryphal. Kiggell was an able and dedicated officer.'

On 31 January 1917, Germany had announced that its U-boats would engage in unrestricted submarine warfare (the subsequent sinking of American merchant vessels had led to the declaration of war by the US on Germany in April 1917). The resulting heavy losses in UK-bound shipping had caused food shortages to which Dorothy Haig was not immune. A letter to Sadie Ryan from Dorothy Haig on 24 December tells that Christmas fare at Eastcott in 1917 came from Ireland.

> Eastcott
> Kingston Hill
> Surrey
> December 24

My dear Mrs Ryan

How awfully kind of you sending me the turkey and butter which arrived this morning. They were both so awfully welcome as food here is not very plentiful at present. ... I hope so much that 1918 will be a happier year for us all. Wishing you & yours the very best of luck & again a thousand thanks for the fare.

> Yours   Dorothy Haig

In France, Ryan again celebrated Christmas with Haig.

IID Tuesday 25 December 1917. ... The thaw was sufficient to admit of me riding this afternoon. All the ADC's mess *[of which Ryan was a member]* came to dinner with me, and the party seemed very cheery.

For Ryan, 1917 ended with his fourth Mention in Dispatches.

Friday 28 December 1917. My name in dispatches. ... Fourth time.
[Field Marshal Sir Douglas Haig's Dispatch of 7 November 1917.]

6
First World War: 1918

Hiatus: January – March 1918

The imminent arrival of American troops into the theatre of war put pressure on the Germans to secure a victory in the spring of 1918. Harris [13, page 432] sets the scene thus. 'From mid-December 1917 GHQ's intelligence staff predicted a large–scale German offensive effort in the following spring with increasing certainty and in increasing detail. From then until it began, on the morning of Thursday 21 March 1918, Haig was trying to get his army ready for the onslaught.'

At this time, Haig was also anticipating the birth of his third child in March.

Haig's letter to his wife, 15 January 1918. I enclose the name of a Dr whom Ryan gave me on his own initiative yesterday. Not that he wanted to upset any of your arrangements but if you thought of calling him in at any time, he would write to him. He is at the head of the profession in these particular matters, & Ryan learnt a great deal from him. His name is Dr Eden[1] of Charing X Hospital. It is just as well to know of a good man & also a very charming fellow Ryan says.

Haig's letter to his wife, 17 January 1917. I saw Ryan this evening as Alan *[Fletcher]* had sprained a tendon in his leg. Ryan will be in London at the end of the month and would very much like to run down to Eastcott to see you and the children. You can then have a good talk with him. But he seems quite satisfied that Lady Barrett will do her work efficiently.

Lady Florence Barrett (1865 – 1945) was an eminent obstetric surgeon and later Dean of the London School of Medicine for Women.

---

[1] Thomas Watts Eden, a renowned obstetrician and gynaecologist.

Haig's letter to his wife, 28 January 1918. Ryan is going on leave today and is to call & see you on his way through London.

Monday 28 January 1918. Left Montreuil with General B *[Major General Richard H K Butler, Deputy Chief of the General Staff]* on leave. Saw Lady Haig & children in town. Air raid on London 8 o'c. Left Euston at 8.45. Reached Dublin 7.30. Went south by 3 o'c train, reaching Mallow 7.40 p.m.

Haig's letter to his wife, 31 January 1918. I am glad you saw Ryan. I hope he also saw the children as he takes such an interest in them too, and is so fond of them.

On 9 February, Haig crossed from France to London.

HD Sunday 10 February 1918. I spent a quiet morning with Doris. A walk in the Park before lunch. Col. Ryan came before 1 o'clock and examined Doris. His report was highly satisfactory ... After lunch he left to see Lady Barrett (the lady Dr. attending Doris). R*[yan]* proposes to return 12th March as probably date will be 15th (about).

Sunday 10 February 1918. Went to Farm Street then on to Eastcott where I lunched with Sir D. & Lady H. Event *[childbirth]* due on March 17th?
Monday 11 February 1918. Left Charing Cross with Sir D & G *[General Sir Hubert Gough]*. Met General B *[Butler]* on board. Reached Boulogne at 7 p.m.

©Author's collection

Haig's letters to his wife.
11 February 1918. Ryan (who travelled with me) was loud in his delight at seeing you so fit, and so free from nerves! He said that he had never seen

you looking so well. That is splendid, is it not? But he hoped that you would not motor in your little car so I felt v. glad that you had used the big car this afternoon.

12 February 1918. Ryan proposes going to you on 10th March (a Sunday).

14 February 1918. I do hope for your sake that your wish to have a son will be granted. ... Ryan who has had much experience has reported to me that he is 'pretty confident that it is a young Field Marshal'.

28 February 1918. I'll see that Col. Ryan brings his ration ticket with him when he goes to Eastcott or possibly it might be better to send it to you beforehand, and when I come, I'll bring some meat with me as butcher's shops here seem to have lots of meat to sell.

3 March 1918. I have just seen Ryan. He will cross to London on Sunday with his ration certificate! I have also ordered our cook to buy half a sheep and some butter to send with him, so as to save you anxiety on the score of meat. He will send you a wire as to hour his train reaches Victoria so that your motor car can meet him. Good luck.

On 6 March 1918, Dorothy Haig wrote to Sadie.

EASTCOTT,
KINGSTON HILL,
SURREY.

March. 6.

My dear Mrs Ryan,

How kind of you sending me the woodcock, which arrived quite allright today. Your husband comes over on Sunday. I must hurry up so as to let him go and see you. It is nice having him, which gives one confidence, although as I expect he has told the lady Dr is conducting the case!!!!!!!! But am going to scream for the chloroform and your husband!!!!!

Again so many many thanks for the woodcock, but, you really must not send all these things. Douglas is sending with your husband some meat from France as we have such difficulties,so, all will be well!

Very Sincerely Yrs,

My dear Mrs Ryan

How kind of you sending the woodcock, which arrived quite allright to-day. Your husband comes over on Sunday. I must hurry up so as to let him go and see you. It is nice having him, which gives one confidence, although as I expect he has told you, the lady Dr *[Lady Florence Barrett]* is conducting the case!!!!! But am going to scream for the chloroform and your husband!!!!!

Again so many thanks for the woodcock, but, you really must not send all these things. Douglas is sending with your husband some meat from France as we have such difficulties, so, all will be well!

Very sincerely yours,
Dorothy Haig

Birth of Haig's son: London, March 1918

Sunday 10 March 1918. Left Montreuil at 7 a.m. & Boulogne at 10 a.m. Came across with General Charteris. Reached Victoria at 2 p.m. & arrived at Eastcott at 3 p.m. & went for a walk with Lady Haig after tea. Found her very well.

Monday 11 March 1918. Motored to London. Went to Holts & Hawkes for uniform. Had lunch with Ford & motored back about 4 p.m.

©Author's collection

Haig's letter to his wife, 10 March 1918. I hope Ryan arrived all safe today. It certainly gives me a great feeling of confidence to know that he is in the house with you and able to help you in any way required. He is so kind and tactful. I am sure you will find him a great comfort.

Tuesday 12 March 1918. ... Sir D. arrived for meeting with War Council ...

HD Tuesday 12 March 1918. I left Beaurepaire at 8.45 a.m. and Boulogne at 10 a.m. for England. I crossed by the ordinary boat service and reached Eastcott about 2 p.m. I found Doris at lunch with Col. Ryan and Col. & Mrs. Fox Pitt.[2] Doris was looking very fit and in the afternoon I took her for a walk in Richmond Park ... Col. Ryan dined out with John Charteris so Doris & I had a quiet evening together.

---

[2]Lieutenant Colonel William Augustus Fox-Pitt and his wife Lily.

Wednesday 13 March 1918. Had a round of golf with Sir D. this afternoon. Lady Haig keeping very well.

HD Wednesday 13 March 1918. I called at War Office ... I got back to Eastcott for lunch and afterwards played golf with Ryan.

Thursday 14 March 1918. Went to London with Sir D. dropping him at 10 Downing St at 10 a.m. [meeting of the Supreme War Council]. Clothes fitted. Lunched with Lumsden. Tea at 21 Prince's Gate with Lady H[aig], D [Haig?] & Lord Sefton.[3]

©Author's collection

HD Thursday 14 March 1918. I visited Downing Street at 10 a.m. ... and at 11.30 the full conference met. ... We adjourned about 6 p.m. ... I called at Prince's Gate for Doris & Col. Ryan, and we all motored back together to Eastcott. We three dined quietly together.

Friday 15 March 1918. Had a game of golf with Colonel Fox Pitt. Lady Haig & self chatted till 10.30. Labour started. Young Douglas born at 11.02 p.m. very quiet. Lady Barrett arrived 11.50 after everything was well over. D.V.

©Author's collection

HD Friday 15 March 1918. I attended conference at Downing Street at 11 a.m. ... returned to Eastcott at about 3.30 p.m. ... Doris complained of pains in her back about 7 p.m. and decided to go to bed for dinner after her bath. So Ryan & I dined alone. I was with Doris bidding her good night at 10.30. She complained of pains she thought due to wind – so I went to ask Ryan to come to see her ... at 10.45 he told me that the child had started to come and at 11.2 p.m. the child was born. "The quickest thing on record" he said afterwards. Lady Barrett arrived at 11.45 p.m. after I had seen Doris.

Haig's reaction to the birth of his son and heir (George Alexander Eugene Douglas – known as 'Dawyck') revealed an uncharacteristic facet of his reserved personality, as recorded by both Charteris and Duff Cooper.

    'During this anxious month of March, Haig's mind was eased of one great

---

[3]Osbert Cecil Molyneux, 6th Earl of Sefton.

burden. While her husband himself was at home on a brief visit Lady Haig gave birth to a son. Haig's mind had been torn between his eagerness for an heir and his concern for Lady Haig's health, and when the doctor *[Ryan]* allayed his fears, bringing the good news that the son and heir he had so much desired was born, the barrier behind which Haig concealed his emotions for once broke down. Impulsively he embraced the doctor, kissing him on each cheek. "Like a damned foreigner!" as the doctor added, in recounting the incident.' [4, page 313]

'On these same ides of March an event occurred of deep importance in the life of Haig. Between eleven o'clock and midnight a son was born to him. Colonel Ryan of the Royal Army Medical Corps, who had been with him during the retreat from Mons and ever since, was in attendance. Haig was now nearly fifty-seven and must have almost given up hope of handing to an heir the ancient name which he had inherited and to which he had added such great renown. When therefore the news was brought that the child was a boy and that all was well, words failed him. He threw his arms round the astonished Colonel and, as the latter has described it, "kissed me like a Frenchman". Very seldom was any man privileged to see behind the mask of stern reserve with which Haig concealed from the world a sensitive and intensely human heart.' [10, page 242]

From a grateful patient – Dorothy Haig – March 15th 1918.   ©Author's collection

Saturday 16 March 1918.
Sir D. returned to France. I went to town. Had clothes fitted. Motored to Mc.D. & returned to Eastcott at 7 p.m. Opened 45 wires of congratulations etc. Telephoned Sir D. about notices.

March 16 .... Saturday

[facsimile of handwritten diary entry]

Sunday 17 March 1918.
Motored to Farm Street, 11 Mass. Lunched at Carlton with Ford & Lumsden.
[On 4 June, Frederick William Lumsden VC was killed in action at Blairville, near Arras.]
Saw Carter at War Department. Returned Eastcott for dinner. Lady Haig & son doing very well.

March 17 .... Sunday
5th Sunday in Lent.
St. Patrick's Day.

[facsimile of handwritten diary entry]

©Author's collection

Haig returned to France on 16 March. The next day, he wrote the following letter to Ryan (who remained at Eastcott until Monday 18 March, when he crossed to Ireland on leave).

Colonel E. Ryan D.S.O.
Eastcott
Kingston Hill
Surrey.

©Author's collection

General Headquarters,
British Armies in France
Sunday 17 March 18

My dear Ryan,

I cannot thank you enough for all your kindness to my wife during the past week and for what you have done to save me anxiety. And I do heartily congratulate you in the skill with which you have attended my wife and saved her much pain and suffering.

I am very anxious to give you ...

©Author's collection

... some present as a mark of our gratitude & regard for you. But cannot think what would be useful to you, and at this time of war it is particularly difficult to get things. I have therefore solved the problem by sending a cheque for £100 to your Bankers,[4] and I hope you will spend it as you think best. Thanking you again for all you have done for us.

I am, yours very sincerely,
  D. Haig

---

[4] A generous gift which, today, would be in excess of £6,000.

On 18 March 1918, Dorothy Haig wrote to Sadie from Eastcott.

Dear Mrs Ryan,

I am so grateful to you for letting me have your skilled husband. Douglas & I feel we owe him the deepest debt of gratitude for what he has done & you for sparing him here. So many thanks for your kind congratulations ...

Well I must stop now & I again repeat, Douglas & I are so grateful. Best wishes to the family.   Very sincerely yours,   Dorothy Haig

P.S. I fear this is a rotten letter, but I am writing it in a hurry, expecting your husband to come in & stop it. He really forbade my writing!!   DH

Haig's letter to his wife, 19 March 1918. I am pleased to hear that Ryan prevented you from dealing with the wires and letters yourself.

On 29 March 1918, Ryan returned to Eastcott from leave in Ireland. He crossed to France on 30 March. On the same day, Dorothy Haig wrote to him.

Dear Colonel Ryan

I forgot yesterday to ask you to be an angel and let me know when you have seen Douglas what you candidly think of him after all this strain.

I know as you said, he will be taking all quietly, still, should just like an honest report. ... I wonder if D. will approve of the Godparents ...

> Lord Derby [Secretary of State for War]
> Lord French [Haig's predecessor as C. in C.]
> Sir Eric Geddes [First Lord of the Admiralty]
> General Neil Haig [Haig's cousin]
> Sir Pratap Singh [Maharajah of Idar]

quite a war Baby!! Thanking you again for all you have done. Mind you tell D. how good I have been about the vexed question 'taking in food'. It's all I can do just now to help Douglas.   Very sincerely yours,   Dorothy Haig

Haig's letter to his wife, 4 April 1918. I am so happy to hear ... that our son is getting on so well. Ryan was full of his good qualities and of you too of course.

In Haig's Dispatch of 7 April 1918, Ryan received his Fifth Mention.

German spring offensives: March – July 1918

The influx of German troops from the Eastern Front (following the withdrawal of Russia from the war) gave the Germans numerical superiority on the Western Front – a superiority which they sought to exploit before the arrival of American troops. In *Forgotten Victory* (Review – Headline Book Publishing, London, 2002, page 223), Sheffield observes: 'Ironically, the fateful decision *[to mount the spring offensives]* was taken at a meeting held at Mons on 11 November 1917. Exactly twelve months later the war ended, in great part as a consequence of the decision taken on that day.'

Michael offensive: March – April 1918

Thursday 21 March 1918.
German spring offensive started today.

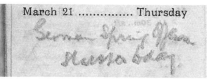

March 21 .... Thursday

©Author's collection

Preceded by a 5 hour bombardment, a German assault was launched on the morning of 21 March 1918 across a 50 mile front from the River Sensée in the Arras region to the Oise in the region of St Quentin. Before midday, the British were in retreat: by the day's end, the Germans had taken approximately 100 square miles of British-held territory.

24 March 1918: British troops retiring near Fricourt, Somme.
©The Ohio State University, Byrd Polar Research Center Archival Program,
Sir George Hubert Wilkins Papers, wilkins52_1_49.jpg

During the next two days, the Germans reached the Somme between Péronne and St Simon: their advance across the old Somme battlefield continued and Albert was taken on 26 March. On the previous day, Charteris [5, page 292] had commented that the 'situation is very serious both in the battle and behind it ... the Germans are still pressing on. The Péronne bridgehead and the line of the canal were given up yesterday, and we shall soon be back to our old line of 1915.' By 28 March, the offensive was losing momentum and Charteris's optimism was mounting. 'The situation is very much better ... I think we can safely say now that this great German effort has failed.' [5, page 294] Harris's assessment [13, page 459] is similar. 'Though it was not clear at the time, by 28 March the Allies had won the opening round. They had lost a lot of ground, but none of it vital.'

Sunday 31 March 1918.
Saw Sir D today looking well, quite satisfied with situation.

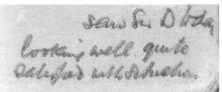

©Author's collection

As Sheffield [18, page 278] notes, the Michael offensive ended in 'one last spasm of action'. 'Between 29 and 31 March the Germans halted to prepare for a major push towards Amiens. ... On 4 April the attack began, to be stopped ... at Villers-Bretonneux by Australian troops newly arrived from Flanders. ... The Germans had not succeeded in reaching Amiens, and they called off the offensive.'

While the Michael offensive was being run down, the Germans were preparing for their next attack, the Georgette offensive, to be directed against the British in Flanders. In a letter to Esher (vide [20, page 72]) at about this time, Haig's private secretary, Philip Sassoon, wrote: 'Here the Spring is come, leaves flowers – birds – but all bloodstained ...'.

Georgette offensive: April 1918
The preliminary bombardment began early in the morning of 9 April 1918, followed by an infantry attack which resulted in immediate German gains. By late afternoon, they had advanced 6 miles and had taken 6,000 prisoners and 100 guns. These initial successes were followed, over the next two days, by the taking of Neuve Chapelle, Messines and Armentières from the British. The situation for the British was critical. On 11 April, with the vital rail and communication centre at Hazebrouck under threat, Haig issued an uncharacteristically emotional appeal to his troops:

TO ALL RANKS OF THE BRITISH FORCES IN FRANCE
Three weeks ago to-day the enemy began his terrific attacks upon us on a 50-mile front. His objects are to separate us from the French, to take the Channel Ports, and to destroy the British Army.

In spite of throwing already 106 divisions into the battle, and enduring the most reckless sacrifice of human life, he has as yet made little progress towards his goals. We owe this to the determined fighting and self-sacrifice of our troops. Words fail me to express the admiration which I feel for the splendid resistance offered by all ranks of our Army under most trying circumstances.

Many among us are now tired. To those I would say that Victory will belong to the side which holds out the longest. The French Army is moving rapidly and in great force to our support. There is no other course open to us but to fight it out! Every position must be held to the last man. With our backs to the wall and believing in the justice of our cause, each one of us must fight on to the end. The safety of our Homes and the Freedom of Mankind alike depend upon the conduct of each one of us at this critical moment.

Sheffield [18, pages 284-5] summarizes subsequent developments as follows. 'In desperate fighting, the Germans were stopped short of Hazebrouck. ... Yet another attempt to break through the Allied positions began on 17 April. Once again the Allies, including by this stage the Belgian army, remained firm. ... Since early April, the Somme front had been fairly quiet, but on 24 April the Germans attacked towards Amiens. Supported by tanks, the Germans made deep gains around Villers-Bretonneux, 10 miles from Amiens, the world's first tank–against–tank combat taking place in the process. An Australian-British counterattack slammed shut the door to Amiens. On the same day, in Flanders, the Germans captured Mount Kemmel *[strategic high ground with a commanding view of the Ypres salient]* from the French. Again the Allies did enough to prevent the attackers from building on their success.'

The Germans were left with exposed flanks: the Georgette offensive – also known as the Battle of the Lys – stalled and was finally called off on 30 April.

Blücher-Yorck offensive: May – June 1918

For the Germans, the strategic objective remained that of driving a wedge between the British and the French to secure victory before the arrival of the full-strength American force. A new attack – the Blücher-Yorck offensive – on the French in the Aisne area was planned. This offensive, launched on 27 May 1918, was the most successful of the German spring offensives. Charteris [5, page 310] comments: 'The Germans have fairly caught Foch napping, and have scored heavily in their last attack; but it cannot go far or last long. They attacked yesterday on the Aisne in great strength against the very part of the line where our exhausted IXth Corps had been sent for a rest! We have very little news yet, but what we have got is serious.'

By mid-morning on 27 May the Germans had crossed the Aisne; on 29 May, they took Soissons and advanced to Château-Thierry on the Marne, where they were held by French and American forces. The Germans had taken 65,000 prisoners and 800 guns, and were within 60 miles of Paris. However, by early June, the offensive had lost momentum. On 9 June, the Germans sought to renew the attack westwards with operation Gneisenau. They succeeded in advancing some 9 miles. On 11 June, the advance was halted at Compiègne by a French counter-attack under General Charles Mangin. On 12 June, operation Gneisenau was called off.

Afterword

The initial successes of the German spring offensives caused recriminations regarding the state of preparedness of the BEF in early 1918. In a letter to *The Times* on 6 May 1918, Major General Sir Frederick Maurice (Director of Military Operations, Imperial General Staff) was highly critical of Lloyd George – accusing him of misleading Parliament on the strength of the BEF and withholding reserves. This precipitated what was essentially a vote of confidence in Parliament, which Lloyd George duly won: Maurice was forced to resign. In letters to Philip Sassoon (vide [20, page 74]), Esher's comments on the controversy serve to underline the disparate personalities of Haig and Lloyd George: 'Whatever happens, *never* permit D.H. to open his mouth. His silence is a tremendous factor'; 'How that little L.G. does love polemics. He gets himself into trouble for the sheer sensual pleasure of getting himself out again.'

Notwithstanding the strength of the BEF in early 1918, the cessation of the German spring offensives in mid-June 1918 marked the turning of the tide for the Allies who, at the same time, were gaining numerical superiority through the arrival of the Americans. Harris [13, page 485] summarizes the situation in the following terms. 'By mid-summer 1918 the Germans on the Western Front were in very serious trouble. Between 21 March and 25 June the length of the front they held had increased from 390 kilometres to 510. Over the same period they had suffered about one million casualties, so the numbers available to hold the extended front had significantly declined. ... The Germans had launched their offensives from sophisticated and powerful systems of fortification ... By contrast, much of the front they occupied in late June, July and early August was fortified only in the most rudimentary way.'

Ryan's GHQ Pass: May – August 1918.   ©Author's collection

The Hundred Days: July – November 1918

The period 18 July – 11 November 1918 is known (with numerical imprecision) as the Hundred Days and saw the final sequence of Allied offensives on the Western Front, culminating in the Armistice.

The first of these was a French counter-attack, on 18 July 1918, on the German positions near Château-Thierry. By the time the French offensive – known as the Second Battle of the Marne – ended on 4 August, the Germans had been pushed back to the Aisne.

Battle of Amiens

The second offensive of the Hundred Days Campaign is known as the Battle of Amiens. It began on 8 August 1918 with a surprise tank attack by the British which forced the Germans back nine miles in one day. By the end of the second phase of the battle (the Battle of Bapaume, also known as the Battle of Albert) on 2 September, the Germans had retreated to the Hindenburg Line (which had been the starting point of the German spring offensives).

Sheffield's [18, page 303] overview of Allied strategy during the Hundred Days is as follows. 'Back in 1915 Haig had talked about his ideal of an offensive over a very wide front. Now, in 1918, Haig had the men, the guns and the logistic support to make it happen. ... Rather than plunging forward until they ran out of steam, as the Germans did in the spring, advances were limited and logistically sustainable. Once resistance stiffened in one sector, the point of attack was switched elsewhere. The German army was always on the back foot, never able to initiate.'

Thursday 8 August 1918. At 4 a.m. this morning battle south of Albert to Montdidier started – a great success, 10,000 prisoners and 200 guns

Friday 9 August 1918. Battle continues. Prisoners 20 000, guns 200 to 300. Advanced 25 kms. Saw Sir D. at Wiry in train. A very good day.

©Author's collection

On 7 August, Haig had moved his Advanced HQ into a special train – which afforded greater mobility and from where he operated for virtually all of the remaining period of the war. 'I have 9 officers living in my train. The General Staff occupy a second one accommodating 8 more. Thus the whole is very long, half a mile about! and all say they are very comfortable.' For the period 8–18 August, the Advanced HQ train was based at Wiry-au-Mont, approximately 20 miles west of Amiens; on 18 August, it moved to Boubers-sur-Canche, about 20 miles west of Arras, where it remained until 4 September.

Saturday 31 August 1918. An excellent month. Advanced all along the line in places 30 miles, taking 57 000 prisoners. Advanced GHQ at present at Boubers [*Boubers-sur-Canche*].

Death of Captain George Balfour Black

Friday 23 August 1918.
Captain Black, 17th Lancers, mortally wounded today near Proyart. Buried on right of road midway between Warfusée-Abancourt [*Lamotte-Warfusée*], & Sailly [*Sailly-Laurette*] .

August 23.................19....Friday
Capt BLACK. 17 Lco: mortally wounded to day near FROYART: buried on right of road midway between WARFUSEE ABLAINCOURT , SAILLY,

©Author's collection

Captain George Balfour Black was a Scottish officer and a highly-regarded personal friend of Haig's who commanded Haig's mounted escort (a detachment of the 17th Lancers) from April 1915 to January 1918 when he transferred to the Tank Corps. He died of his wounds on 23 August 1918, aged 29. In 1915, Haig had noted Black's arrival in his diary.

HD Tuesday 20 April 1915. Captain Egerton[5] 17th Lancers (Com[*mandin*]g the Escort Troop) returned to the regiment for duty today. Having been on the staff in Bombay and away from reg[*imenta*]l duty for 2 to 3 years, his brother officers thought he should go back. He has been replaced by Lt George Black, who joined the regt. 3 years ago from Oxford University O.T.C.. He came to Aldershot for training when I was in command there.
HD Saturday 24 August 1918. I received news of George Black's death yesterday. No details, only that he was badly wounded with his Tank and died in the Casualty Clearing Hospital at Daours ... He was with me from April 1915 until the beginning of this year in charge of the 17th Lancers troop (my mounted escort). He insisted on going to the Tank Corps as 'he wanted to fight'! He is a great loss to me and all of us. Always so cheerful and happy even when things looked darkest ...

Wednesday 11 September 1918. Put a wreath on Black's grave today from Sir D. & Personal Staff. Place of interment P18. 13.40. near three trees on right of road at 2 km stone between Warfusée & Sailly.
[*After the war, Black was re-interred in Villers-Bretonneux Military Cemetery.*]

September 11 ...... Wednesday
Put a wreath on BLACKS. grave to-day from Sir D , Personal Staff . Place of interment P18. 13.40. near 3 trees on right of road at 2 KM. stone between WARFUSEE, SAILLY,

©Author's collection

On his transfer to the Tank Corps in January 1918, Captain Black had been replaced by Major Ivor Hedley of the 17th Lancers, who took charge of Haig's

---

[5]Captain Edward Brassey Egerton died on 1 September 1916 of wounds received at Arras.

mounted escort. Hedley was acutely aware that Black was a hard act to follow, as the latter had become a personal friend of 'the Chief'. In Hedley's diaries [*Imperial War Museum, Ref IWM 3151*], he records an encounter with Ryan.

Ivor Hedley's diary, Thursday 24 January 1918. ... Motored back with Ryan & stopped at his billet for a 'small one'. He was most interesting about the Chief – what a big man he is & how human 'He's all right if ye only treat him as a man & not as a bloody Field Marshal'. A most pleasant Irishman. Told me how wonderful George [*Black*] was with the Chief – a tonic to him & far more use than he, Ryan the M.O.. I have always felt that I am attempting to replace the irreplaceable. But Ryan said very kindly 'ye're all right me bhoy'. Lifted a weight from my mind.

Leave & CMG: September 1918

In the Birthday Honours List of June 1918, Ryan had been nominated Companion of the Order of St Michael & St George (CMG), an order of chivalry established in 1818 by the Prince Regent, later King George IV.

Monday 3 June 1918. Got C.M.G. in birthday honours of today.

On 17 September 1918, Ryan left Boulogne on a period of leave in London and Ireland. On 18 September, he received the CMG at Buckingham Palace.

Wednesday 18 September 1918.
Went to Levee [*at Buckingham Palace*] this morning. Got C.M.G. from H.M. Crossed to Dublin by night mail. A good crossing.

©Author's collection

Assault on the Hindenburg Line

A three-pronged Allied assault on the Hindenburg line was planned for the end of September 1918. In the north, the Belgians, with British and French support, would attack through Flanders. In the centre, Haig would command three British armies and one French army in an attack on the heart of the Hindenburg line between Cambrai and St. Quentin. To the south, the French and Americans would attack on the front between Reims and Verdun. The southern component of the attack was the Meuse River/Argonne Forest offensive of 26 September – 11 November 1918. The first phase of this battle began on 26 September. The Americans advanced two miles through the difficult Argonne Forest and five miles along the Meuse: to the west the French pushed forward nine miles. In the second phase, by 17 October the Americans had breached the main German defences, and by the end of October had cleared the Argonne forest: the French meanwhile had advanced twenty miles, reaching the Aisne. By the end of the Hundred Days, the French and Americans had reached Sedan and had cut the Sedan-Metz railway line, one of the main supply lines to the German front. The northern attack (sometimes referred to as Fourth Ypres) began on 28 September: its first phase was a marked success. The Belgian, British and French forces advanced across the old Ypres battle-fields and recaptured all of the ground lost during the German spring offen-sives. In three days, the Allies advanced some 10 miles: the Menin Road and Passchendaele Ridges were retaken. Adverse weather then stalled the offen-sive for 2 weeks.

On 2 October 1918, Dorothy Haig wrote (from Eastcott) to Ryan:

Dear Colonel Ryan

A thousand thanks to you for the letter, how kind of you thinking of it and also for the photo, which I shall value very very much, of a real kind friend and also the precious Baby's what shall I call you "Protector". I always feel you saved his little life & he is so everything for Douglas and me. ...
The letter finishes with a reference to Haig's recent successes.
... How just grand the news is.   Ever yours very sincerely,   Dorothy Haig

The second phase of the northern component of the Allied assault (Battle of Courtrai) began on 14 October 1918 and continued until the end of the war. On 17 October 1918, Lille, Ostend and Douai were liberated and on 19 Octo-ber, Zeebrugge and Bruges were taken. By 11 November 1918, the Allies had advanced fifty miles.

In command of the central component of the three-pronged attack, Haig's was a daunting prospect: on this part of the front, the Germans enjoyed nu-merical superiority and their defences took advantage of a series of wide canals in the area. The central attack began on 27 September 1918 with an assault on the Canal du Nord (Battle of Cambrai - St. Quentin), followed, two days later, by an attack on the St. Quentin Canal: a key bridge over the canal, at Riqueval, was taken. A further attack on 3 October met with more success: the Hindenburg line was breached. The Germans fell back to a new line running south from Cambrai, forcing another set-piece action by Haig. On 8 October, the British, with French support, attacked along a seventeen mile front ex-tending south from Cambrai. The town was taken on 9 October: the Germans again fell back and took up another position on the Selle, which, in turn, was attacked on 17 October (Battle of the Selle). The Germans retreated to yet an-other line on the river Sambre. On 4 November 1918, Haig initiated the final British set-piece of the war, with an assault on a thirty mile front along the Sambre. In Sheffield's words [18, page 333]: 'It was the end. The Battle of the Sambre dispelled any lingering illusions among the German leadership. The war had to be ended before the German army collapsed.'

The final days: November 1918

Wednesday 6 November 1918. Went to Paris to see Alan Fletcher. Day very wet. Arrived about 4.30. Stayed at Crillon Hotel. Alan coughing a lot.

Thursday 7 November 1918. Returned leaving Paris at 12. ... Called at 18 Casualty Clearing Station to see Corporal Putland.

Friday 8 November 1918. Corporal Putland died today. General Burtchaell[6] lunched with me at Bertincourt.

Corporal George Putland served with GHQ Troops Mechanical Transport Company, Army Service Corps. His connection with Ryan is unknown (but it is plausible that Putland was a GHQ staff car driver). Putland was a victim of the 1918 influenza pandemic and is buried in Rocquigny–Equancourt Road British Cemetery, Manancourt.

Saturday 9 November 1918. Reported that German Emperor & Crown Prince have got the Order of the Boot & that Baravia has declared itself Republic.

Sunday 10 November 1918. Left Bertincourt today for Iwuy, North-East of Cambrai.
[For the period 10–19 November, Haig's Advanced HQ train was based at Iwuy, approximately 5 miles north east of Cambrai.]

By early November 1918, German negotiations with the Allies were under way. On 10 November Kaiser Wilhelm II went into exile in Holland.

One of the closing actions of the war was the liberation of Mons on the morning of 11 November 1918, 'the lead troops halting just a few yards from where the 4th Dragoon Guards had launched the BEF's first action of the war back in August 1914' ([18, page 335]).

Armistice: 11 November 1918

The Armistice was signed at 5am on Monday 11 November 1918. At 11am on 11 November 1918 fighting ceased on the Western Front.

©Author's collection

Monday 11 November 1918. Cessation of hostilities today at 11. The Armistice was signed at 5 am this morning.

---

[6]Lieutenant General Charles Burtchaell, Director General of Medical Services since June 1917.

OPERATIONS SPECIAL PRIORITY.

First Army.	E.-in-C.
Second Army.	D.R.T.
Third Army.	D. Sigs.
Adv. Fourth Army.	I.G. Training.
Fifth Army.	D.G.S.
Cavalry Corps	M.S.
Adv. Operations, R.A.F.	G.H.Q. Troops.
Tank Corps.	D.G.M.S.
Communications.	British Mission, French G.Q.G.
M.G.G.S., (S.D.).	British Mission, Belgian G.Q.G.
A.G.,	Brit.Mission, H.A.E.F.,
Q.M.G.,	General DuCane, C/o E.M. Bacon.
D.G.T.,	General Cavendish, C/o E.M., Conde.

------------------------------- *Colonel Ryan*

O.A.D. 953.   11th November   AAA

                Hostilities will cease at 1100 to day, November

11th AAA   Troops will stand fast on the line reached at

that hour, which will be reported by wire to Adv. G.H.Q.

AAA   Defensive precautions will be maintained AAA   There

will be no intercourse of any description with the enemy

until the receipt of instructions from G.H.Q. AAA   Further

instructions follow AAA   ACKNOWLEDGE AAA

                Addressed all Armies, Cavalry Corps and Adv.

Operations, R.A.F., repeated all concerned.

                                        W.P. Dobbie
                                          Lt.Col
                                        _____

Adv. G.H.Q.   General Staff.
0650

Copies :-

        G.S., I. (Adv.).
        M.G.R.A., (Adv.).

OPERATIONS SPECIAL PRIORITY

Hostilities will cease at 1100 to-day, November 11. Troops will stand fast on the line reached at that hour, which will be reported by wire to Adv. G.H.Q.

Defensive precautions will be maintained. There will be no intercourse of any description with the enemy until the receipt of instructions from G.H.Q. Further instructions follow. ACKNOWLEDGE

Addressed all Armies, Cavalry Corps and Adv. Operations, R.A.F., repeated all concerned.

W.G.S. Dobbie
Lt.Col.
General Staff

As Staff Officer on duty at Advanced GHQ early on 11 November 1918, it fell to Lieutenant Colonel William George Shedden Dobbie (1879 – 1964) to sign the order to cease hostilities at 11am. This fortuitous signing justly entitled Dobbie to describe his role in the Great War as having 'stopped the beastly thing!'.

HD Monday 11 November 1918. Day fine but cold and dull. Reports from Foch's HQ state that meeting with the German delegates (which took place in train in Forest of Compiègne, not in Château as previously reported) began at 2 am and at 5 am the Armistice was signed. ... The Armistice came into force at 11 am. The state of the German Army is said to be very bad, and the discipline seems to have become so low that the orders of the officers are not obeyed ... We heard this morning that the Kaiser is in Holland. If the war had gone against us no doubt our King would have had to go, and probably our Army would have become insubordinate like the German Army! cf. John Bunyan's remark on seeing a man on his way to be hanged, 'But for the Grace of God, John Bunyan would have been in that man's place!'.

On 13 November 1918, Dorothy Haig wrote to Ryan:

Eastcott
Kingston Hill
Surrey
Nov 13, 1918

Dear Colonel Ryan

Thank you most awfully for your kind letter. You have just helped enormously to carry through Douglas [sic.] the anxious days you have all been through, by your kind care of him. From the wife please accept oh such grateful thanks. ...

Forgive the hurried line, have letters galore to answer. I feel so proud of Douglas.

Very sincerely yours
Dorothy Haig

Saturday 16 November 1918. F.M. Foch lunched with Sir D. today.
Tuesday 19 November 1918. Left Iwuy today & returned to Brimeux *[Château de Beaurepaire]*.

With the Armistice came some relief for Haig from the strain of command. Ryan's diary records two rounds of golf with Haig (the existence of a functioning golf course in north-eastern France in November 1918 is somewhat surprising). The location was Le Touquet which boasted a golf links inaugurated in 1904 by the British Prime Minister, Arthur Balfour, an enthusiastic golfer and former captain of the Royal & Ancient Golf Club of St. Andrews. Haig shared Balfour's enthusiasm for golf and was himself captain of the Royal & Ancient Golf Club of St. Andrews in 1920-21.

Saturday 23 November 1918. Had a round of golf with Sir D., Alan F. *[Fletcher]* & Botha.

Captain Louis Botha was ADC to Haig and the son of the Prime Minister of the Union of South Africa, General Louis Botha. During the Second Anglo–Boer War, General Botha was Commander-in-Chief of the Boer forces. His son Louis – then only ten years old – was with his father at the Battle of Onverwacht, an action fought during the closing stages of the war on 4 January 1902. With the granting of dominion status in 1910, the Union of South Africa was formed with General Botha as its first Prime Minister. At the outbreak of the First World War, Botha pledged support for Britain. With a hint of irony, 1918 found Botha's son acting as ADC to Haig, whose 2nd Army was under the command of General Sir Herbert Plumer who, in turn, some 16 years earlier was one of the British commanders in the action at Onverwacht.

HD Saturday 23 November 1918. ... Morton brought a number of papers before lunch. He, Ryan & Botha came to lunch. The latter two played in a foursome after lunch against Alan & me. We were beaten!

Captain Desmond Morton (1891 – 1971) was ADC to Haig. On 28 March 1917, near Arras, Morton had been hit by a machine gun bullet which lodged in his spine close to his heart. The position of the bullet prevented its removal; nevertheless, Morton was deemed fit for appointment as ADC to Haig. In the Second world War, Morton was Personal Assistant to Winston Churchill.

Monday 25 November 1918. Golf. Lunch with Sir D., Gen. Lawrence *[Chief of the General Staff]* & Alan F.

HD Monday 25 November 1918. ... Ryan came to lunch and afterwards we played a foursome R*[yan]* & Lawrence against Alan & myself. Ryan started very confident & backed his side with Alan for 10frcs ... At one time we were 7 up. Eventually we won 5 up & 4 to play.

To/Mickie Ryan
    With heartfelt gratitude for what he has done to keep myself & staff fit from date of mobilisation to the end!
        D.Haig F.M.
         Xmas 1918

Excerpts from Haig's final dispatch.

'At 11.00 on the 11th November, 1918, at which hour and date the armistice granted to Germany by the Allies took effect, the British front extended over a distance of about 60 miles from the neighbourhood of Montbliart, East of Avesnes, to just North of Grammont. This front from South to North was held by troops of the Fourth, Third, First, Fifth and Second British Armies, all of whom were in hot pursuit of the enemy at the moment when the armistice came into operation. ...

Troops were at once directed not to advance East of the line reached by them at the time when hostilities ceased, and certain parties of Germans taken prisoner after that hour were returned to the enemy. Outposts were established along this line both for the sake of military security and in order to prevent all possibility of fraternisation. ...

In order to permit the enemy to withdraw his troops from the area immediately in front of us, our positions were maintained unchanged until the morning of the 17th November. Thereafter, to avoid all possibility of collision be tween the opposing forces, the movement of troops towards the frontier was regulated so as to preserve a safety zone of 10 kilometres in depth between our advanced detachments and the enemy's rearguards. The general advance into Germany was directed to begin on the 1st December. On the 12th December, French, American and British forces would cross the Rhine at Mayence [Mainz], Coblentz [Koblenz] and Cologne [Koeln], and commence the occupation of bridgeheads having a radius of 30 kilometres from the crossings ...

During this period large numbers of released prisoners of war, French and British, came through our lines and were passed back to collecting stations. The enemy seems to have liberated the majority of the Allied prisoners west of the Rhine without making any provision for their feeding and conveyance. The result was that much unnecessary suffering was caused to these unfortunate individuals, while a not inconsiderable additional burden was placed upon our own transport and supplies. ...

Throughout the whole of the advance, and especially in the stage which followed the crossing of the German frontier, very great, but unavoidable, difficulties were encountered in connection with supply. At the time of the armistice railheads were on the general line Le Cateau, Valenciennes, Lille, Courtrai, and for many miles in front of them bridges had been broken and track torn up or destroyed by mines. Even after the cessation of hostilities delay action mines, which the enemy had laid in the course of his retreat without preserving exact record of their location, went up from time to time, causing serious interruption to traffic.'

7

The Postwar Years: 1919 – 1951

Ryan remained in France, on Haig's Personal Staff, until 5 April 1919 when both he and Haig returned to England. Haig became Commander-in-Chief of the Home Forces and Ryan took command of Bethnal Green Military Hospital, London.

Prior to their final departure from France, Haig and Ryan spent a period of leave in England: 5–19 March 1919.

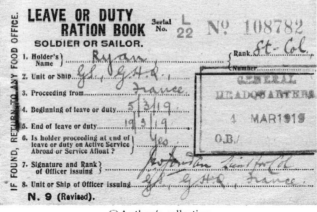

©Author's collection

Haig's diary, Tuesday 18 March 1919. Doris & I ... played golf in afternoon on small course at back of Eastcott. ... While playing, Col. Ryan joined us. He thought our son 'a very fine child & in excellent health'. He left after tea and returns to France tomorrow.

In Haig's Dispatch of 19 March 1919, Ryan received his seventh Mention.

Battlefields tour: March – April 1919

Haig, together with his wife Dorothy (Doris) and Dorothy's sister, Lady Alexandra Worsley, crossed to France on Thursday 20 March 1919.

HD Thursday 20 March 1919. Beaurepaire was reached about 7.30 pm. Doris & her sister in great spirits ... Col. Ryan R.A.M.C. came to dinner.

On the following day, a party – consisting of Haig, his wife & sister-in-law, Lieutenant Colonel Christopher Heseltine (ADC), and Ryan – embarked on a pilgrimage to the battlefields of the Western Front. This must have been a cathartic experience for all.

HD Friday 21 March 1919. ... About 3 p.m. we left by motor for Cassel. The party is Doris, myself, & Heseltine in first motor. Alexandra Worsley (1914 widow) & Col. Ryan in second one.
HD Saturday 22 March 1919. ... We got away about 10 a.m. ... From Messines we motored to Wytschaete and continued some two miles towards Ypres. Unfortunately the near fore-wheel slipped into a shell hole and we spent an hour and a half getting it out. Then we retraced our steps to Wytschaete as Ryan reported that the direct route to Ypres was impassable, and took the Kemmel–Ypres road. ... Registration officer to guide us to Lord Worsley's grave tomorrow. On return to Cassel, Heseltine rejoined and reported that he had found a good track to Zandvoorde and the grave.

Lord Worsley, Charles Sackville Pelham (1887 – 1914). At First Ypres on 30 October 1914, Pelham had been killed, at the age of 27, his machine gun section having been isolated at Zandvoorde by a German attack. Worsley's body had been buried by the Germans: the British were notified of his burial location via diplomatic channels.

Dorothy Haig kept a diary of the pilgrimage [*National Library of Scotland: Acc. 3155, No. 347/48*]. On 21–23 March, the party toured the Ypres salient. On 22 March, Dorothy Haig wrote: 'Douglas was very interested going down the Menin Road, he had not been there since 1914 during the very anxious days. ... We also passed his old H.Q. by Hell Fire Corner ... White Château at the Menin Road Crossing, nothing left standing at all.' On Sunday 23 March, they located the grave of Alexandra's husband, Lord Worsley. In her diary, Dorothy Haig records that 'Alexandra was upset at first but was very delighted with the peacefulness of the ground Worsley lies in.'

HD Sunday 23 March 1919. We left Cassel about 10 a.m. and went straight via Ypres to Gheluvelt. ... Heseltine led us to the grave (Worsley's) which we had been in search of yesterday. ... It was nerly 2 p.m. before we got back to the cars. ... On the way back we looked at the H.Q. of 1st Corps in Oct. 1914 but it was difficult to recognise where Hooge Château, the White Château and the house at X roads Ypres–Menin–Zonnebeke stood! All so destroyed by shell fire as to be most difficult to find.

Tuesday 25 March saw the party visit, inter alia, Hinges, Béthune and Aubers Ridge. 'Then ... on to Neuve Chapelle, passing through Fauquissart (road where Gen. Gough was wounded). Then from Neuve Chapelle to Estaires where we saw Gen. Gough's grave' [from Dorothy Haig's diary].

Brigadier General John Gough VC, Haig's Chief of Staff, First Army, had died on 22 February 1915, having been been mortally wounded two days earlier.

HD Tuesday 25 March 1919. We left at 10 a.m. and motored via Hazebrouck & St. Vennant to Hinges where we spent some time looking at the château and one of the trees which I had taken much trouble to preserve when I had my H.Q. (1st. Army) there from Sept to Dec 1915. ... The château front is standing, but the back wall is greatly damaged, and the rooms quite opened up with gaping rents. ... We next passed through La Bassée ... to Aubers village. Here we had lunch under the shelter of a concrete block house on the slope looking over towards Fauquissart. ... We walked round Neuve Chapelle and then visited Gen. Johnnie Gough's grave at Estaires. It was in good order but two shrapnel bullets had grazed and dented the cross & railing.

Wednesday 26 March included visits to Loos, Lens, Vimy Ridge and Arras.

HD Wednesday 26 March 1919. ... we spent some time walking about over the scene of the Battle of Loos. ... After lunch we motored through Lens. The destruction here is indescribable. ... We next visited Vimy Ridge. ... The Canadians have already erected some very simple, but solid monuments to their dead in the battle of April 1917 on this ground. We continued our journey through Arras to Bavincourt.

On 27 March, Haig and his ADC, Lieutenant Colonel Heseltine, left to attend to matters in Cologne and Brussels, and the party was joined by another of Haig's ADCs, Captain Desmond Morton.

HD Thursday 27 March 1919. I left Bavincourt about 9.30 a.m. leaving Doris with Gen Travers Clarke (QMG), Ryan R.A.M.C. and Capt. Morton R.A. who joined today.

Lieutenant General Travers Edward Clarke (1871 – 1962). Quartermaster General to the Armies in France from 1917 to 1921.

Over the following three days, the battlefields tour continued, with focus on Cambrai, the Somme and Amiens. The party returned to Montreuil on 1 April, and again met up with Haig. By this stage, the demobilization of Haig's GHQ was more or less complete. On 2–4 April, Haig visited Paris and Chaumont to bid farewell to his French and American allies. He returned to Boulogne on 5 April and crossed to England on the same day.

Haig took command of the Home Forces on 15 April 1919.

Bethnal Green Military Hospital: April – October 1919

Ryan also left France on 5 April 1919 and took command of Bethnal Green Military Hospital, London, on 13 April.

On 11 October 1919, Ryan was requested to hold himself 'in readiness to proceed to India at an early date'.

©Author's collection

To/Mickie Ryan
With all good wishes for the future
from D.H.
October 1919

Ryan sailed from Devonport on 1 November, and reached Army Headquarters in Delhi on 28 November 1919.

India: November 1919 – January 1925

Inspection Tour: January – April 1920

Ryan spent the four-month period of January to April 1920 on an inspection tour of Military Hospitals in India and Burma. In a gruelling schedule, he travelled the length and breadth of India, from Simla in the north to Madras (now known as Chennai) in the south, and from Bombay (now known as Mumbai) in the west to Calcutta (now known as Kolkata) in the east, with a Burmese excursion taking in Rangoon (now known as Yangou) and Mandalay.

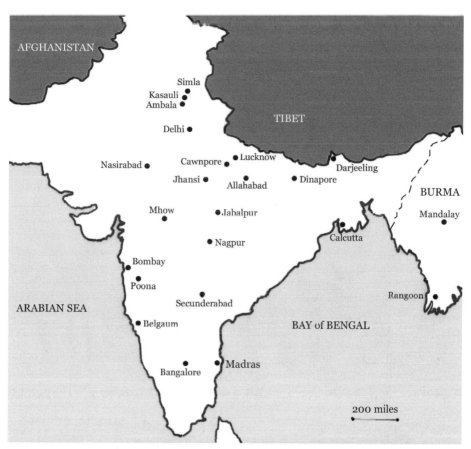

Locations visited on inspection tour: January – April 1920. ©Author's collection

The following selection from Ryan's 1920 diary provides an indication of the extent of the inspection tour (placenames as given in the diary) – during which Ryan returned periodically to Delhi to write his reports.

January 1: Kasauli. January 3: Delhi. January 8: Cawnpore. January 11: Lucknow. January 14: Delhi. January 18: Ambala. January 22: Delhi. January 30: Rangoon. February 2: Mandalay. February 9: Rangoon. February 13: Calcutta. February 15: Darjeeling. February 20: Dinapore. February 21: Allahabad. February 22: Delhi. March 1: Nasirabad. March 4: Mhow. March 5: Bombay. March 7: Poona. March 10: Belgaum. March 13: Secunderabad. March 15: Bangalore. March 20: Madras. March 24: Nagpur. March 26: Jabalpur. March 29: Jhansi. March 31: Kalka. April 1: Simla.

Escorting Prince Carol of Roumania: April – May 1920

On 9 April 1920, Ryan received orders to escort Carol, the Crown Prince of Roumania, on a tour of India. On completion of this duty, he was to take command of the British Station Hospital, Kasauli.

©Author's collection

'Will you please note that you have been selected to accompany His Royal Highness the Crown Prince of Roumania during his forthcoming visit to India.

On completion of this duty you will proceed to Kasauli for command of the British Station Hospital there ... '

These orders came from the Director of Medical Services in India, who at that time was Lieutenant General Sir Charles Burtchaell, an erstwhile RAMC colleague of Ryan's from France & Flanders.

Crown Prince Carol was the eldest son of Ferdinand I, King of Roumania, and Queen Marie, a daughter of the second son (Prince Alfred, Duke of Edinburgh) of Queen Victoria. His first marriage (to Zizi Lambrino in August 1918) was annulled in 1919. His tour of India took place between the annulment and his next marriage, in 1921, to Princess Helen of Greece and Denmark. The second marriage broke down owing to Carol's affair with Elena Lupescu. As a result of the scandal, he renounced his right to the throne in 1925 in favour of his son Michael by Crown Princess Helen. Michael duly became King in 1927. Carol unexpectedly returned to his country on 7 June 1930: he reneged on his renunciation of his right and was proclaimed King on 8 June 1930. He reigned as King Carol II of Roumania from then until forced into exile in 1940. Carol died in Portugal in 1953.

In his diary, Ryan records receiving 'orders to accompany the Crown Prince of Roumania round India with Major Bailey'. The Major (later Lieutenant Colonel) referred to was Frederick Marshman Bailey.

Lieutenant Colonel Frederick Marshman Bailey (1882 – 1967) was a truly remarkable and colourful character. As soldier, linguist, explorer, botanist, ornithologist, intelligence officer, secret agent and diplomat, his life reads like a story from the *Boy's Own Paper* and would be regarded as impossibly far-fetched were it not true. Born at Lahore, he was commissioned into the Indian Army in 1901. He was with the Tibet Expedition to Lhasa 1903-04 and again with an exploring party in western Tibet in 1904-05. He became an expert on Tibet and its culture, and a personal friend of the Dalai Lama. Bailey's feats as an explorer won him the Gold Medal of the Royal Geographical Society. In 1915, Bailey was with the Indian Expeditionary Force, first in Flanders where he was wounded and later in Gallipoli where he was again wounded. Bailey returned to India and served as Political Officer on the Northwest Frontier 1916-17. An intelligence assignment to Turkestan 1918-20 followed, his brief being to investigate the intentions of the new Bolshevik government in relation to India. Working incognito in Tashkent and elsewhere, Bailey adopted different identities and languages. This culminated in an extraordinary episode in which he was recruited to the Bolshevik counter-espionage service and given the task of uncovering a rogue British agent, in the *Scarlet Pimpernel* mould, named Bailey! In January 1920, Bailey had to flee, making his escape through Bokhara (in modern-day Uzbekistan) and Meshed (in modern-day Iran), eventually arriving in Delhi on 9 February. Bailey described his exploits in his book *Mission to Tashkent* (Jonathan Cape, London, 1946). Within 10 weeks of his safe return to Delhi, Bailey was again on the move – accompanying Ryan and Crown Prince Carol on their tour of India (a photographic record of the tour is held in the Bailey Collection at the British Library).

Ryan's diary Monday 19 April 1920. The Crown Prince arrived at 16.40. Drove around Bombay. Left Victoria in special at 18.40. A good dinner in train.

Wednesday 21 April. Motored ... 80 miles to Mahabaleshwar to country house of Governor of Bombay. Met H.E. George Lloyd.[1] ... HRH, Lady Lloyd, Bailey & I played bridge after dinner.

Friday 23 April. Left Mahabaleshwar at 15.30. Arrived at Poona about 19.30. A nice drive of 80 miles. Left Poona at 19.35 for Agra.

Sunday 25 April. Arrived at Agra about 6 a.m. Was met at the Station by a crowd of flunkeys. Drove in motors about 15 miles to Circuit House for breakfast. Saw the Taj & Fort in the afternoon. Dined at the Circuit House & left about 23.30 for Delhi.

Monday 26 April. Arrived at Delhi at 6.30. Motored to the Fort. Spent about 2 hours there. Came back to Alipore Hospital for breakfast. Went to see New

---

[1]Governor of Bombay: George Ambrose Lloyd, 1st Baron Lloyd of Dolobran.

Delhi etc. in the afternoon. Dined at Alipore Hospital. Left at 23 hrs for Patiala's place.

Maharaja of Patiala.   ©Author's collection

Tuesday 27 April. Arrived at Patiala's place at 6 hrs. Red carpet & guns galore. Met by H H Patiala. Drove to one of his places where we put up & had breakfast. Went to the Fort to see the Crown Jewels which were beautiful & historic. After lunch we went black buck shooting.
Wednesday 28 April. Left for Pinjaur at 15 hrs. Arrived there at 18 hrs. A beautiful place about 3 miles from Kalka.
Thursday 29 April. Left Pinjaur at 6. Motored a mile & then got onto elephants & made for the jungle. Got back to Pinjaur at 20 hrs.
Friday 30 April. Left Pinjaur at 11 hrs for Simla. Arriving at Simla at 15 hrs. Stayed at Grand Hotel.
Saturday 1 May. Lunched at the Gymkhana Club at the invitation of the Viceroy.
Monday 3 May. A dinner & dance was held at Viceregal Lodge.
Tuesday 4 May. Left by motor rail at 16.20 bound for Kashmir.
Wednesday 5 May. Arrived at Pindi about 15 hrs. Left at 17 hrs with the Prince and two Condescus in a motor reaching Tret about 19 hrs.
Thursday 6 May. Left Tret at 9 hrs reaching Uri at 19 hrs where we were joined by the rest of party. Had a good dinner. Crossed the frontier *[Punjab-Kashmir]* over the Jhelum about 4 p.m. Ran along by the left bank of the Jhelum. Hills snow-capped all round and river muddy & turbulent. The air delightful & the country beautiful.
Friday 7 May. Left Uri at 13. Motored to Baramula where we met the Governor. Then on to the capital Srinagar where we were met by the Resident

Colonel Bannerman. The Prince inspected the Guard of local soldiers who were rather good. They played a kind of Scotch pipe. The river looks beautiful. Houseboats line the two banks. We had tea in the Resident's Garden: Lady Ridley & daughter & Miss Anderson & Mrs Bannerman.

The British Residency of Jammu & Kashmir was the Office of the Viceroy's Representative in that Princely State. From 1917 to 1921, the British Resident was Lieutenant Colonel Sir Arthur D'Arcy Bannerman.

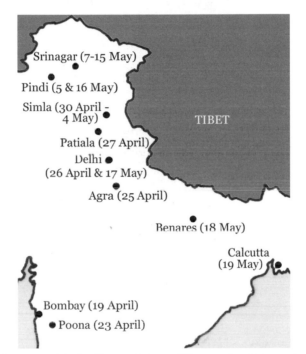

Ryan's itinerary with the Crown Prince of Roumania. ©Author's collection

Saturday 15 May. Left Srinagar at 8 hrs. Arrived at Tret at 19 hrs - where we stayed the night.
Sunday 16 May. Reached Pindi at 11 hrs. Lunched in train. Motored 20 miles out of Pindi to see some Buddhist old temples. Left Pindi at 20 hrs - pretty hot.
Monday 17 May. Reached Delhi at 15 hrs. HRH presented me with the Order of the Star of Roumania.
Tuesday 18 May. Arrived Benares about 6 hrs. Saw the Hindoos incinerate their dead, etc.
Wednesday 19 May. Arrived at Calcutta at 5.40. Introductions etc. Stayed at Grand Hotel.
Saturday 22 May. HRH left Calcutta at 8 hrs & I at 20 hrs.

©Author's collection

Kasauli: June 1920 – January 1925

On 29 June 1920, Ryan took command of the British Station Hospital, Kasauli (Himachal Pradesh), in the foothills of the Himalayas about 150 miles north of Delhi and close to Simla. He remained in command until 23 January 1925.

On 18 May 1921, Ryan was appointed Honorary Surgeon to the Viceroy of India (Rufus Isaacs, 1st Marquess of Reading).

Ryan and staff at the British Station Hospital, Kasauli.
©Author's collection

Continued contact with Haig

As early as 1917, Haig was warning the government in London that, at the end of the war, demobilization and the issue of ex-servicemen's pensions would require sensitive handling if disciplinary problems and social unrest were to be avoided. In February 1919, Winston Churchill, the newly-appointed Secretary of State for War, commented: 'It is surprising that the Commander-in-Chief's prescient warnings were utterly ignored'. On his return from France in April 1919, Haig was appointed Commander-in-Chief of the Home Forces and found a Britain greatly troubled by disenchantment, unemployment, industrial unrest and strikes. Indeed, in the immediate postwar years, many feared the unthinkable – a revolution in Britain. In a letter of 4 January 1921 to Ryan, Haig voiced his concern that '[t]here is much unemployment at home and I am afraid that there may be trouble'.

With the abolition of the post of Commander-in-Chief of the Home Forces on 31 January 1920, Haig effectively retired from the Army, but, as Field Marshal, remained on the Active List. From then until his death eight years later, Haig tirelessly campaigned for the well-being of ex-servicemen, both officers and other ranks. He sought to amalgamate the many postwar ex-servicemen associations into a single organization – this he refers to in the following letter to Ryan. The efforts of Haig and others to foster unity among ex-servicemen gave rise to the British Legion, of which he became the first President.

©Author's collection

Eastcott, Kingston Hill, Surrey.
Tuesday 4 Jan -1921

My dear Micky Ryan

I was delighted to get your kind letter of 28th Nov just before Xmas and thank you ever so much for all your good wishes. My wife & I heartily reciprocate them & hope that this New Year will bring you & yours much joy & happiness & still more success. We have sent you some photos. I am glad to say all the family are very well. The 2 little ones are wonderfully strong & fit and Xandra has benefitted all round by her life at the Broadstairs School. We are going to send Doria there also this next term. The latter is wonderfully good at golf and drives quite a long ball: often as far as I can!

On 4th Feb my wife and I sail for Capetown. I have accepted an invitation to attend a conference there at the end of Feb. of ex-servicemen from all parts of the Empire. We hope to be back at the end of April. We are sending the 2 little ones to Cornwall to my wife's brother (Lord Vivian). He has a big house & lots of room for them all. We have taken a house near the North Foreland again for the summer.

There is much unemployment at home & I am afraid that there may be trouble as Govt. has been too slow in tackling the question. We have got all the ex-servicemen to unite into one Empire Organisation and a "unity committee" directing its affairs is now sitting in the Officers Association, Grosvenor Square! ...

All good wishes & hoping to hear from time to time how you are getting on. I am, Yours ever   Haig

EASTCOTT,
KINGSTON HILL,
SURREY.

We are thinking of old friends at this season, and send this card to you with our heartiest greetings for Xmas, and to hope that the New Year maybe a very prosperous one for you.

Haig of Bemersyde

December 1922.

Dorothy Haig

We are thinking of old friends at this season, and send this card to you with our heartiest greetings for Xmas, and to hope that the New Year may be a very prosperous one for you.

Haig of Bemersyde
Dorothy Haig

December 1922

Ryan's Service Record indicates that he left India on 22 November 1922 for a period of leave in England: this is consistent with Haig's letter of 28 December 1922.

Eastcott, Kingston Hill, Surrey
28th December 1922

My dear Mickie Ryan

Have just heard that you are home! Please let us know when you are to be in London. My wife & I much hope that you will come & spend a few days with us here.

We hope to give up this house in March and to take up my residence at Bemersyde during the summer.

I hope that your wife & family are all very well, and hoping to see you soon.

I am, Yours very sincerely,
Haig

EASTCOTT,
KINGSTON HILL,
SURREY.

28th Dec. 1922.

My dear Mickie Ryan

Have just heard
that you are home!
Please let us know
when you are to be
in London — my
wife & I much hope
that you will come
& spend a few days

with us here —
We hope to give up
this house in March
and to take up my
residence at Bemersyde
during the summer.

I hope that your
wife & family are
all very well, and
hoping to see you soon
I am,
Very sincerely
Haig.

Edinburgh: April 1925 – January 1927

On 23 January 1925, Ryan relinquished command of Kasauli with orders to embark for the UK. He sailed from Bombay on the Hospital Troopship *Assaye* and disembarked on 17 February.

In April 1925, Ryan was posted to the Scottish Command as Officer Commanding the Military Station Hospital, Edinburgh Castle. No papers from 1925 survive.

On 18 February 1926, Ryan was appointed Honorary Physician to the King and promoted to Brevet Colonel.

The Services.

THE KING has approved of the appointment of Lieut.-Colonel E. Ryan, C.M.G., D.S.O., R.A.M.C., to be Honorary Physician to His Majesty, and to be promoted to the brevet rank of colonel, with effect from February 18th, 1926, in succession to Lieut.-Colonel and Brevet Colonel Sir Edward S. Worthington, Kt., K.C.V.O., C.B., C.M.G., C.I.E., R.A.M.C., who has retired.

© British Medical Journal, page 926, 29 May 1926.

©Author's collection

Bemersyde, St Boswells, Scotland
30 May 1926

My dear Ryan

Please accept my heartiest congratulations on your well deserved promotion. I had nothing really to do with it. You owe it all to ownself.

The 2 little kids are very well indeed. I took Dawyck to Folkestone on the 20th. The School Mistress thought him the picture of health. Rene too is v. fit and well again, all thanks to your skilful handling of them.

Xandra left for London on Friday - she stays with an aunt until we arrive. We go South about 10th June. All good wishes.

>   Yours ever
>   Haig

Diary Thursday 22 July 1926. Buckingham Palace *[Garden Party]*. Lunched at Haigs. Met Laws, Unwins, General & Lady Jacob.

The Jacobs referred to in the diary entry were General (later Field Marshal) Sir Claud and Lady Clara Jacob. Ryan would have known Claud Jacob from his time on the Western Front (in 1916, Jacob was in command of II Corps). Their paths again crossed in Kasauli, India, in 1921, as the following letter indicates. Jacob was Chief of the General Staff, India, 1920-24.

The Kasauli Club, 13.4.21

Dear Ryan,

I enclose a cheque for Rs 500/- as a donation to your Family Hospital Fund for you to spend in any way you think fit.

I cannot tell you how grateful I am to you for all you have done for my

wife. It is entirely due to you & the Sisters that she has made such a wonderful recovery. You yourself have done wonders & I cannot say too much in
gratitude for all your kindness to us both. ...

You have been a perfect brick –
Yours ever
Claud W. Jacob

For Dorothy Haig, November – December 1926 was a period of ill health (in [4,
page 375], Charteris comments: 'Lady Haig's health gave him [Haig] anxiety
during the years 1926 and 1927'). Ryan was in attendance and, on Saturday
13 November, she was admitted to a clinic at 14 Drumsheugh Gardens, Edinburgh.

Diary Saturday 13 November 1926. Sent Lady Haig into 14 Drumsheugh Gardens.
Thursday 18 November 1926. Lady Haig still in Home.

On 25 November, Haig wrote to Ryan.

Bemersyde, St Boswells, Scotland
Thursday 25 Nov. 1926

My dear Micky Ryan
I was delighted to see so much improvement in my wife's condition
y[ester]day ... you are a wonderful fellow!!
I hope to be back by the 4th Dec and will be in Edinburgh on the 5th. but
the massage seems to be doing so much good that I suggest keeping Lady
Haig in the Home until Sat 11th Dec. which will be four weeks exactly from
the day she went there.
A thousand grateful thanks to you.
I am, yours ever
D.H.

On 20 December 1926, Haig again wrote (from Ireland) to Ryan.

©Author's collection

St Marnock's, Portmarnock, Co. Dublin
Monday 20 Dec 1926

My dear Micky Ryan

I arrived here Friday night with my wife & Dawyck and I feel I must send you a few lines of very grateful thanks for your most kind & most skilful attention to my wife. She is now better than I have seen her for many months, and I feel sure that but for your taking hold of her at the right moment she must have suffered a very severe break down. I can't tell you all I feel about your care & kindness & can only say I thank you a thousand times. ...

I hope that Mrs Ryan & all your children are very well and with hearty good wishes for Xmas.　　　　Believe me, Yours very sincerely,　Haig F.M.

Hong Kong & Shanghai: January – November 1927

In 1912, a revolution deposed the Emperor of China and a Republic was proclaimed. Thereafter, China entered a period of internal anarchy, with no effective central government. Warlords, Nationalists and Communists struggled for control. After the First World War, anti-foreign sentiment grew, much of which was directed against Britain as the largest foreign holder of property in China. In 1926, concern for the safety of the large international population in Shanghai – then the wealthiest city in China – precipitated international intervention as part of which Britain dispatched a substantial force, the Shanghai Defence Force.

Ryan was ordered to take command of a general hospital of 600 beds: he embarked for China on 28 January 1927 on the *Assaye*, the same ship on which he had returned from India two years earlier.

The Services.

MEDICAL ARRANGEMENTS FOR THE SHANGHAI DEFENCE FORCE.

THE following are the medical arrangements which have been made for the troops composing the Shanghai Defence Force:

Colonel H. Ensor, C.B., C.M.G., D.S.O., Deputy Director of Medical Services of the Western Command, has been appointed A.D.M.S., with Major D. G. Cheyne, *M.C.*, R.A.M.C., from the Royal Army Medical College, as D.A.D.H. Lieut.-Colonel S. Boylan Smith, D.S.O., O.B.E., R.A.M.C., Senior Medical Officer at Hong-Kong, will act as temporary D.A.D.M.S.

Colonel Ensor will have under his administration a general hospital of 600 beds, a field ambulance, and a field hygiene section, all of which have left England. Brevet Colonel E. Ryan, C.M.G., D.S.O., R.A.M.C., is in command of the general hospital, Lieut.-Colonel S. L. Pallant, D.S.O., R.A.M.C., of the field ambulance, and Captain G. O. F Alley, *M.C.*, D.P.H., R.A.M.C., of the hygiene section.

© British Medical Journal, p.316, February 12, 1927.

'Colonel Ensor[2] will have under his administration a general hospital of 600 beds, a field ambulance, and a field hygiene section, all of which have left England. Brevet Colonel E. Ryan, C.M.G., D.S.O., R.A.M.C., is in command of the general hospital ... '

---

[2]Colonel Howard Ensor RAMC.

Bemersyde, St Boswells, Scotland
Monday 25 Jan 1927

My dear Micky Ryan

Just a few lines of very hearty congratulations on your good fortune in being selected for Service in China, and to wish you every success & a safe return home again. It must be a great upset to Mrs Ryan & your family, and if my wife can be of any help in any way I trust you will let me know. Lady Haig returns tomorrow from London.

Again all good wishes & the very best of good luck.

Yours most sincerely

Haig. F.M.

©Author's collection

On the eve of his departure for Shanghai, Ryan stayed with his old friend and RAMC colleague, John Southey Bostock. He wrote to Sadie:

Crookham Camp,
Thursday 27th 11 a.m.

My own darling

I arrived here yesterday morning at 10 a.m. Met most of my officers and old John Bostock who has been a brick in getting my show ready. I was hard at it until 6.30 when Bostock took me to his place where I dined & slept. ...

I have just now made my will and am sending it on to Holt & Co. for safe custody so it washes out any other wills made. Now I know you are good and that you will be careful in everything.

I have no time to write any more I am perpetually being interrupted. ...

Your loving Jane

On 28 January 1927, Ryan embarked for China on HMT *Assaye*. He arrived in Hong Kong on 3 March, where he disembarked awaiting further orders. On

21 March, Ryan was ordered to proceed to Shanghai with a section (200 beds) of his hospital. In a letter to Sadie on 21 March, he comments: 'The number of orders and counter orders we got since our arrival here would fill a page and make some very interesting reading. In fact they would suffice to drive an ordinary man off his chump. Whether I will stay at Shanghai or return here to where the other 400 beds will be will all depend on circumstances. Ensor states he has nobody to give him any advice at Shanghai and wants me there to get the show started and going.'

Ryan boarded the *Herminius* in Hong Kong on 23 March and arrived in Shanghai on 28 March.

The following are excerpts from Ryan's letters to Sadie over the period April to September 1927.

2 April. We are located here in quite a big building which will soon be a very fine hospital. We started to take in cases yesterday & have about 25 in at present. I expect to have my surgical crowd working in a few more days. ... I have only been practically out of this building 3 or 4 times, twice to Army Headquarters and twice to the Club to play squash rackets. We always go in uniform with a revolver & change there and again change into uniform to return which is a d[amned] nuisance. ... The people here are getting much easier in their minds but the people in the French Concession are windy and clearing out and moving in here. The Cantonese Army or some of them are within spitting distance of ours. This state of affairs cannot last long as they the Cantonese will have to get away from this area or else ...

10 April. We had a visit from the GOC [*Major General Sir John Duncan (1872 – 1948)*] this morning. We found out we knew each other in Malta [*1903*]. He and his Chief of Staff went all round the building, saw the patients, swapped a word with each and when leaving said he was delighted with my show. So far so good. I do hope we won't have any more moves and I am doing my best to get the remainder of my unit up from Hong Kong. I have already 180 beds equipped here and expect to have about 300 in a week or ten days as soon as I can get the other people out of the building.

22 April. The people are showing their gratitude to the troops whose presence undoubtedly saved their lives and times. I have met some of the refugees from Nanking who tell harrowing tales.

28 April. It does not look as if there is going to be much fighting here as I believe our presence here has put the wind up the Cantonese blokes.

2 May. There is a puff in the local papers this morning with caricatures of my officers. Mine is a terrible caricature. ...

©Author's collection

I have never seen such a transformation in any place in a month. The Chinese have completely changed. This place was a mass of communistic flags on our arrival. Today there are none to be seen, and instead of tin hats etc people go around in the ordinary way. Curfew is now midnight. I have only been out one night till 12 and that was last Thursday when I dined with Ensor & some of his staff. On my way home the streets were as silent as a desert.

6 May. We passed through a bunch of the Cantonese Army. They are a terrible looking lot of guys. At present it does not look as there will be any fighting here. They are quite tame at present but people seem to think if the Army leaves here there will be the old trouble all over again.

1 June. The remainder of my unit joined here yesterday from Hong Kong. I think they were sorry to leave there as one has more freedom of movement, bathing etc at Hong Kong, though the weather is much nicer here and the people are most hospitable.

29 August. A letter from War Office stating the Queen Alexandra Military Hospital becomes vacant in January & that Fell was very anxious that I should take it, if so to wire and I have just now wired accepting it. So with any hope I will be home by Xmas.

29 September. I have got my birthday present from the War Office in the shape of my orders for home. Ensor is away at Hong Kong so I have ordered myself home on the *Karmala* troopship which is due from here on 14 or 15 Oct ... I expect to reach London end of 3rd week in Nov & hope to hear what your ideas are before I leave here. Have just wired Ensor at Hong Kong telling him of my intentions. He is expected back here about that date but whether he is or not I am off.

Ryan left Shanghai on the Troopship *Karmala* on 15 October 1927. He disembarked at the Royal Albert Docks, London, on 25 November and reached Edinburgh on 29 November 1927.

Haig: the final contact

Bemersyde: December 1927

Public subscriptions in 1920 had provided a fund for the purchase of Bemersyde, a house in the Scottish Borders long associated with the Haig family (the motto *Tyde what may betyde, Haig shall be Haig of Bemersyde* is attributed to Thomas the Rhymer, a 13th century poet and reputed prophet). The house had been presented to Haig in 1921. Haig had moved into a renovated Bemersyde in March 1924.

Following Ryan's return to Edinburgh from Shanghai in late November 1927, he and his wife Sadie were invited to spend some days with the Haigs at Bemersyde in December. This was probably the last occasion on which Ryan and Haig met: Ryan moved to London to take command of the Queen Alexandra Military Hospital at Millbank in January 1928; Haig died of a heart attack on the night of 29 January 1928.

Diary Friday 2 December 1927. Had a phone message from Lady Haig asking us to go there on 6th.

Wednesday 7 December 1927.
Went to Bemersyde yesterday. Had a day with the Buccleugh Hounds.
Thursday 8 December 1927.
Rode with Earl & Lady Haig about 10 miles.
Friday 9 December 1927.
Returned from Bemersyde.

DECEMBER, 1927.

8 Thurs.
Rode with Earl Lady Haig about 10 mile

9 Fri.
Returned from Bemersyde

Haig's death: January 1928

On his effective retirement from the army in January 1920, Haig devoted himself to the care and well-being of ex-servicemen, both officers and other ranks. In [10, pp.422-423], Duff Cooper records Haig's dedication to this task.
'Henceforth that work became unremitting, and it would probably not be an exaggeration to say that at no period of his life did he work harder than during the last years of it. Nor was the work congenial to him. ... he was condemned to spend long hours at the writing table, varied by visits of ceremony and the making of speeches. Public speaking is a strain even on those to whom it comes easily; but for those who hate it, as Haig did, it is pain and travail. ... He would not spare himself. In France he had kept regular hours throughout the war and taken regular exercise ... But now he would sit far into the night replying to a host of correspondents - old soldiers and widows of old soldiers who brought their troubles to him with the certain knowledge that they would not be neglected. His old friend and medical adviser throughout the war, Colonel Ryan, on one occasion warned him solemnly that he was overworking and that the consequences might be serious. He suggested at the

same time that his labours would be considerably lightened if he would dictate his letters instead of writing them all with his own hand. Haig replied that he thought people preferred to get letters written in his own hand, that in many cases there was so little he could do for those who appealed to them and that he believed in maintaining the human touch.'

Douglas Haig suffered a heart attack and died on the evening of Sunday, 29 January 1928, whilst in London staying at his brother-in-law's house in Prince's Gate. Haig's coffin lay in state in St. Columba's Church, London, until 3 February when it was carried – via Whitehall – to a memorial service in Westminster Abbey. It then went by train to Edinburgh where again it lay in state in St. Giles' Cathedral.

Haig's funeral cortège: Whitehall, London, 3 February 1928
From *The British Legion Journal*, March 1928. © Copyright expired

Duncan [11, page 98], described a spontaneous manifestation of public grief. 'It is hard to convey to a later generation the emotion that swept the country when the news went out that Haig was dead. Not within living memory had the nation accorded to any of its sons such a demonstration of loyalty, gratitude and affection. Day after day thousands filed reverently past the body as it lay in state, first in London and then in Edinburgh. Vast crowds lined the London streets as the funeral procession went on its way from St Columba's ... to Westminster Abbey, and then to Waterloo Station, from which the body was to go by train to Edinburgh. It arrived there at midnight ... the route [to St. Giles'] was lined by denser crowds than had ever been seen ... '

Haig was buried in a private ceremony (at which Ryan and his wife Sadie were present) at Dryburgh Abbey, near Bemersyde, on 7 February 1928. In accordance with his wishes, Haig's grave is marked by the same simple headstone as adopted by the Commonwealth War Graves Commission for the graves of those soldiers buried in France and Flanders.

Mrs Ryan

BEMERSYDE
ST BOSWELLS

3rd February 1928

MADAM,

I am instructed by Lady Haig to request the honour of your company at a Private Service in St Giles' Cathedral, Edinburgh, on Tuesday, 7th instant, at 11.15 a.m., and afterwards to Dryburgh Abbey, where the interment of her late husband will take place at 3.35 p.m.

I am further to say that Lady Haig very much regrets that, owing to the serious illness of her son, she is unable to provide Luncheon at Bemersyde for those attending the ceremony.

A note of the arrangements is appended for your guidance.

I am, Madam,

Your obedient Servant,

W. K. O. SHEPHERD

Please retain this invitation as it is necessary for admission to St Giles' Cathedral and the private enclosure at Dryburgh Abbey.

In March 1928, the British Legion issued a Commemorative Issue of its Journal dedicated to Field Marshal Earl Haig, to which Ryan was invited to contribute.

272   BRITISH LEGION   March, 1928.

THE EX-SERVICE MAN'S BEST FRIEND
By COLONEL E. RYAN, C.M.G., D.S.O., R.A.M.C.

IT is difficult for one who, as the writer did, lived in close intimacy with the late Lord Haig to transfer to paper his thoughts so soon after his lamented death, and the loss of such a great friend.

I first met the late Field-Marshal at Aldershot in 1912, and from that time until his death was either with or in touch with him.

His wonderful military career is known to everybody, but a few words as to his personality as a Commander and a friend might be appropriately addressed to the Legion, to which he was the greatest friend of all.

The outstanding feature of his character was his great loyalty to the cause he had at heart, and loyalty to the men who had given him all that was in them to bring the struggle in which they were engaged to a successful conclusion.

Whether it was in 1914, when he went to France in command of the 1st Corps, during those dark and desperate days when everything appeared lost, or during the triumphant days from August 1918 onwards, he was the same, calm, cool, and never dismayed, solicitous for everyone's welfare but his own, and never doubting the ultimate success of a cause which he was convinced of in his own mind was the right one.

The strain which he had to bear during these years was such as has never been borne by any Commander in the history of the world.

To me as his personal Medical Officer his health naturally at times caused anxiety, and attempts were made to induce him to take up some form of relaxation after his hard day's work. Bridge after dinner was suggested, but he definitely refused, stating that after he had formulated his schemes he found all the relaxation he required in meditating upon and trying to improve them.

It seems to me that it was given to few men, however brilliant and to whatever heights they rose, to inspire in men, many of whom had never seen him, such deep respect and whole-hearted confidence.

They say that no man is any good among men until he has been given a name. The name of " our Duggie " was used by everyone, from the highest to the lowest throughout the vast legions which he commanded in France.

Loyalty, I have said, was the outstanding feature of his character, and where is it better known than in the laborious and worrying work which he undertook after the war ? Not for him was the rest he so richly deserved after his strenuous times, but work and still more work, into which he put his whole heart in an endeavour to show those who had helped him that he would never forget, and would, God helping him, repay the debt.

I have not the slightest doubt that the continuous strain of war accelerated his death. His loss to the country, to the ex-soldier, to the officer ex and present, is irreparable.

We shall not see his like again—such a lovable character, such a great chief, an ideal husband and a most affectionate father.

His best epitaph might be :—

" A great man, a loyal, trusting and considerate gentleman, the great friend of all ranks and the best friend an ex-soldier and the Legion ever had."

E. Ryan.

British Legion Journal, March 1928. © Copyright expired

THE EX-SERVICE MAN'S BEST FRIEND
By Colonel E. Ryan, C.M.G., D.S.O., R.A.M.C.

It is difficult for one who, as the writer did, lived in close intimacy with the late Lord Haig to transfer to paper his thoughts so soon after his lamented death, and the loss of such a great friend.

I first met the late Field-Marshal at Aldershot in 1912, and from that time until his death was either with or in touch with him.

His wonderful military career is known to everybody, but a few words as to his personality as a Commander and a friend might be appropriately addressed to the Legion, to which he was the greatest friend of all.

The outstanding feature of his character was his great loyalty to the cause he had at heart, and loyalty to the men who had given him all that was in them to bring the struggle in which they were engaged to a successful conclusion.

Whether it was in 1914, when he went to France in command of the 1st Corps, during those dark and desperate days when everything appeared lost, or during the triumphant days from August 1918 onwards, he was the same, calm, cool, and never dismayed, solicitous for everyone's welfare but his own, and never doubting the ultimate success of a cause which he was convinced of in his own mind was the right one.

The strain which he had to bear during these years was such as has never been borne by any Commander in the history of the world.

To me as his personal Medical Officer his health naturally at times caused anxiety, and attempts were made to induce him to take up some form of relaxation after his hard day's work. Bridge after dinner was suggested, but he definitely refused, stating that after he had formulated his schemes he found all the relaxation he required in meditating upon and trying to improve them.

It seems to me that it was given to few men, however brilliant and to whatever heights they rose, to inspire in men, many of whom had never seen him, such deep respect and whole-hearted confidence.

Loyalty, I have said, was the outstanding feature of his character, and where is it better shown than in the laborious and worrying work which he undertook after the war? Not for him was the rest he so richly deserved after his strenuous times, but work and still more work, into which he put his whole heart in an endeavour to show those who had helped him that he would never forget, and would, God helping him, repay the debt.

I have not the slightest doubt that the continuous strain of war accelerated his death. His loss to the country, to the ex soldier, to the officer ex and present, is irreparable.

We shall not see his like again - such a lovable character, such a great chief, an ideal husband and a most affectionate father.

His best epitaph might be:-
"A great man, a loyal, trusting and considerate gentleman, the great friend of all ranks, and the best friend an ex-soldier and the Legion ever had."

E Ryan

An unlikely alliance

The words of Sir Philip Sassoon again come to mind: 'Sir Douglas Haig did not choose his friends lightly; but once made he remembered them'.

My dear Micky Ryan

Haig's death brought down the curtain on his enduring friendship with Ryan. This was an unlikely alliance, given the disparate nature of their personalities and backgrounds – the taciturn Haig, a staunch Scottish Presbyterian and devotee of Empire, and the jovial Ryan, a Catholic from an Irish Nationalist milieu. Yet theirs was a friendship based on mutual trust and respect.

Douglas Haig in 1920

'Micky' Ryan in 1932

©Author's collection

Somewhat serendipitously, the equestrian statue of Haig, which had been located on the Esplanade of Edinburgh Castle, was re-sited, in March 2011, in the forecourt of Ryan's former command – the Military Hospital: the statue now stands close to the entrance thereto.

©Author's collection

To my dear friend Mrs Ryan from Dorothy Haig, Christmas 1928.
©Author's collection

Dorothy, Countess Haig, died on 18 October 1939.

©Author's collection

Bemersyde, St Boswells, Scotland
17-3-29

My dear Col Ryan,

Thank you so much for your kind wire wishing me a happy birthday, and it was very kind of you remembering me.

I am here for the day from school, and am enjoying it very much. Mummy gave me a lovely gramophone for my birthday.

I hope you are quite well.

With love
  from
  Dawyck

Following the death of his father, George Alexander Eugene Douglas (known to his family and friends as Dawyck) inherited the Earldom of Haig of Bemersyde. On graduating from Christ Church Oxford in 1939, he was immediately involved in World War 2, being commissioned into the Royal Scots Greys. He was captured in North Africa in 1942 and after incarceration in PoW camps in Italy, he was transferred to Colditz Castle in Saxony. During his time in captivity, he developed a talent for painting and drawing. Back in London in 1945, he enrolled at Camberwell School of Art. A career as a professional artist followed. The Second Earl Haig died on 10 July 2009.

Haig: a controversial figure

No narrative on Douglas Haig should close without reference to the polarization of opinion on his reputation as Commander-in-Chief in France & Flanders, 1915 – 1918. Haig was lionized during the immediate post-war years: his death and funeral were marked by a public outpouring of sympathy and mourning, both in England and Scotland. His loyal staff officer, John Charteris, was an early biographer and chronicler of Haig's career [4, 5].

The erosion of Haig's reputation gathered momentum with the publication, in the mid 1930s, of David Lloyd George's *War Memoirs* (Ivor Nicholson & Watson, London, 1933-6). As Secretary of State for War and later as Prime Minister, Lloyd George's views on the conduct of the war were frequently at variance with those of Haig (whose distrust is encapsulated in his diary description of Lloyd George as 'astute and cunning ... but ... shifty and unreliable'). In his memoirs, Lloyd George was highly critical of Haig's leadership: 'Haig undoubtedly lacked those highest qualities which were essential in a great Commander in the greatest war the world has ever seen. ... It was far beyond his mental equipment.' The vitriolic comment that Haig was 'brilliant to the top of his army boots' is also attributed to Lloyd George. In his biography of Haig (*Douglas Haig*, Weidenfeld & Nicolson, London, 1976), E K G Sixsmith regards Lloyd George's *War Memoirs* as an illustration of William Blake's maxim:

> *A truth that's told with bad intent*
> *beats all the lies you can invent.*

Sixsmith also offers the view that it 'was a tragedy that Haig and Lloyd George did not get on better with each other'.

Lloyd George's negative assessment of Haig's command was countered by the publication of Duff Cooper's two-volume biography *Haig* [9, 10]. Thus began the schism of opinion into the 'anti-Haig' and 'pro-Haig' camps. In relation to the former camp, the slow transformation of Haig from war hero to villain continued into the 1960s. The publication of Alan Clark's book *The Donkeys* (Hutchinson, London, 1961) led to the popularization of the phrase 'lions led by donkeys' to describe the rank and file under British generalship (a remarkable *volte face* given Haig's lionization immediately following the war). Clark's book is generally regarded as providing the inspiration for the 1963 musical *Oh! What a Lovely War*, which, in 1969, was made into a film with John Mills playing Haig in a highly unflattering light (the attendant myth of the Château general – ensconced in luxury remote from the front line and indifferent to the fate of the Tommy – percolated down to the 1990s and re-emerged, in the BBC television series *Blackadder*, in the character of General Melchett). It is ironic that, in his book (which dwells on the years 1914-15), Clark reflects neither on Haig's performance as Commander-in-Chief nor on the battles of 1916 and 1917 (the Somme and Third Ypres/Passchendaele in particular) but nevertheless the film, which the book inspired, served to plant in the public mind the caricature of Haig as the 'butcher of the Somme'. The publication, in 1963, of John Terraine's authoritative biography *Douglas Haig: the Educated Soldier* [21] served to redress the balance and dispel the myth of the ambitious, callous, technophobic, cavalry-obsessed Château general. In a later work, *The Smoke and the Fire* (Sidgwick & Jackson, London, 1980, p.173), Terraine observes that, in the First World War, British military and naval leaders had to face 'the first war of aviation ..., the first real under-sea war ..., the first war of the internal combustion engine ..., the first war of wireless telegraphy ..., the first of two great artillery wars ..., the first chemical war ..., the first war of modern mass production ...'. He draws the following conclusion. 'The truth is that those ruddy-cheeked, bristling-moustached, heavy-jawed, frequently inarticulate generals rose to challenge after challenge, absorbed weapon after weapon into their battle systems, adapted themselves to constant change with astonishing address. But no one cared to make a legend out of that.'

Haig was a strong supporter of new technologies – tanks and aircraft in particular. Following a meeting with General Sir John Stephen Cowens (Quartermaster General to the Forces) on 16 August 1917, Haig mused in his diary: 'he [Cowens] has an idea that "Tanks" will never be of any use, when as a matter of fact they have already accomplished so much as to show that they have come to stay!'. Haig maintained a close working relationship with Hugh Montague Trenchard, the 'Father of the Royal Air Force', based on mutual respect and admiration. In his diary entry for 19 September 1917, Haig commented: 'General Trenchard stated that airoplanes were not coming as well as he hoped. The Army seems to suffer, he thinks, from the lack of someone at the War Office to press our special needs in aircraft, and to see that they are provided in proper time. In June 1916 I asked for 56 air squadrons. In November 1916 for 20 more, total 76. We today have 51 squadrons, i.e. 25 short!'.

The perception of Haig as a callous commander insensitive to the suffering of the Tommy does not square with Ryan's period of command of No 18 Casualty Clearing Station (only one of many such stations), to which Haig was a regular visitor. Reid [16, page 400] comments that it 'is true that he did not show his emotions ... The culture of his background and the ethos of his class was to maintain an aspect of imperturbability ...'. In his book *Great Contemporaries* (Reprint Society, 1941, page 190), Winston Churchill reflects on Haig's pent-up emotions. 'The Furies indeed contended in his soul; and that arena was large enough to contain their strife.' It should also be borne in mind that the British Army under Haig's command did not act as an independent autonomous unit. In the words of Richard Holmes (*Tommy*, Harper-Collins, London, 2004, page 30) 'they had to fight a coalition war, difficult, frustrating and costly that it so often was. The timing and location of the British offensives at Loos in 1915 and the Somme in 1916 were the direct result of French pressure, and the state of the mutiny-struck French Army in 1917 was an element in the decision-making process which led Haig to attack at Ypres that summer.'

The myth of the 'Château general' also falters under scrutiny. Reid [16, page 452] makes the following observations. 'As is now sometimes grudgingly acknowledged, the generals did not have the cushy time in their safe billets which was an essential part of 1960s prejudice. Four lieutenant-generals, twelve major-generals and eighty-one brigadier-generals died or were killed in the course of the war ... . These figures are far higher than in the Second World War ... .'

That Haig was ambitious is unquestionable: what is open to question is the nature of that ambition. It can be argued that Haig's ambition was fuelled, to a large extent, by a strong Victorian concept of duty which, today, is difficult to fathom. In a letter to his nephew (vide [16, page 106]), Haig is effusive on this theme: 'Don't let ... mediocrities about you deflect you from your determination to belong to the few who can command or guide or benefit our great Empire ... it behoves everyone to do his little and try and qualify for as high a position as possible. It is not ambition. This is duty.' From a modern-day perspective, it is all too easy to dismiss such sentiments as jingoism in the Colonel Blimp mould: however, from the viewpoint of the early years of the twentieth century when they were written, they convey (laying aside the filter of hindsight) an unmistakable sense of responsibility and obligation. To paraphrase Sheffield's words [18, page 7], Haig should be judged by the standards of his own time, not ours.

In the article *He had hatred thrust upon him* (Times Higher Education, 26 July 1996), Gerard DeGroot seeks to explain the transformation of Haig from war hero to villain: 'When the British felt the need of a scapegoat, they created one in Haig. ... Far better that a million men should have died because of one man's stupidity than because of the irresistible arithmetic of modern technological war.' The latter theme is also taken up in the Editors' Foreword in [1]: Haig 'has become synonymous with the huge organization and its complex operations for which no single person can realistically be held responsible, whether in the allocation of blame or the bestowal of praise'.

Queen Alexandra Military Hospital, Millbank: Jan 1928 – Sept 1930

7 November 1928. Ryan with staff of Queen Alexandra Military Hospital
& No 18 Company RAMC.   ©Author's collection

On 16 January 1928, Ryan took up his final appointment as Officer Commanding the Queen Alexandra Military Hospital, Millbank, London (named after the wife of King Edward VII and built on the site of the 19th century Millbank

Penitentiary: first opened in 1905, the hospital closed in 1977 – its buildings now form part of Tate Britain and the Chelsea College of Art & Design).

Wednesday 27 November 1929. Edward, Prince of Wales, leaves the Queen Alexandra Military Hospital at Millbank after opening a new wing. (Ryan and Sadie – third and fourth from right.)　©Author's collection

Retirement: September 1930 – April 1951

Ryan was in command of the Queen Alexandra Military Hospital until his retirement from military service on 30 September 1930 (he remained in the Regular Army Reserve of Officers until his 60th birthday on 29 September 1933). After his retirement, Ryan acted as Recruiting Medical Officer with the London Recruiting Depot until 1938.

He and Sadie moved from London back to their native Cork in 1942. Sadie died on 18 April 1943. Ryan died on 11 April 1951.

Eugene 'Micky' Ryan, 1873 – 1951
Sarah 'Sadie' Ryan (née O'Connor), 1884 – 1943

(Shamrock on their lapels suggests that the photograph was taken on St Patrick's Day,
the year and the location are unknown.)
©Author's collection

From the frontispiece of Ryan's copy of John Charteris's book *At G.H.Q.*

To Micky
In friendship - 1912 to 1931 & onwards
from
John Charteris
Xmas 1931

Bibliography

[1] Bond, B. & Cave, N., *Haig: a Reappraisal 70 Years on*, Pen & Sword, Barnsley, 1999.

[2] Bourne, J., *Who's Who in World War One*, Routledge, London, 2001.

[3] Brereton, F.S., *The Great War and the R.A.M.C.*, Constable, London, 1919.

[4] Charteris, J., *Field-Marshal Earl Haig*, Cassell & Co., London, 1929.

[5] Charteris, J., *At G.H.Q.*, Cassell & Co., London, 1931.

[6] Churchill, W.S., *The Great War*, Vol. 2, George Newnes, London, 1933.

[7] Davidson, J., *Haig: Master of the Field*, Pen & Sword, Barnsley, 2010. (First published by Peter Nevill, London, 1953.)

[8] De Croÿ, Princess M., *War Memories*, MacMillan & Co., London, 1932.

[9] Duff Cooper, A., *Haig*, Vol. 1, Faber & Faber, London, 1935.

[10] Duff Cooper, A., *Haig*, Vol. 2, Faber & Faber, London, 1936.

[11] Duncan, G.S., *Douglas Haig As I Knew Him*, Allen & Unwin, London, 1966.

[12] French, J., *1914*, Constable & Co., London, 1919.

[13] Harris, J.P., *Douglas Haig and the First World War*, Cambridge University Press, Cambridge, 2008.

[14] Harrison, M., *The Medical War - British Military Medicine in the First World War*, Oxford University Press, Oxford, 2010.

[15] Lees-Milne, J., *The Enigmatic Edwardian – The Life of Reginald, 2nd Viscount Esher*, Sidgwick & Jackson, London, 1986.

[16] Reid, W., *Douglas Haig - Architect of Victory*, Birlinn, Edinburgh, 2006.

[17] Secrett, T., *Twenty Five Years with Earl Haig*, Jarrolds, London, 1929.

[18] Sheffield, G., *The Chief: Douglas Haig and the British Army*, Aurum Press, London, 2011.

[19] Sheffield, G. & Bourne, J. (editors), *Douglas Haig: War Diaries and Letters 1914–1918*, Weidenfeld & Nicholson, London, 2005.

[20] Stansky, P., *Sassoon – The Worlds of Philip and Sybil*, Yale University Press, New Haven, 2003.

[21] Terraine, J., *Douglas Haig - The Educated Soldier*, Cassell, London, 2005. (First published by Hutchinson, London, 1963.)

Index

TANGLED LIVES